Assessing and Managing Suicide Risk

Guidelines for Clinically Based Risk Management

Assessing and Managing Suicide Risk

*Guidelines for
Clinically Based Risk Management*

Robert I. Simon, M.D.

Clinical Professor of Psychiatry
Director, Program in Psychiatry and Law
Georgetown University School of Medicine, Washington, D.C.

Chairman, Department of Psychiatry
Suburban Hospital, Bethesda, Maryland

American Psychiatric Publishing, Inc.

Washington, DC
London, England

Copyright © 2004 American Psychiatric Publishing, Inc.
ALL RIGHTS RESERVED

Manufactured in the United States of America on acid-free paper
07 06 05 04 03   5 4 3 2 1
First Edition

Typeset in Adobe's BaskervilleBE Regular and Frutiger55 Roman

American Psychiatric Publishing, Inc.
1000 Wilson Boulevard
Arlington, VA 22209-3901
www.appi.org

Library of Congress Cataloging-in-Publication Data
Simon, Robert I.
   Assessing and managing suicide risk : guidelines for clinically based risk management / Robert I. Simon.—1st ed.
      p. ; cm.
   Includes bibliographical references and indexes.
   ISBN 1-58562-122-6 (alk. paper) — ISBN 1-58562-170-6 (alk. paper)
      1. Suicide. 2. Suicide—Prevention. 3. Suicide—Risk factors. 4. Suicidal behavior—Prevention. 5. Risk assessment. I. Title.
      [DNLM: 1. Suicide–prevention & control. 2. Emergency Services, Psychiatric. 3. Malpractice—legislation & jurisprudence. 4. Psychotherapy. 5. Risk Management. WM 165 S596a 2004]
   RC569.S556 2004
   362.28' 7—dc22   2003057840

British Library Cataloguing in Publication Data
A CIP record is available from the British Library.

To be or not to be: that is the question:
Whether 'tis nobler in the mind to suffer
The slings and arrows of outrageous fortune,
Or to take arms against a sea of troubles,
And by opposing end them? To die: to sleep;
No more; and, by a sleep to say we end
The heartache and the thousand natural shocks
That flesh is heir to, 'tis a consummation
Devoutly to be wish'd. To die, to sleep;
To sleep: perchance to dream: ay, there's the rub;
For in that sleep of death what dreams may come
When we have shuffled off this mortal coil,
Must give us pause.

William Shakespeare, *Hamlet,* Act III, Scene 1

There is but one truly serious philosophical problem
and that is suicide.

Albert Camus, *The Myth of Sisyphus*

To Professor Ralph Slovenko, J.D., Ph.D.

Your wit,
your excellence of scholarship and elegance of writing,
your generosity of spirit
kindled my interest in psychiatry and the law

CONTENTS

FOREWORD

Suicide is a catastrophic human event, a shattering blow to families and friends, an ending of life by the person's own hands. It is the foolish surrender to a warped view of the world, or it is the ultimate expression of the human striving for autonomy. It has engrossed, captivated—and, ultimately, mystified—creative artists and philosophers, from classic Greek tragedians describing the mighty Ajax, driven mad and falling on his own sword, to Albert Camus, pondering the ultimate existential issue.

But suicide is not only the province of artists and philosophers. Because suicide and depression are closely linked, and depression has become a more treatable disorder, the mental health professions have targeted suicide as an unfortunate outcome to be combated through the treatment of mental illness. But like all treatments, treatment of suicidal illness may fail. When this happens, survivors may initiate a lawsuit, blaming the mental health professionals for malpractice. This presents a paradox.

Because suicide is "self-murder," why should anyone else, other than the perpetrator, be held accountable for it? Indeed, prior to the Second World War, the law agreed with this position: whatever may have gone amiss with the treater's approach, the patient's suicidal act—seen then as, indeed, autonomous—was the ultimate, defining cause of death. Consequently, the doctor could not be held liable. Subsequent shifts in legal theory came to hold treaters accountable for the suicide, using the rationale "Had it not been for the negligent treatment, the suicide would not have occurred."

Although the certainty implicit in this assumption may bemuse the reader familiar with what one scholar described as the "web of cause and chance" that leads to suicide, current malpractice litigation against mental health providers in cases of suicide now follows this reasoning. Some background may be useful here.

In purely legal terms, medical malpractice has taken place when, as a direct result of medical negligence, some harm occurs. Four elements are required for a finding of malpractice: a duty of care existed, the care was negligent, harm resulted, and the negligence directly (the law says "proximately") caused the harm.

But this technical description scants the emotional wellsprings of such litigation. Those who understand and work in the litigation arena know well that many acts of negligence go unlitigated, or even unnoticed. Actual malpractice litigation appears empirically to result from the malignant synergy of a bad outcome, for any reason, and what might be termed *bad feelings*. If, for the moment, we assume this to be true, we can readily see that suicide is certainly one of the worst human outcomes and one that is likely to leave some of the worst possible feelings in its wake. Thus, we can grasp the reason for the finding by malpractice insurers that the most common grounds for malpractice litigation in the mental health fields is suicide.

What sorts of "bad feelings" are brought by suicide? One is guilt. Survivors berate themselves: "We should have done more, acted sooner." Another is rage at clinician unavailability, insensitivity, and lack of response; suits have been filed over doctors' failure to return telephone calls. Grief after suicide is normal but not, for many, tolerable; blaming, distraction, and defensive reactions are familiar grief alternatives, realizable through litigation.

Surprise is another bad feeling. Baffled by the ultimate human mystery, survivors of suicide may say, "We knew he was depressed, but it never occurred to us he would kill himself." Being surprised may make people angry; litigation may express the feeling. Finally, families who have suffered a suicide describe the withdrawal of friends and colleagues who "don't know what to say" to the survivors. Clinicians in emotional conflict and distress about a patient's suicide also may withdraw, leaving the survivors emotionally abandoned. This bad feeling may also trigger litigation.

An important but complex response to suicide is the clinician's outreach to the family or other survivors. Such "debriefing" may help the survivors to resolve some of the bad feelings and to further the normal grief process that constitutes the core of recovery from the loss. Risk managers and malpractice defense attorneys often maintain a jaundiced view of this intervention, fearing that—should litigation ensue—the case may be compromised: the grief-stricken treater, swept away by emotion, may blurt, "It's all my fault!" or "It was your abuse that killed him!" or "Don't blame us, we did everything we could!" or some other nonhealing response. Yet experienced risk managers understand the value of such outreach in defusing the passions aroused by suicide. Clearly, the risk managers or insurers should be consulted before such outreach, but the value of the practice is well established, not only in risk management terms but also as a humanitarian aid to the grief-stricken.

Clinicians know well that the most closely watched patient can still commit suicide, that patients do not always reveal their intentions, and that all the medical and psychological treatments in the world may not suffice. Yet the larger society seems to make a curious distinction between medical and psychiatric problems. If someone dies of a serious form of cancer, no one is particularly surprised; the public understands that cancer's effects are, at present, more powerful than the bulk of our treatment armamentarium. But when someone commits suicide—even though the underlying illness may be the psychiatric equivalent of cancer—the public often assumes that it was somehow preventable, or at least that "someone should have done something." This popular attitude may, of course, constitute part of a jury's reasoning during a malpractice trial.

Clinicians have attitudes of their own that may pose problems. Asking about suicide—indeed, thinking about suicide—raises anxiety, and clinician denial may prevent appropriate exploration of the issue. Because some patients use suicidal threats to manipulate or control clinicians, resentment toward the patient may cloud clinical judgment. The patient's depressive posture of hopelessness may be associated with a curious contagion: despite the general treatability of depression, the clinician comes to feel hopeless about the patient's treatment and fails to follow through on necessary interventions. Involuntary hospitalization, required in some instances, is always a coercive and uncomfortable step for treaters, who may attempt to avoid it inappropriately.

One subtle pitfall is created by the common human reactions of identification. A patient who seems to be a solid citizen with a secure job and family has led the clinician in some cases to identify with the patient and falsely assume that such a person could not commit suicide.

The present volume, by one of the giants in the field of forensic psychiatry, attempts to place all the aforementioned considerations into a cohesive whole, to aid the clinician to cope effectively with both the risk of suicide and the risks of subsequent litigation. Rich in clinically based advice and drawing from vast clinical experience, this textbook will prove an essential aid to clinicians confronting the ultimate.

Thomas G. Gutheil, M.D.
Professor of Psychiatry
Harvard Medical School

PREFACE

This book is written by a clinician for clinicians who evaluate and treat patients at risk for suicide. It is indeed the rare clinician who does not struggle, even agonize, over the complex, difficult task of assessing and managing the risk of suicide in such patients.

The case examples are fictional, distilled from more than 40 years of clinical practice. The discussion that follows each case example is based on my clinical experience and a thorough examination of peer-reviewed and evidence-based suicide literature and research. Writing about suicide is a task made daunting by the availability of too much information. I have relied on my review of the professional literature and the publisher's extensive peer review process to temper the inevitable clinical biases that accompany a single-author book.

I employ the format of a detailed case example followed by a clinical discussion and clinically based risk management guidelines. In each chapter, a case example is presented in some detail as a full complement to the discussion that follows, rather than merely serving as an introduction. Clinical misadventures are avoided as a means of illustration. I much prefer to demonstrate sound clinical suicide risk assessment and management through the provision of good patient care.

Relying on the evidence-based literature and research, I try to present the best clinical practices in assessment and management of patients at risk for suicide. I do not, however, arrogate to myself the role of arbiter regarding what constitutes best clinical practice. Best practice is often a moving target. It is, to a significant extent, defined by the individual clinician based on training, knowledge, and experience as well as the severity and complexity of the patient's illness. Nonetheless, basic principles of clinical assessment and management exist that apply to the care of patients at risk for suicide.

Thus, it should be understood that I am not proposing a standard of care by which clinicians should be held responsible. States vary in their definition of the standard of care required of a mental health professional. The specific legal language, usually "care ordinarily employed" or the "reasonable, prudent practitioner," is applied to the unique fact pattern of individual cases. The law does not require the mental health professional to provide ideal, best practice or even good patient care. The clinician's legal duty is to provide adequate patient care.

The book suggests guidelines for clinical risk management whose primary purpose is to enhance and support good patient care. These guidelines may also help the clinician to avoid litigation or provide a sound legal defense, if the clinician is sued for malpractice. Although it is a reality that clinicians are frequently sued after a patient attempts or commits suicide, there is no place for destructive defensive practices that demean the clinician's professionalism and potentially harm patients.

It is my desire that the case examples, the discussion, and the clinically based risk management guidelines will prove helpful to practitioners in the challenging clinical task of assessing and managing the patient at risk for suicide.

ACKNOWLEDGMENTS

Every book is a struggle, every line a labor of love. Yet no book can be born without the help of others.

I want to express my sincere appreciation to Robert E. Hales, M.D., Editor-in-Chief of American Psychiatric Publishing, Inc., for his unstinting support of my authorship.

Many thanks to Carol A. Westrick, my administrative and editorial assistant, for her diligence and competence, which made the production of this book possible.

I would like to recognize Lynne Lucas-Dreiss, A.P.R.N.-P.M.H., and Susanne Goetz, L.C.S.W.-C., for their review of portions of the manuscript.

My deepest gratitude I extend to my wife, who, with great patience and constant support, has enabled my recidivist penchant to write.

Robert I. Simon, M.D.

SUICIDE AND MALPRACTICE LITIGATION

Errors in judgment must occur in the practice of an art which consists largely of balancing probabilities.

  Sir William Osler, *Aequanimitas,* 38

As a litigant I should dread a lawsuit beyond almost anything short of sickness or death.

  Justice Learned Hand, Before the Association of the
  Bar of the City of New York, 1926

Litigation, n. A machine which you go into as a pig and come out as a sausage.

  Ambrose Bierce, *The Devil's Dictionary*

INTRODUCTION

It is said that there are only two kinds of clinical psychiatrists: those who have had patients commit suicide and those who will. The assessment and management of suicide risk is one of the most complex, difficult, and challenging clinical tasks in psychiatry. When a patient commits suicide, a lawsuit may follow. Patient suicides account for a large number of malpractice suits filed against psychiatrists and the highest percentages of settlements and verdicts

1

covered by professional liability insurers (American Psychiatric Association–Sponsored Professional Liability Insurance Program 2002). Patient suicide is an unavoidable occupational hazard of psychiatric practice that is accompanied by increased malpractice liability exposure. Although the potential for malpractice suits remains high for psychiatrists who treat suicidal and violent patients, the plaintiff's success rate of these and other malpractice actions is only 2 or 3 out of every 10 litigated claims.

A Psychiatrist's Purchasing Group workshop presented at the American Psychiatric Association (2002) annual meeting identified patient suicide as the most common insurance loss from April 2001 through March 2002. The categories of claims involving suicide or attempted suicide were as follows:

- Failure to provide proper assessment and management in high-volume patient settings
- Failure to construct a comprehensive treatment plan
- Failure to perform comprehensive suicide risk assessment
- Failure to obtain past treatment records
- Failure to hospitalize
- Failure to make a rational diagnosis based on the history and evaluation
- Failure to record suicide risk assessments

Generally, malpractice claims against psychiatrists for a patient's suicide are brought under the following theories of negligence:

- Failure to properly diagnose the patient's condition
- Failure to adequately assess suicide risk
- Failure to implement an appropriate treatment plan (use reasonable treatment interventions and safety precautions)

Ordinarily, only the patient with whom the psychiatrist has established a doctor-patient relationship can file a malpractice claim. No duty is owed to any family members. However, wrongful-death statutes allow survivors to recover money damages for a death caused by another person's wrongful act. The right to sue for wrongful death belongs to individuals who suffer financial or other loss because of the patient's death.

Families may bring malpractice suits under the Federal Tort

Claims Act if the decedent was employed by the United States government and the government is accused of wrongdoing. This federal statute permits the government to be sued like any citizen in similar circumstances and is an exception to the doctrine of sovereign immunity.

UNDERSTANDING MALPRACTICE CLAIMS

Courts evaluate the psychiatrist's assessment and management of the patient who attempts or commits suicide to determine the *reasonableness* of the suicide risk assessment process and whether the patient's suicide attempt or suicide was foreseeable (Simon 2001). Courts generally assume that if the suicide was foreseeable, it was preventable. Foreseeability is a legal term of art rather than a scientific construct. It is a commonsense, probabilistic concept. There is, however, an imperfect fit between legal and medical terminology. *Foreseeability* is defined as the reasonable anticipation that harm or injury is likely to result from certain acts or omissions (Black 1999). The law does not require defendants to "foresee events which are merely possible but only those that are reasonably foreseeable" (*Hairston v. Alexander Tank and Equip. Co.* 1984). Foreseeability is not to be confused with the predictability of suicide, for which no professional standard exists. Moreover, foreseeability is not the same as preventability. In hindsight, a suicide may have been preventable, but not foreseeable at the time of the assessment.

Psychiatric malpractice is medical malpractice. Malpractice lawsuits are civil, not criminal, actions. Malpractice suits allege negligence, not intentional wrongdoing. A malpractice claim contains four basic elements, sometimes referred to as the "four D's" (see Table 1–1).

DUTY OF CARE

A legal duty of care derives from the existence of a doctor-patient relationship. Usually, a psychiatrist-patient relationship is created knowingly and voluntarily by both parties. No duty of care is owed to a patient unless a psychiatrist-patient relationship exists. However, a psychiatrist-patient relationship may be established unwittingly. Unless working in an emergency department or a similar setting where

Table 1–1.   Basic elements of a malpractice claim

A doctor-patient relationship must exist, creating the following components:

- **DUTY** of care
- **DEVIATION** from the standard of care
- **DAMAGE** to the patient
- **DIRECT** damage caused by the deviation from the standard of care

Source.   Adapted from Simon RI: *Concise Guide to Psychiatry and Law for the Clinician,* 3rd Edition. Washington, DC, American Psychiatric Publishing, 2001. Used with permission.

psychiatrists are legally obligated to treat all individuals who seek help, the psychiatrist owes no duty of care to a prospective patient.

A court will determine whether a psychiatrist-patient relationship existed if a malpractice suit is brought. A number of actions may be construed as creating a doctor-patient relationship (see Table 1–2). Online consultations may create a doctor-patient relationship with a duty of care. Individuals at risk for suicide should not have their conditions assessed or managed online. Face-to-face psychiatrist-patient interaction is necessary. Psychiatrists may also be vicariously liable for the negligence of others under their supervision or employ. Vicarious liability is discussed further in Chapter 5, "Collaborative Treatment."

CASE EXAMPLE

A psychiatrist conducts a pre-employment examination of a 48-year-old single man. The examinee has been unemployed for more than a year. He admits to depression and to loss of appetite and weight but denies any suicidal intent, ideation, or plan. The psychiatrist provides some samples of antidepressant medications and refers the patient for psychiatric treatment. Two weeks following the interview, the examinee commits suicide by overdose. Empty containers of antidepressant sample packets are found in his apartment.

If a lawsuit is brought against the psychiatrist, the court may find that the psychiatrist created a doctor-patient relationship with a continuing duty of care based on the provision of medication.

Table 1–2. Actions by therapists that may create a doctor-patient relationship

- Practicing online consultation
- Giving clinical advice to prospective patients, friends, and neighbors
- Making psychological interpretations
- Writing a prescription or providing sample medications
- Supervising treatment by a nonmedical therapist
- Having a lengthy telephone conversation with a prospective patient
- Treating an unseen patient by mail
- Giving a patient an appointment
- Telling walk-in patients that they will be seen
- Covering for a psychiatrist or other mental health professional
- Providing treatment during an evaluation or consultation

Source. Adapted from Simon RI: *Clinical Psychiatry and the Law,* 2nd Edition. Washington, DC, American Psychiatric Press, 1992. Used with permission.

STANDARD OF CARE

The standard of care, like the duty of care, is a legal concept. States define by statute the standard of care required of physicians. The precise definition of the standard of care varies for each state. The specific statutory language is applied to the facts of a malpractice case to determine whether the patient's treatment was negligent. For example, in *Stepakoff v. Kantar* (1985), the standard of care applied by the court in a suicide case was the "duty to exercise that degree of skill and care ordinarily employed in similar circumstances by other psychiatrists." The duty of care was that of the "average psychiatrist." The standard of care for assessing and managing suicide risk is discussed in greater detail in Chapter 2, "Suicide Risk Assessment."

The standard of care is determined by expert testimony, practice guidelines, the psychiatric literature, hospital policies and procedures, and authoritative sources. Managed-care protocols and utilization review procedures are entrepreneurial-based; they are not necessarily clinically authoritative.

Guidelines and policies are general concepts that must be applied to highly specific fact patterns of complex cases in litigation. The standard of care is not a fixed legal concept.

Official practice guidelines are not static but evolve and change according to new developments in practice and science, requiring frequent updating. Studies show that no more than 90% of practice guidelines are valid after 3.6 years (Shekelle et al. 2001). At 5.8 years, half of such guidelines are outdated. Thus, sponsoring organizations issue disclaimers that practice guidelines do not represent the standard of care. The American Psychiatric Association (2003) has published "Practice Guideline for the Assessment and Treatment of Patients With Suicidal Behaviors."

The standard of care must be distinguished from the quality of care (Simon 1997). Quality of care refers to the adequacy of total care that the patient receives from the psychiatrist and other health care professionals and providers, including third-party payers. The quality of care is also influenced by the patient's health care decisions and the allocation and availability of psychiatric services. The quality of care that is provided by the psychiatrist may be below, equal to, or even exceed the acceptable standard of psychiatric care.

CASE EXAMPLE

A psychiatrist is treating a 34-year-old female patient with bipolar disorder. The patient is seen once a week for supportive psychotherapy and medication management. A working alliance is present. A number of medication regimens have been tried, producing only moderate improvement. The patient is referred for consultation regarding other possible psychopharmacological interventions. Adequate suicide risk assessments are performed and documented that indicate that the patient is at moderate risk for suicide. The psychiatrist considers hospitalizing the patient. However, the patient rejects hospitalization. She does not meet commitment criteria for involuntary hospitalization. A second consultation is obtained. Based on the psychiatric consultant's suggestions, the psychiatrist and patient agree to continue outpatient treatment, implementing changes in medications and in the frequency of visits. Within hours of the session, the patient commits suicide. A malpractice suit is filed against the psychiatrist for negligent treatment.

Generally, a psychiatrist who exercises the "skill and care ordinarily employed" by the "average psychiatrist" will not be held liable for any resulting injury. Mistakes alone are not a basis for liability, if the standard of care has not been breached. In the case example, the judge or jury will consider that the psychiatrist documented adequate suicide risk assessments, obtained consultations regarding treatment, considered both voluntary and involuntary hospitalization, and maintained a therapeutic alliance with the patient. If the court finds that the psychiatrist did not deviate from the standard of care, then no basis for a malpractice claim exists.

Although a lawsuit may follow a patient's suicide, the suicide by itself does not establish that the psychiatrist was negligent. In *Siebert v. Fink* (2001), the court held that a clinician is not automatically liable when a patient commits suicide, provided that careful examination and assessment took place that directed the decision-making process. Experts for the plaintiff (estate of deceased patient) and for the defendant psychiatrist will testify regarding the standard of care provided by the psychiatrist.

The "skill and care ordinarily employed" standard is undergoing change. Tort law generally allows physicians to set their own standard of care; for example, the practice of the "average physician" is the measure applied to negligence claims. Defendants in ordinary tort claims are expected to use reasonable care under the same or similar circumstances. Physicians, however, have needed only to conform their provision of care to the customs of their peers (Peters 2000).

An increasing number of states are rejecting the "medical custom" standard in favor of the "reasonable, prudent physician" standard (Peters 2000). This standard goes beyond a statistical "head count." For example, even if 99 of 100 psychiatrists do not perform and document adequate suicide risk assessments, such omission still would be negligent practice and potentially harmful to patients. Courts have held that negligence cannot be excused simply because others practice the same kind of negligence (Simon 2002). Thus, actual practice must bear a relationship to a reasonable, prudent standard of care.

RESPECTED-MINORITY RULE

Innovation is critically important to new diagnostic and treatment developments in psychiatry (Simon 1993). American psychiatry has welcomed credible treatments and procedures that have held promise for the alleviation of mental suffering. The causes of most mental disorders are unknown. A professional climate that encourages innovation in research and treatment offers the most productive opportunities for progress.

In some jurisdictions, it is sufficient to show that a treatment or procedure is supported by a respectable minority of therapists (Reisner and Slobogin 1990). Unless egregious, treatments and procedures that would not be employed by most psychiatrists may fall within the *respected-minority rule*. This rule states that a psychiatrist is free to choose from any of the available schools of treatment, even ones that most psychiatrists would not use, if a respected minority of psychiatrists would employ the same treatment and procedures (Malcolm 1988). If the psychiatrist deviates from recognized guidelines and procedures, the reason for the deviation should be documented.

DIRECT CAUSATION

If a psychiatrist deviates from the standard of care in the diagnosis and treatment of a patient, no malpractice liability can be found unless the harm to the patient is the direct result of the deviation from the standard of care.

CASE EXAMPLE

A therapist who is treating a 28-year-old female patient with borderline personality disorder leaves for a vacation. The therapist asks a psychiatrist to cover her practice while she is away. The therapist provides the covering psychiatrist with a brief history of the patient. The patient has had suicidal ideation from time to time but has made no suicide attempts.

The patient, upset by the therapist's absence, calls the covering psychiatrist frequently. Exasperated by the number of telephone calls, the psychiatrist stops returning the calls from the patient. The psychiatrist's answering machine directs patients to the nearest emergency facility if a "true emergency arises." The patient becomes frantic, drinks three double martinis, and, for the first time, uses cocaine. She attempts to drown herself in a bathtub. The patient is found by friends, is brought to an emergency department, and is hospitalized. Six weeks later, a malpractice suit is filed against the therapist and the psychiatrist, alleging negligent treatment and abandonment.

Although the defense attorney concedes that the psychiatrist's failure to respond to the patient's calls may constitute substandard care, he argues that the patient's suicide attempt was the result of combining alcohol with the first-time use of an illegal "street drug," cocaine. The combination of alcohol and cocaine was an "intervening, superseding" cause that led to destabilization of the patient, for which the psychiatrist cannot be held responsible. The patient had access to emergency care, if she felt she required it. The defense attorney claims that the psychiatrist's failure to respond to the patient's telephone calls was not the direct cause of the patient's suicide attempt. However, the plaintiff's attorney argues that "but for" the psychiatrist's negligent coverage of the patient, the patient would not have attempted suicide. The patient's suicide was the direct result of the "double abandonment" by the therapist and the covering psychiatrist. The case settles for a nominal amount of money.

In *Paddock v. Chacko* (1988/1989), a Florida appeals court concluded that the psychiatrist was not liable for the self-inflicted injuries of a patient he had seen only once. The patient had placed herself in her parents' care and custody. The parents disregarded the psychiatrist's recommendation that their daughter be hospitalized. The parents' unwillingness to heed the psychiatrist's recommendation represented a "superseding" factor that intervened between the patient's injuries and the psychiatrist's care.

DAMAGE

Even if a deviation in the standard of care occurs, legal liability cannot be assessed when there is no harm to the patient. The courts rely on the testimony of expert witnesses to determine the presence or absence of harm to the plaintiff. However, the determination of emotional injury can be difficult because psychiatric disorders or conditions often preexist. Also, the emotional injury claimed may be the result of the natural progression of the patient's psychiatric disorder rather than harm caused by the psychiatrist's alleged negligence.

CASE EXAMPLE

A 53-year-old woman experiences recurrent major depression and suicidal ideation. She is being treated in a "split treatment" arrangement by a psychiatrist, who monitors medication, and a master's-level psychologist, who conducts the psychotherapy. The psychiatrist has a high-volume practice in which he sees a patient for medication management every 15 minutes from 8:00 A.M. to 5:00 P.M., with an hour off for lunch and for returning telephone calls.

The psychiatrist has had a difficult day, falling behind in his appointments. The patient is angry, having waited for more than an hour. The psychiatrist determines that the patient is stable and quickly renews her medications. Because the psychiatrist is rushed, he erroneously prescribes an antihypertensive medication instead of her usual antidepressant drug. The names of the two drugs are very similar.

The patient does not recognize the error until after she takes a few doses. She notices an increase in her depression and suicidal ideation. She is unable to go to work. The patient discovers that the medication differs in color and shape from her usual prescription. She calls the psychiatrist, who, upon checking his records, acknowledges the error and apologizes. He orders a refill of the correct medication. The patient's depression improves, and her suicidal ideation subsides.

The psychiatrist's failure to check the patient's medication records before writing a prescription is a deviation in the standard of care. However, if a malpractice suit were to be brought, the damage (physical and psychic harm) experienced, although significant to the patient, would be insufficient to support monetary damages. Most lawyers would not accept such a case.

If the patient is successful in suing a psychiatrist, the damages awarded are commensurate with the extent of the injury sustained. The harm may be physical, psychological, or both. Damages are usually classified as compensatory, nominal, or financial (Simon 1992). In a successful malpractice action, compensatory damages are normally awarded. This type of award represents the amount of compensation necessary to replace and restore the loss or injury to the plaintiff. Compensatory damages include, among other awards, payment for impairment of work ability, for past and future loss of earnings, for caregiving, for medical expenses, and for intangible damages such as physical and mental pain and suffering, loss of normal life, inconvenience, and humiliation.

The courts may make a distinction between general and special damages. Special damages include medical expenses, past and future lost wages, and other out-of-pocket expenses. The cost of litigation and attorney's fees are borne by the litigants separately and are not part of the damages assessed, unless otherwise provided by law.

Nominal damages are awarded in cases in which an actual or technical wrong has been suffered that cannot be translated into dollar terms, such as when certain legal rights are violated. The fact finder may make a symbolic award of one dollar. Wrongdoers are legally responsible for all of the natural and direct consequences of their acts. In some extreme situations, punitive damages may be awarded.

In a malpractice action, punitive damages are awarded only when the defendant's conduct is considered willful, wanton, malicious, or reckless. The purpose of punitive damages is to punish the wrongdoer rather than to compensate the victim. Mere negligence is insufficient to merit an award of punitive damages.

Malpractice suits require plaintiffs to prove their allegations by a preponderance of the evidence. Preponderance of the evidence is defined as the weight of evidence (51% versus 49%) for the plaintiff to prevail. However, the law does not attempt to assign a percentage to the standard of proof.

Because malpractice cases are determined by a preponderance of the evidence, the outcome of these suits is often difficult to predict. Defendants who perceive themselves to be vulnerable to heavy damages may choose to settle for a given amount rather than risk open-ended liability.

In summary, a malpractice suit brought against a psychiatrist for an attempted or actual suicide of a patient must contain all four basic elements (the four D's) to prevail.

"VOLITIONAL ACTS" OF SUICIDE

When patients kill themselves, are they not the agents of their own deaths, regardless of negligence (Appelbaum 2000)? In malpractice claims arising out of attempted or actual suicide, the patient or a representative must establish that the psychiatrist's negligence was the proximate cause of the suicide or attempted suicide. A patient's "volitional act" of suicide may be considered an intervening factor, thus relieving the psychiatrist of liability, if the patient's act was not reasonably foreseeable.

For instance, after conducting a thorough assessment of a patient, including reviewing past records and consulting with other knowledgeable sources, a psychiatrist could reasonably conclude that the patient does not represent a significant suicide risk. If the patient were to commit suicide without a warning or a reasonable sign of intent, then the death would likely be considered "unforeseeable." The patient's unexplained behavior could be considered an "intervening cause," severing the chain of causation between the psychiatrist and the patient's suicide.

A patient may be considered contributorily negligent if he or she fails to participate reasonably in treatment and that failure is the proximate cause of injury or death. For example, in *Skar v. City of Lincoln* (1979), the patient failed to cooperate in any manner, preventing the psychiatrist from obtaining a case history or assessing the actual suicide risk. The patient injured his spine after attempting to jump out of a window. The court refused to hold the psychiatrist liable for the patient's injuries, stating that the patient has a duty to cooperate with the psychiatrist to the extent he is able.

In *Weathers v. Pilkinton* (1988), the majority opinion of the Court of Appeals of Tennessee held that a patient's suicide was an independent, intervening cause unless the patient "did not know and understand the nature of his suicidal act and, therefore, did not have willful and intelligent purpose to accomplish this." In this case, a wrongful-death action was brought against a physician who allegedly failed to take appropriate steps to prevent his patient from committing suicide. The trial judge held that the suicide of the patient was an independent, intervening cause and directed a verdict for the physician. The appeals court affirmed.

Beahrs (1990) stated that psychiatric patients incur legal duties in the health care context. These duties include the provision of accurate and complete information and cooperation with treatment within the boundaries of informed consent. General duties that apply to all citizens, but are particularly applicable to patients in the mental health context, include respect for the physical integrity of oneself, respect for others and for their property, and obeying the law.

However, because of psychiatric impairment, there are limits to how much responsibility the law will impute to a patient. Such limits are illustrated in the case of *Cowan v. Doering* (1987/1988). In *Cowan,* the trial judge refused to submit to the jury the question of the patient's contributory negligence toward her own injuries. The patient, diagnosed as having a borderline personality disorder, jumped from her hospital window. She sued, contending that her physician was negligent for not ordering a "suicide watch." The experts all agreed on her diagnosis, but differed in their opinions concerning whether the patient made a genuine suicide attempt or a manipulative gesture to gain attention. The jury awarded the plaintiff $600,000 in compensatory damages. This decision was affirmed on appeal. The court noted that suicidal patients whose judgment is adversely affected by mental illness cannot have their conduct judged by the standards of care and risk assessment used for rational adults. The physician had a duty to prevent or at least guard against the patient's suicidal act, including the anticipation of irrational behavior such as jumping from a window.

In *Hobart v. Shin* (1998), the Illinois Supreme Court held that a patient who committed suicide by overdose of a prescribed antidepressant was contributorily negligent in her death. The court opined that Ms. Hobart's behavior was premeditated and deliberate in leaving her home to check into a motel using a fictitious name and refusing to contact her doctors. The court further held that severe mental illness that makes the patient incapable of being contributorily negligent precludes inquiry into the patient's contribution to negligent behavior. In Illinois, if a person behaves negligently and is more than 50% responsible for the injury suffered, recovery for damages is not permitted.

Benke (2000) noted that competence, the capacity to make autonomous decisions for which one may be held legitimately responsible, is the central issue in contributory negligence. The fact that the patient is mentally ill, involuntarily hospitalized, or engaged in violent acts related to mental illness does not necessarily equate with the legal capacity to be contributorily negligent. The law's presumption favors patient autonomy. Benke suggested that the trier of fact should be instructed to assess the individual's capacity to act autonomously and to determine whether the individual acted according to the appropriate standard of care.

From a risk management perspective, psychiatrists should not look to the suicidal patient's "volitional" act as a defense in a malpractice suit. The psychiatric patient's mental impairment almost always voids the psychiatrist's defense of contributory negligence. Timely, contemporaneously documented systematic suicide risk assessments combined with appropriate clinical interventions provide the best malpractice defense.

DEFENSES TO A MALPRACTICE CLAIM

The best defenses to a malpractice claim are preemptive. Gutheil and Appelbaum (2000) identified the basis of malpractice litigation to be the result of a synergy between a bad clinical outcome for any reason and bad feelings. They found that bad feelings leading to litigation include guilt, particularly in survivors of suicide; rage; surprise; betrayal; and psychological abandonment. Good care may trigger a lawsuit in the presence of a patient's bad feelings. On the other hand, substandard care may not evoke litigation in the presence of a working alliance with the patient.

Psychiatrists, perhaps more than any other medical specialists, should be expert in establishing good working alliances with patients. This, however, may not always be possible. For example, financial hardship for the survivors may lead to a malpractice suit, especially if life insurance coverage is unavailable because of a suicide exclusion clause in the policy. When suicide occurs during the first episode of a patient's depression, the family is unprepared and shocked, underscoring the element of surprise in initiation of a lawsuit. Of course, any patient can sue, for rational or irrational reasons.

A number of valid legal defenses may be available against a malpractice claim for patient suicide (see Table 1–3). Although each legal defense is case specific, two of the more common defenses deserve mention. First, all civil lawsuits are subject to a statute of limitations requiring that legal action be commenced within a prescribed period of time following the discovery or occurrence of the alleged negligent act. If a lawsuit is not filed within the requisite time period, the suit is barred unless a recognized exception exists that suspends the statute of limitations (*Bolen v. United States* [1989]).

Table 1–3.   Legal defenses in malpractice litigation
of suicide cases

• Exercise of reasonable professional judgment and compliance
with the standard of care
• Determination of suicide not foreseeable
• Justified allowance of movement ("open-door policy")
• Least restrictive alternative
• Superseding, intervening acts
• Government immunity
• Statute of limitations expiration
• Contributory negligence
• Other[a]

[a]Depending on fact-specific case pattern.

The time within which a lawsuit can be filed is governed by the laws
of the state where the suit is being brought (King 1986).

The use of reasonable professional judgment is a mainstay defense. The credibility of this defense depends on compliance with
the standard of care as documented by the psychiatrist's own
records. For example, in *Centeno v. City of New York* (1975/1976), the
court ruled that the decision to release a patient from the hospital
and place him on convalescent outpatient status, during which time
he committed suicide, was not negligent but an act of reasonable
medical judgment. As a general rule, a psychiatrist who exercises
reasonable judgment and care in compliance with accepted medical practice will not be held liable for a resulting injury (Simon
2001).

If after adequate psychiatric evaluation no evidence of a foreseeable suicide risk is found, courts have held in favor of the clinician.
For example, in *Wilson v. State* (1985), the court held that no liability
could be imposed for the granting of grounds privileges to a patient
who later committed suicide. The defendant knew the patient's history through prior treatment records. Nothing in his current behavior indicated that the patient was contemplating suicide.

In recent years, a more liberal, open-door policy has evolved in
the treatment and management of suicidal patients. The open-door
policy is one aspect of the greater autonomy accorded all patients,
but especially psychiatric patients. Some courts have not imposed
liability because of the reasonableness of the decision to implement

the open-door policy with certain patients. These courts have viewed the open-door policy, when reasonably used, as an extension of professional judgment and a viable treatment approach. For instance, in *Johnson v. United States* (1976/1978/1981), a discharged patient committed suicide after killing his brother-in-law and wounding his wife. Although the court acknowledged that an open-door policy creates a higher potential for danger, it noted that

> The court is aware that some psychiatrists adhere to the older, more custodial approach. However, it has been proved to the court's satisfaction that the open door policy and the judgment balancing test are an accepted method of treatment. Therefore, no liability can arise merely because a psychiatrist favors the newer over the older approach.

The least restrictive alternative, a related concept, may be a valid defense in suicide litigation. A number of states require that patients be treated in the least restrictive treatment environment consistent with their clinical needs (Perlin 1989). Robertson (1991) identifies two other defenses, contributory and comparative negligence, that can serve as either a complete or a partial bar to defendant liability. The theory of *contributory negligence* states that if the plaintiff was negligent to any degree, he or she is barred from recovery. Because of the harshness of this rule, only a few states still use contributory negligence. As noted previously, Illinois enacted a modified contributory negligence statute. If a person is more than 50% contributorily negligent, damages cannot be recovered. The modern trend has been toward *comparative negligence,* which reduces the plaintiff's recovery by the percentage of his or her fault. With the shift from contributory to comparative negligence, there is a greater tendency to consider the patient's behavior and responsibility in committing suicide (Slovenko 2002). Under a comparative negligence statute, an accident victim receiving a $1,000 award who was 20% at fault would recover only $800.

Governmental immunity is a defense in some suicide cases. It is an expression of the traditional legal principle that federal and state governments cannot be sued without their consent. Professionals employed by federal, state, or municipal agencies or facilities may be protected from liability by some form of governmental immunity (Reisner and Slobogin 1990; see, e.g., *Miller v. State* [1987]).

Whether absolute or qualified, governmental immunity is governed by statute.

OTHER LEGAL ACTIONS

Although civil claims typically arise because of negligence, they may also result from a breach of contract or from an intentional tort. A *breach of contract* can occur if a patient undertakes treatment based on an agreement in which the psychiatrist promises some result but then fails to produce it. An *intentional tort* is any act willfully committed that the law has declared as wrong (e.g., treating patients without their consent). A claim may be based on violation of a patient's civil rights pursuant to federal and state law (e.g., discriminatory treatment practices against institutionalized patients). Psychiatrists can also become embroiled in administrative, licensure, and ethics proceedings.

NATIONAL PRACTITIONER DATA BANK

On September 1, 1990, the National Practitioner Data Bank, established by the Health Care Quality Improvement Act of 1986, went into effect. The data bank tracks disciplinary actions, malpractice judgments, and settlements against physicians, dentists, and other health care professionals (Johnson 1991).

Hospitals, health maintenance organizations (HMOs), managed-care organizations (MCOs), professional societies, state medical boards, and other health care organizations are required to report any disciplinary action taken against providers lasting more than 30 days. MCOs do not report physicians to the data bank if they do not follow treatment protocols. When a physician is deselected for a quality-of-care issue, the MCO must report it (American Psychiatric Association 1999). Disciplinary actions include limitation, suspension, or revocation of privileges or professional society membership. Medical malpractice payments account for approximately three-quarters of reports made to the data bank. Under the Health Care Quality Improvement Act, immunity from liability is granted for health care entities and providers making peer review reports in good faith (Walzer 1990).

Hospitals are required to request information from the data bank concerning all physicians applying for staff privileges. Every 2 years, a query of the data bank is required concerning each physician or other practitioner on the hospital staff. Hospitals that do not comply with this requirement face loss of immunity for professional peer review activities.

The public does not have access to the data bank. Plaintiff's attorneys can have access to the data bank only if they prove that the hospital failed to query the data bank about the physician in question. The information obtained can be used only to sue the hospital for negligent credentialing. Physicians can request information from the data bank about their own files. A recent study found that hospital reporting of actions taken regarding clinical privileges from 1991 to 1995 declined, raising concerns about underreporting (Baldwin et al. 1999).

IMPORTANCE OF CLINICALLY BASED RISK MANAGEMENT

Risk management is a reality of psychiatric practice, especially in the assessment and management of patients at risk for suicide. Risk management guidelines usually recommend *ideal* or *best* practices, whereas the actual standard of care is ordinary or reasonable care. Moreover, suicide cases are challenging, multifaceted, and nuanced, making it difficult to provide precise assessment and management guidelines.

Clinically based risk management is patient centered. It supports the treatment process and the therapeutic alliance (see Table 1–4). At a minimum, it follows the fundamental ethical principle in medicine of "first do no harm." A working knowledge of the legal regulation of psychiatry enables the psychiatrist to manage clinical-legal issues more effectively. Clinically based risk management also provides the psychiatrist with a significant measure of practice comfort that permits continued maintenance of the treatment role with patients at risk for suicide.

Good clinical care is always the best risk management. For example, performing systematic suicide risk assessments that inform

Table 1–4. Basic elements of clinically based risk management

• Patient centered
• Clinically appropriate
• Supportive of treatment and the therapeutic alliance
• Working knowledge of legal regulation of psychiatry
• Clinical management of psychiatric-legal issues
• Wellness, not legal agenda
• "First do no harm" ethic

treatment and management interventions is good clinical care and the essence of clinically based risk management. Documentation of the risk assessments supports good patient care and substantiates clinical judgment (American Psychiatric Association 2002). It is also useful to know that courts have held that what is not recorded by a physician is considered not to have been performed (Simon 2001). Good clinical care of patients at suicidal risk requires full clinical commitment to the patient's evaluation, treatment, and management. This principle holds true for collaborative treatment relationships with other mental health professionals.

Defensive practices that are not clinically tempered usually interfere with the patient's treatment and undermine the therapeutic alliance. Defensive psychiatry may involve acts or omissions that are not for the benefit of the patient but are undertaken to avoid malpractice liability or to provide a legal defense against a malpractice claim. For example, an excessive reliance on suicide prevention contracts ("no-harm contracts") may be the result of the clinician's attempt to reduce the anxiety associated with treating suicidal patients (Miller et al. 1998). Some clinicians erroneously believe that the suicide prevention contract legally binds the patient to refrain from self-harm. The instrument is a clinical, not a legal, contract (Simon 1999). Moreover, there is no evidence that such contracts reduce suicide risk. Suicide prevention contracts may falsely reassure the clinician, taking the place of adequate suicide risk assessment and thereby increasing the patient's risk for suicide (see Chapter 3, "Suicide Prevention Contracts").

Defensive practices can be divided into so-called positive and negative practices (Simon 1985). Positive defensive practice involve procedures and treatments designed to prevent or limit liability, such as hospitalizing a patient at risk for suicide who could be effectively treated as an outpatient. Negative defensive practices are attempts to avoid procedures or treatments out of a fear of being sued, even though the patient may benefit from these interventions. For example, forgoing the use of electroconvulsive therapy (ECT) when it is indicated for a severely depressed patient at high risk for suicide is unduly defensive, even unethical. In fact, the number of lawsuits brought for ECT use is low. The American Psychiatric Association Professional Liability Insurance Program does not charge higher premiums for psychiatrists who use ECT (Simon 1992). Psychiatrists should consider the liability risk of not using ECT when it is indicated for selected patients at high risk for suicide (see Chapter 6, "Inpatients").

Consulting with a colleague is good clinical practice when the clinician is confronted with complex diagnostic, treatment, and management issues regarding patients at significant risk for suicide. As a clinically based risk management technique, it supports and guides good clinical care by providing "a biopsy" of the standard of care. Moreover, the clinician's uncertainty, even anxiety, must be contained within reasonable limits in order to be an effective treater. The clinician should "never worry alone" (T.G. Gutheil, personal communication, December 2002). It also may be necessary to consult with a risk manager or an attorney.

Clinically based risk management helps the psychiatrist avoid defensive practices that are harmful to both the patient and the clinician. Each of the following chapters concludes with clinically based risk management guidelines.

CLINICALLY BASED RISK MANAGEMENT

- The psychiatrist must fully commit to the overall care and treatment of the patient at risk for suicide.
- Documentation of adequate suicide risk assessment supports good patient care and substantiates clinical judgment.
- Care must be exercised not to unwittingly create a doctor-patient relationship.

- Online assessment and management with respect to patients at risk for suicide should not be done. Face-to-face evaluation is clinically necessary.
- Mistakes alone are not a basis for liability, if the standard of care has not been breached.
- The psychiatrist should never worry alone. He or she should consider obtaining consultation when confronted by complex, difficult problems in treatment and management of patients at risk for suicide.
- Risk management should be clinically based and patient centered. It supports both the treatment process and the therapeutic alliance. At a minimum, it should not interfere with patient treatment.
- A working knowledge of the legal regulation of psychiatry enables the psychiatrist to manage clinical-legal issues more effectively.
- Some courts have held that what was not recorded was not done: document, document, document.
- Defensible cases are settled or lost as the result of inadequate or absent documentation.

REFERENCES

American Psychiatric Association: The National Practitioner Data Bank and MCOs, in Psychiatric Practice and Managed Care, Vol 5, No 5. Washington, DC, American Psychiatric Association, 1999, pp 1, 9–10

American Psychiatric Association: Risk management issues in psychiatric practice. Workshop presented at the American Psychiatric Association Psychiatrist's Purchasing Group, Inc. Component Workshop, 155th Annual Meeting, Philadelphia, PA, May 20, 2002

American Psychiatric Association–Sponsored Professional Liability Insurance Program: Retaining and discarding psychiatric records. Rx for Risk 10:1, 6–7, 2002

American Psychiatric Association: Practice guideline for the assessment and treatment of patients with suicidal behaviors. Am J Psychiatry 160 (suppl):1–60, 2003

Appelbaum PS: Patients' responsibility for their suicidal behavior. Psychiatr Serv 51:15–16, 2000

Baldwin LM, Hart LG, Oshel RG, et al: Hospital peer review and the National Practitioner Data Bank. JAMA 282:349–355, 1999

Beahrs JO: Legal duties of psychiatric patients. Bull Am Acad Psychiatry Law 18:189–202, 1990

Benke SH: Suicide, contributory negligence, and the idea of individual autonomy. J Am Acad Psychiatry Law 28:64–73, 2000

Black HC: Black's Law Dictionary, 7th Edition. St Paul, MN, West Group, 1999

Bolen v United States, 727 F. Supp. 1346 (D. Idaho 1989)

Centeno v City of New York, 48 A.D.2d 812, 369 N.Y.S.2d 710 (N.Y. App. Div. 1975), *aff'd,* 40 N.Y.2d 932, 358 N.E.2d, 520, 389 N.Y.S.2d 837 (1976)

Cowan v Doering, 215 N.J. Super. 484, 522 A.2d 444 (1987), *aff'd,* 111 N.J. 451, 545 A.2d 159 (1988)

Gutheil TG, Appelbaum PS: Clinical Handbook of Psychiatry and the Law, 3rd Edition. Philadelphia, PA, Lippincott Williams & Wilkins, 2000

Hairston v Alexander Tank and Equip. Co., 310 N.C. 227, 234, 311 S.E.2d 559, 565 (1984)

Hobart v Shin, 185 Ill. 2d 283, 705 N.E.2d 907 (1998)

Johnson ID: Reports to the National Practitioner Data Bank. JAMA 265:407–411, 1991

Johnson v United States, 409 F. Supp. 1283 (M.D. Fla. 1976), *rev'd,* 576 F.2d 606 (5th Cir. 1978), *cert. denied,* 451 U.S. 1019 (1981)

King JF: The Law of Medical Malpractice. St Paul, MN, West Group, 1986

Malcolm JG: Treatment choice and informed consent: current controversies, in Psychiatric Malpractice Litigation. Springfield, IL, Charles C Thomas, 1988, pp 49–50

Miller MC, Jacobs DG, Gutheil TG: Talisman or taboo: the controversy of the suicide prevention contract. Harv Rev Psychiatry 6:78–87, 1998

Miller v State, 731 S.W.2d 885 (Mo. Ct. App. 1987)

Paddock v Chacko, 522 So. 2d 410 (Fla. Dist. Ct. App. 1988), *review denied,* 553 So. 2d 168 (Fla. 1989)

Perlin ML: Mental Disability Law: Civil and Criminal, Vol 1. Charlottesville, VA, Michie, 1989

Peters PG: The quiet demise of deference to custom: malpractice law at the millennium. Wash Lee Law Rev 57:163, 2000

Reisner R, Slobogin C: Law and the Mental Health System, 2nd Edition. St Paul, MN, West Group, 1990

Robertson JD: The psychiatrist in the courtroom: suicide litigation—the trial of a suicide case, in American Psychiatric Press Review of Clinical Psychiatry and the Law, Vol 2. Edited by Simon RI. Washington, DC, American Psychiatric Press, 1991, pp 423–441

Shekelle PG, Ortiz E, Rhodes S, et al: Validity of the Agency for Healthcare Research and Quality clinical practice guidelines: how quickly do guidelines become outdated? JAMA 286:1461–1467, 2001

Siebert v Fink, 280 A.D.2d 661, 720 N.Y.S.2d 564 (2d Dep't 2001)

Simon RI: Coping strategies for the "unduly" defensive psychiatrist. Int J Med Law 4:551–561, 1985

Simon RI: Clinical Psychiatry and the Law, 2nd Edition. Washington, DC, American Psychiatric Press, 1992

Simon RI: Innovative psychiatric therapies and legal uncertainty: a survival guide for clinicians. Psychiatr Ann 23:473–479, 1993

Simon RI: Discharging sicker, potentially violent psychiatric inpatients in the managed care era: standard of care and risk management. Psychiatr Ann 27:726–733, 1997

Simon RI: The suicide prevention contract: clinical, legal and risk management issues. J Am Acad Psychiatry Law 27:445–450, 1999

Simon RI: Psychiatry and Law for Clinicians, 3rd Edition. Washington, DC, American Psychiatric Publishing, 2001

Simon RI: Suicide risk assessment: what is the standard of care? J Am Acad Psychiatry Law 30:340–344, 2002

Skar v City of Lincoln, 599 F.2d 253 (8th Cir. 1979)

Slovenko R: Law in Psychiatry. New York, Brunner-Routledge, 2002

Stepakoff v Kantar, 473 N.E.2d 1131, 1134 (Mass. 1985)

Walzer RS: Impaired physicians: an overview and update of legal issues. J Leg Med 11:131–198, 1990

Weathers v Pilkinton, 754 S.W.2d 75 (Tenn. Ct. App. 1988)

Wilson v State, 112 A.D.2d 366, 491 N.Y.S.2d 818 (N.Y. App. Div. 1985)

SUICIDE RISK ASSESSMENT

Medicine is a science of uncertainty and an art of probability.
Sir William Osler, *Aphorisms,* 129

Doubt is not a very pleasant condition, but certainty is absurd.
Voltaire, Letter to Frederick the Great

INTRODUCTION

Suicide risk assessment is a complex, difficult, and challenging clinical task that informs treatment and management issues for patients at risk for suicide (Simon 2001). For example, modifiable, treatable risk factors can be identified (see Table 2–1) and the patient's safety requirements determined. In this book, the term *suicidal patient* is used sparingly. In one sense, there is no such thing as a "suicidal patient," unless one is speaking generically. Patients are at varying risk for suicide, and the risk can change rapidly.

No standard of care exists for the prediction of suicide (Pokorny 1983, 1993). Suicide is a rare event. It is the result of multidimensional factors, including diagnostic (psychiatric and medical), psychodynamic, genetic, familial, occupational, environmental, social, cultural, existential, and chance factors at any point in time. Stressful life events have a significant association with completed suicides (Heila et al. 1999). Attempts to predict who will commit suicide lead

Table 2–1. Examples of modifiable and treatable
suicide risk factors

Depression	Impulsivity
Anxiety	Agitation
Panic attacks	Physical illness
Psychosis	Difficult situation (e.g., family, work)
Sleep disorders	Lethal means (e.g., guns, drugs)
Substance abuse	

to a large number of false-positive and false-negative predictions. General suicide risk factors occur in many depressed patients who do not commit suicide. Suicide risk factors have high sensitivity in identifying suicidal patients, but low specificity in determining which patients will commit suicide. Sensitivity is the rate in which a prediction of suicide was made for an actually suicidal patient. Specificity is the rate in which a prediction of nonsuicide was made for a nonsuicidal patient.

There is no standardized suicide risk prediction scale to identify which patients will commit suicide (Busch et al. 1993). Single scores from suicide risk assessment scales and inventories cannot be relied on by clinicians as the sole basis for clinical decision making. Structured or semistructured suicide scales may complement, but should not substitute for, systematic suicide risk assessment. Malone et al. (1995) found that semistructured screening instruments improved routine clinical assessments in the documentation and detection of lifetime suicidal behavior. Research scales for the assessment of suicide risk are of value in studying large groups of subjects about lifetime risk. However, they do not provide reliable assessment of the imminence of suicide risk (Oquendo et al. 2003).

Self-administered suicide scales tend to be overly sensitive but lack specificity. Moreover, checklists cannot encompass all the pertinent suicide risk factors for a specific patient. A checklist may not contain the patient's unique suicide risk factors. Moreover, suicide risk factor that a patient does display may be overlooked and not checked. Plaintiff's attorneys are quick to point out the omission of suicide risk factors on checklists that were used to assess patients who committed suicide. No standard of care exists that requires specific psychological tests or checklists to be used as part of the systematic assessment of suicide risk (Bongar et al. 1992).

Most depressed patients do not kill themselves. The national suicide rate in the general population for 2000 was 10.6 per 100,000 (Silverman 2003). The suicide rate or absolute risk of suicide for individuals having bipolar disorder is estimated to be 193 per 100,000, a relative risk 18 times that of the general population (Baldessarini et al. 2003). Turning this statistic around, 99,807 patients with such a disorder do not commit suicide in a given year. Thus, on a statistical basis alone, the vast majority of bipolar patients will not commit suicide. The same statistical analysis can be applied to other psychiatric disorders. Although the suicide rate for individuals with mood disorders, schizophrenia, or alcohol and drug abuse is 18 times the 2000 national suicide rate of 10.6, suicide remains a low-base-rate event. The clinical challenge is to identify those patients with depression who are at significant risk for suicide at any given time (Jacobs et al. 1999).

The standard of care requires psychiatrists and other mental health professionals to adequately assess suicide risk, when indicated. An adequate risk assessment systematically evaluates both risk and protective factors (see Table 2–2). Perfect assessments of suicide risk are not possible; exhaustive assessments are not necessary. Systematic suicide risk assessment is an inductive process, using specific patient data to arrive at a clinical judgment that informs appropriate treatment and management. Systematic assessment refers to the identification and the weighing of patient-specific suicide risk and protective factors. Suicide risk assessment based on current research enables the clinician to make evidence-based treatment and safety management decisions.

Professional organizations recognize the need for developing evidence-based and clinical consensus recommendations that can be applied to the management of various diseases, including behavioral states such as suicide (Simon 2002). The American Academy of Child and Adolescent Psychiatry (2001) has published practice parameters for the assessment and treatment of children and adolescents with suicidal behavior. The American Psychiatric Association Work Group on Suicidal Behaviors has developed practice guidelines for the treatment and management of patients at risk for suicide (American Psychiatric Association 2003).

Table 2–2.   Admission suicide risk assessment: sample form

Assessment factors[a]	Risk	Protective
Individual		
Clinical features (e.g., psychodynamics)		
Clinical		
Current attempt (lethality)		
Panic attacks[b]		
Psychic anxiety[b]		
Loss of pleasure and interest[b]		
Alcohol abuse[b]		
Depressive turmoil (mixed states)[b]		
Diminished concentration[b]		
Global insomnia[b]		
Suicide plan		
Suicidal ideation (command hallucinations)[c]		
Suicide intent[c]		
Hopelessness[c]		
Prior attempts (lethality)[c]		
Therapeutic alliance		
Psychiatric diagnoses (Axis I and Axis II)		
Symptom severity		
Comorbidity		
Recent discharge from psychiatric hospital (within 3 months)		
Drug abuse		
Impulsivity		
Agitation		
Physical illness		
Family history of mental illness (suicide)		
Mental competency		
Childhood abuse		
Interpersonal relations		
Work or school		
Family		
Spousal or partner		
Children		

Table 2–2. Admission suicide risk assessment: sample form *(continued)*

Assessment factors[a]	Risk	Protective
Situational		
Living circumstances		
Employment or school status		
Financial status		
Availability of guns		
Managed-care setting		
Statistical		
Age		
Gender		
Marital status		
Race		
Overall risk rating[d]		

[a]Rate risk and protective factors present as low (L), moderate (M), high (H), nonfactor (0), or range (e.g., L–M, M–H).
[b]Risk factor statistically significant within 1 year of assessment.
[c]Associated with suicide 2–10 years following assessment.
[d]Judge overall suicide risk as low, moderate, high, or a range of risk.

Official practice guidelines are not static but evolve and change according to new developments in practice and science, requiring frequent updating. Studies show that no more than 90% of practice guidelines are valid at 3.6 years after introduction (Shekelle et al. 2001). At 5.8 years, half of the guidelines are outdated. Sponsoring organizations issue disclaimers stating that practice guidelines do not represent the standard of care. Official practice guidelines have limited applicability to fact-specific cases in malpractice litigation.

CASE EXAMPLE

Mr. Mathews, a 22-year-old fourth-year college student, is brought to an urban community hospital emergency department after ingesting an unknown quantity of aspirin tablets and slashing his arms with a knife. He is severely agitated and is responding to command hallucinations that tell him to kill himself. No specific suicide plan is directed by the auditory hallucinations. Mr. Mathews became acutely depressed and agitated after the breakup of a brief relationship with a girlfriend, his first "serious" intimate relationship.

At age 16 he made a few superficial wrist scratches with a razor, following a "disappointment" with a young woman he idolized. During the week prior to admission, he abused alcohol and cocaine. An admission drug screen is positive for alcohol and cocaine. The salicylate level is 70 mg/dL (moderate toxicity).

On admission to the psychiatric unit, Mr. Mathews is "zoned to the couch" in front of the nurses' station for one-to-one safety management. His agitation and disruptive behaviors become so severe that he is placed in open-door seclusion with an attendant sitting by the door. Nursing staff protocol requires that all patients be presented with a suicide prevention contract to sign. Mr. Mathews is unable to comprehend the purpose of the contract. He signs the contract anyway. Psychiatric examination by Dr. Anderson reveals a thought disorder, severe agitation, bizarre facial grimaces and mannerisms, confusion, hopelessness, command hallucinations, flat affect, insomnia, and inability to interact with the psychiatrist, the unit staff, and the other patients.

Dr. Anderson and the psychiatric unit's social worker speak with Mr. Mathews's mother and siblings at the time of admission. Dr. Anderson invokes the emergency exception to consent in speaking to family members without the patient's authorization. He learns that Mr. Mathews's parents were divorced when he was 7 years old. He sees his father infrequently. Mr. Mathews has a close relationship with his mother, older brother, and younger sister. There is no history of physical or sexual abuse.

The mother reveals that her son is a good student, excelling in mathematics. His relationship with teachers and professors has been excellent. He has had few friends. Mr. Mathews is described by his siblings as a "loner." He has reacted to major disappointments with depression and suicidal thoughts, often accompanied by "strange" facial movements and grimaces. The family history is positive for mental illness. A paternal uncle, diagnosed as "manic-depressive," committed suicide with a shotgun. A maternal aunt is a recluse. She has been diagnosed as a "chronic schizophrenic."

Dr. Anderson asks about guns in the home. Mr. Mathews's brother reveals that there is a shotgun at the home used for skeet shooting. The brother agrees to remove the gun from the home. A follow-up call by the social worker confirms that the gun was removed from the home and secured in a safe place. Dr. Anderson's systematic suicide risk assessment of Mr. Mathews on admission is rated as high (see Table 2–3).

Dr. Anderson makes a diagnosis of schizophrenia, disorganized type, and substance abuse disorder (alcohol and cocaine). Treatment is started with an atypical antipsychotic medication, a benzodiazepine for control of severe agitation, and a sleep medication.

Table 2–3.   Admission suicide risk assessment

Assessment factors[a]	Risk	Protective
Individual		
Clinical features (grimacing)	H	
Clinical		
Current attempt (lethality)	H	
Panic attacks[b]	0	
Psychic anxiety[b]	0	
Loss of pleasure and interest[b]	H	
Alcohol abuse[b]	H	
Depressive turmoil (mixed states)[b]	0	
Diminished concentration[b]	H	
Global insomnia[b]	M–H	
Suicide plan	0	
Suicidal ideation (command hallucinations)[c]	H	
Suicide intent[c]	H	
Hopelessness[c]	M–H	
Prior attempts (lethality)[c]	L	
Therapeutic alliance	H	
Psychiatric diagnoses (Axis I and Axis II)	H	
Symptom severity	H	
Comorbidity	H	
Recent discharge from psychiatric hospital (within 3 months)	0	
Drug abuse	H	
Impulsivity	M–H	
Agitation	H	
Physical illness	0	
Family history of mental illness (suicide)	H	
Mental competency (poor)	M	
Childhood abuse	0	
Interpersonal relations		
Work or school		L
Family		M
Spousal or partner	H	
Children	0	

Table 2–3. Admission suicide risk assessment *(continued)*

Assessment factors[a]	Risk	Protective
Situational		
Living circumstances		M
Employment or school status		L
Financial status		L–M
Availability of guns	H	
Managed-care setting	0	
Statistical		
Age	M	
Gender	H	
Marital status	L	
Race	0	
Overall risk rating[d]	High	

[a]Rate risk and protective factors present as low (L), moderate (M), high (H), nonfactor (0), or range (e.g., L–M, M–H).
[b]Risk factor statistically significant within 1 year of assessment.
[c]Associated with suicide 2–10 years following assessment.
[d]Judge overall suicide risk as low, moderate, high, or a range of risk.

He assesses Mr. Mathews's acute suicide risk factors over the course of the hospitalization. In his initial suicide risk assessment, Dr. Anderson evaluates both acute and chronic risk factors as well as preventive factors.

On the day following admission, Mr. Mathews is less agitated. He no longer requires seclusion. On the third day of hospitalization, command hallucinations are muted. Mr. Mathews is more communicative with the hospital staff and other patients. By the fifth day of hospitalization, Mr. Mathews states the command hallucinations "have gone away." No agitation is present. Suicidal ideation continues but without intent or plan. Mr. Mathews's bizarre facial grimaces and mannerisms observed on admission are no longer present. Hopelessness and bewilderment diminish.

Mr. Mathews attends all group therapies. He benefits from individual and group supportive therapies. Mr. Mathews develops a therapeutic alliance with Dr. Anderson and the treatment team. His affect remains flat. His thought processes are logical, but abstracting ability for proverbs is poor. Mild insomnia is present. Concentration is poor. Mr. Mathews willingly takes his medication, although he experiences mild to moderate side effects. Mr.

Mathews feels well enough to announce that he would like to see his "girlfriend."

Dr. Anderson had recently reviewed the psychiatric literature regarding the factors associated with an increased risk of suicide in schizophrenic patients. These include a previous suicide attempt (a robust predictor of eventual completed suicide); substance abuse; depressive symptoms, especially hopelessness; male sex; an early stage in the illness; a good premorbid history and intellectual functioning; and frequent exacerbations and remissions (Meltzer 2001). Dr. Anderson also read the International Suicide Prevention Trial (InterSePT) study, which found that significant risk factors for suicide in patients with schizophrenia include the diagnosis of schizoaffective disorder, current or lifetime alcohol/substance abuse or smoking, hospitalization in the previous 3 years to prevent a suicide attempt, and number of lifetime suicide attempts (Meltzer et al. 2003a).

A systematic suicide risk assessment is performed on day 6 (see Table 2–4). It is compared with the admission suicide risk assessment (Table 2–3). Although most of the acute psychotic symptoms have improved or remitted, suicidal ideation continues. The overall risk of suicide is assessed at moderate on day 6. Dr. Anderson determines that Mr. Mathews needs an additional week of inpatient treatment. However, because of Mr. Mathews's overall improvement, the managed-care organization authorizes insurance coverage for only 1 additional day after a doctor-to-doctor appeal. Most patients at moderate suicide risk are treated as outpatients. Dr. Anderson crafts an outpatient treatment plan based on Mr. Mathews's clinical and safety needs.

The postdischarge plan calls for Mr. Mathews to continue once-per-week supportive psychotherapy and medication management with Dr. Anderson. Mr. Mathews is also referred to the hospital's partial hospitalization and substance abuse programs, to begin the day after discharge. Mr. Mathews has arranged with the university to complete his coursework in physics through a home study program. He hopes to graduate in 6 months. While living at home, he plans to work at odd jobs to earn additional tuition money. Financial assistance is also available through an educational trust fund established by his grandparents. His mother and siblings are very supportive of Mr. Mathews, which is a major protective factor. Dr. Anderson assesses other protective factors, including the patient's ability to form a therapeutic alliance, adherence to prescribed medications, plans for completing college, and socializing with other patients. Dr. Anderson's discharge diagnosis is schizophrenia, single episode in partial remission, and substance abuse disorder (alcohol and cocaine).

Table 2–4. Discharge suicide risk assessment

Assessment factors[a]	RISK	PROTECTIVE
Individual		
Clinical features (no grimacing)	0	
Clinical		
Current attempt (lethality)	H	
Panic attacks[b]	0	
Psychic anxiety[b]	0	
Loss of pleasure and interest[b]	L	
Alcohol abuse[b]	M	
Depressive turmoil (mixed states)[b]	0	
Diminished concentration[b]	H	
Global insomnia[b]	L	
Suicide plan	0	
Suicidal ideation (command hallucinations)[c]	M	
Suicide intent[c]	0	
Hopelessness[c]	L	
Prior attempts (lethality)[c]	L	
Therapeutic alliance		M
Psychiatric diagnoses (Axis I and Axis II)	H	
Symptom severity	L–M	
Comorbidity	H	
Recent discharge from psychiatric hospital (within 3 months)	0	
Drug abuse	M	
Impulsivity	L	
Agitation	0	
Physical illness	H	
Family history of mental illness (suicide)	H	
Mental competency (improved)	L	
Childhood abuse	0	
Interpersonal relations		
Work or school		H
Family		H
Spousal or partner	L–M	
Children	0	

Table 2–4.   Discharge suicide risk assessment *(continued)*

Assessment factors[a]	Risk	Protective
Situational		
Living circumstances		M
Employment or school status		H
Financial status		M
Availability of guns		0
Managed-care setting	L–M	
Statistical		
Age	M	
Gender	H	
Marital status	L	
Race	0	
Overall risk rating[d]	Moderate	

[a]Rate risk and protective factors present as low (L), moderate (M), high (H), nonfactor (0), or range (e.g., L–M, M–H).
[b]Risk factor statistically significant within 1 year of assessment.
[c]Associated with suicide 2–10 years following assessment.
[d]Judge overall suicide risk as low, moderate, high, or a range of risk.

DISCUSSION

STANDARD OF CARE

Each state defines the standard of care required of physicians. For example, in *Stepakoff v. Kantar* (1985), a suicide case, the standard applied by the court was the "duty to exercise that degree of skill and care ordinarily employed in similar circumstances by other psychiatrists." The duty of care established by the court was that of the "average psychiatrist." In an increasing number of states, the standard of care is the "reasonable, prudent practitioner" (see Chapter 1, "Suicide and Malpractice Litigation").

In a suicide case, the courts evaluate the psychiatrist's management of the case of the patient who attempts or commits suicide to determine whether the suicide risk assessment process was reasonable and if the patient's attempt or suicide was foreseeable. The law generally assumes that if suicide is foreseeable, it is preventable. However, an imperfect fit exists between medical and legal terminology. Foreseeability is a legal term of art. It is a commonsense, probabilistic concept, not a scientific construct. *Foreseeability* is defined as the reasonable anticipation that harm or injury is likely to result from certain acts or omissions (Black 1999). Foreseeability should not be confused with predictability, for which no professional standard exists. Foreseeability also must be distinguished from preventability. For example, a patient's suicide may have been preventable in hindsight but not foreseeable at the time of assessment.

The law does not require the defendant to "foresee events which are merely possible but only those that are reasonably foreseeable" (*Hairston v. Alexander Tank and Equip. Co.* [1984]). Only the risk of suicide can be assessed. Therefore, only the risk of suicide is foreseeable. The prediction of suicide is opaque, but there is reasonable visibility for assessing suicide risk. The performance and contemporaneous documentation of systematic suicide risk assessment that informs patient treatment and safety management should more than meet foreseeability criteria.

Incomplete assessments, such as the assessment of isolated risk factors (e.g., demographic factors), will likely be dismissed by courts as "simply insufficient" in establishing foreseeability. In *Williamson v. Liptzin* (2001), a former patient sued the psychiatrist for not foreseeing the murderous rampage perpetrated by the patient 8 months after the termination of treatment. The appellate court held that "evidence of 'risk factors' for potential violence, such as gun ownership, being under a certain age, or being of certain gender, implicates a large portion of our population and is simply insufficient in and of itself to prove foreseeability." However, a history of violence or threats of violence may have "personalized" the risk assessment, leading to a conclusion that the violence was foreseeable. This is not possible with demographic factors alone.

Although *Williamson* is a case about the foreseeability of violence toward others, the court's analysis can be applied to suicide risk assessment in suicide cases. Contemporaneously documented systematic suicide risk assessments help provide the court with guidance. When suicide risk assessments are not performed or documented, the court is less able to evaluate the clinical complexities and ambiguities that exist in assessment, treatment, and management issues for patients at risk for suicide.

SYSTEMATIC SUICIDE RISK ASSESSMENT

Systematic suicide risk assessment identifies acute, modifiable, and treatable risk factors essential to the psychiatrist's treatment and safety management of patients at risk for suicide. It is easy to overlook important risk and protective factors in the absence of systematic assessment.

Suicide risk assessment is an integral part of the psychiatric examination, yet it is rarely performed systematically or, when it is performed, it is not contemporaneously documented. A review of suicide cases in litigation reveals that the extent of suicide risk assessment usually is no more than "Patient denies HI, SI, CFS" (homicidal ideation, suicidal ideation, contracts for safety). Frequently one finds only "patient denies suicidal ideation." This is simply insufficient. Also, a talismanic "no-harm contract" is no substitute for an adequate suicide risk assessment. Laypersons could just as easily ask these same questions and obtain a "no-harm contract." In the case example, systematic suicide risk assessment supplanted the use of a suicide prevention contract.

Approximately 25% of patients at risk for suicide do not admit to suicidal ideation to clinicians but do tell their family (Fawcett et al. 1993). The majority of patients who commit suicide do not communicate their suicide intent during their final appointment (Isometsa et al. 1995). In a retrospective study of 76 inpatient suicides, Busch et al. (2003) found that 77% of the patients denied suicidal ideation in their last recorded communication. Hall et al. (1999) found that 69 of 100 patients had only fleeting or no suicidal thoughts before they made a suicide attempt. None of these patients reported a specific plan before the impulsive suicide. Also, because this was the first attempt for 67% of these patients, no history of prior suicide attempts existed. Moreover, patients who are determined to commit suicide regard the psychiatrist or other mental health professional as the enemy (Resnick 2002). Therefore, just asking the patient at suicide risk about the presence of suicidal ideation, intent, and plan and receiving a denial cannot be relied on by itself. Even when the patient is telling the truth, it is unwise to equate the patient's denial of suicidal ideation with an absence of suicide risk. If possible, family members or significant others should be consulted.

The Principles of Medical Ethics With Annotations Especially Applicable to Psychiatry (American Psychiatric Association 2001) states, "Psychiatrists at times may find it necessary, in order to protect the patient or community from imminent danger, to reveal confidential information disclosed by the patient" (Section 4, Annotation 8). Management for patients at high risk for suicide may require breaking patient confidence and involving the family or significant others (e.g., to obtain vital information, to administer and monitor medications, to remove lethal weapons, to assist in hospitalization). Statutory waiver of confidential information is provided in some states when a patient seriously threatens self-harm (Simon 1992).

Observational information obtained from the psychiatric examination may provide objective information about suicide risk factors, obviating the need for total reliance on the patient's reporting. It may be possible to speak with others who know the patient, if the patient consents. If the severely disturbed patient lacks the mental capacity to consent, a substitute health care decision maker should be consulted. In a number of states, proxy consent by next of kin is not permitted for patients with mental illness. If an emergency exists, as in the case example, the emergency exception to patient consent may be invoked (see Chapter 7, "Emergency Psychiatric Services").

Suicidal ideation is a key risk factor. In the National Comorbidity Survey, the probability for transition from suicide ideation to suicidal plan was 34% and from plan to attempt was 72% (Kessler et al. 1999).The probability of transition from suicidal ideation to an unplanned attempt was 26%. In this study, approximately 90% of unplanned and 60% of planned first attempts occurred within 1 year of the onset of suicidal ideation. The clinician should not be deterred from performing a systematic suicide risk assessment when the patient reports passive rather than active suicidal ideations (e.g., "I hope God takes me" versus "I'm going to kill myself"). When evaluating a patient's suicidal ideation, the clinician should consider specific content, intensity, duration, and prior episodes. Mann et al. (1999) found that the severity of an individual's ideation is an indicator of risk of attempting suicide. Beck et al. (1990) found that when patients were asked about suicidal ideation at its worst point, those patients with higher scores were 14 times more likely to commit suicide compared with patients with lower scores. Beck et al. (1998) defined suicide intent as the intensity or seriousness of the patient's desire to commit suicide. The intensity may vary from passive thoughts of death to a potentially lethal plan. An investigation of suicide intent should include questions about the details of a current plan, perception of lethality, methods considered, and death arrangements (e.g., preparation of a will or recent purchase of life insurance).

There is no pathognomonic risk factor for suicide. A single suicide risk factor does not have adequate statistical power on which to base an assessment. The amount of variance (deviation from the mean) carried by any risk factor is so small that suicide risk assessment cannot be predicated on any one factor (Meltzer et al. 2003b). The assessment of suicide risk is multifactorial.

Why do many psychiatrists, sued or not sued, fail to perform or document adequate suicide risk assessments? When this question is posed to colleagues, a variety of answers are given: the clinician does not know how to perform a systematic suicide risk assessment; the clinician simply does not do suicide risk assessments, usually delegating it to others; the clinician performs systematic risk assessments but does not document them, usually because of a high-volume practice; the anxiety produced by patients at substantial risk for suicide creates denial and minimization of the risk, resulting in the inability to perform an adequate assessment; the clinician fears that documenting the risk assessment process creates legal exposure if the assessment is wrong and the patient commits suicide. In inpatient settings, the short lengths of stay and the rapid turnover of seriously ill patients may distract the clinician from performing adequate suicide risk assessments.

Suicide risk assessment is analogous to weather forecasting (Monahan and Steadman 1996; Simon 1992). Astronomical events such as eclipses can be predicted with 100% accuracy. Weather forecasts can be made only within certain probabilities. Suicide risk assessments are "here and now" determinations whose reliability diminishes over time. Short-term suicide assessments are more reliable than long-term assessments. Psychological and environmental risk factors that influence future occurrences can be specified with more precision in the short term. Similar to weather forecasts, suicide risk assessments should be frequently updated.

The clinician can determine the confidence he or she places in the adequacy of the suicide risk assessment, based on the data-gathering process that forms the foundation for the patient evaluation. Determining the clinician's level of confidence in the available patient data is essential for the treatment and management of those at suicide risk. Table 2–5 contains a suicide risk assessment data checklist that can be used by clinicians. The standard of care requires that the clinician gather sufficient information on which to base an adequate suicide risk assessment. The checklist can alert the clinician to deficiencies in the data collection.

Table 2–5. Suicide risk assessment data checklist

- Identify suicide risk factors unique to the individual
- Identify acute suicide risk factors
- Identify protective factors
- Evaluate status of therapeutic alliance
- Obtain treatment team information
- Interview patient's family or significant others
- Speak with current or prior treaters
- Review patient's daily hospital records

Note. Modify table for outpatient use.
Source. Adapted from Simon RI: "Suicide Risk Assessment in Managed Care Settings." *Primary Psychiatry* 7:42–43, 46–49, 2002. Used with permission.

A systematic risk assessment itself is the impetus to gather information about a patient's level of suicide risk. The checklist reminds the clinician to consider multiple data sources that create the foundational basis for the overall evaluation of the patient's suicide risk and the continuing suicide risk assessment process. When the weather turns stormy, clinicians, like pilots, must rely on their instruments. A systematic suicide risk assessment is such an instrument.

SUICIDE RISK FACTORS

Short-term suicide risk factors derived from prospective studies of patients with major affective disorders are statistically significant within 1 year of assessment (Fawcett et al. 1990). Short-term risk factors include panic attacks, psychic anxiety, loss of pleasure and interest, moderate alcohol abuse, depressive turmoil (mixed states), diminished concentration, and global insomnia. Short-term risk factors are predominantly severe, anxiety driven, and usually treatable by a variety of psychotropic drugs (Fawcett 2001). Patients with major depression and generalized anxiety disorder (GAD) have higher levels of suicidal ideation compared with depressed patients without GAD (Zimmerman and Chelminski 2003). The combination of severe depression and anxiety or panic attacks can prove lethal. A patient may be able to tolerate depression. When anxiety is also present, the patient's life may become unbearable, making suicide a devoutly desired escape. Anxiety (agitation) symptoms should be treated aggressively.

Long-term suicide risk factors in patients with major affective disorder are associated with suicides completed 2–10 years following assessment (Fawcett et al. 1990). Long-term suicide risk factors are derived from community-based psychological autopsies and the retrospective study of psychiatric patients who have committed suicide (Fawcett et al. 1993). Long-term suicide risk factors include suicidal ideation, suicide intent, severe hopelessness, and prior attempts. Suicide risk increases with the total number of risk factors, providing a quasi-quantitative dimension to suicide risk assessment (Murphy et al. 1992).

Patients from diagnostic groups such as major affective disorders, chronic alcoholism and substance abuse, schizophrenia, and borderline personality disorder are at increased risk for suicide. Roose et al. (1983) found that delusional depressed patients were five times more likely to commit suicide than depressed patients who were not delusional. Busch et al. (2003) found that 54% of 76 inpatient suicides had an association between psychosis and suicide. In the Collaborative Study of Depression, no significant difference in suicide was found between depressed and delusionally depressed patients. However, patients who had delusions of thought insertion, grandeur, and mind reading were significantly represented in the suicide group (Fawcett et al. 1987). The majority of follow-up studies do not find that patients with psychotic depression are more likely to commit suicide than patients with nonpsychiatric depression (Coryell et al. 1996; Vythilingam et al. 2003). Suicidal patients with melancholic depression may be at increased risk for suicide in the morning, when their depression is worse. Supervision should be increased accordingly.

Although it is not possible to identify precisely which patients will commit suicide, patients often display unique, individualized suicide risk and preventive factor patterns. Understanding a patient's psychodynamics and psychological responses to past and current life stressors is important. In the case example, the patient displayed bizarre facial mannerisms when he was depressed and at risk for suicide. Other clinical examples of unusual premonitory suicide risk factors that occurred only when the patient became suicidal include the stuttering patient whose speech would become clear, the patient who would compulsively whistle, and the patient who would self-inflict facial excoriations. Other patients may experience more conventional suicide risk patterns, such as suicidal ideation within a few hours or days following the onset of early morning awakening. Knowing a patient's suicide risk factor pattern along with his or her psychodynamics is very helpful in treatment and management.

Actuarial (static) suicide risk factors include age, gender, socioeconomic status, demographics, intelligence, educational level, family history, the patient's past, marital status, and race. The suicide rate for white men older than 65 years is elevated. The suicide rate for white men older than 85 years is among the highest. Males commit suicide at a rate three to four times that of females. Females, however, make suicide attempts at a rate three to four times that of males. Divorced individuals are at significantly increased risk for suicide compared with married individuals. Racially, the suicide rate is higher among white individuals (except in young adults) (National Institute of Mental Health 2003). Actuarial suicide risk factors, although important, supplement the assessment of individual risk factors. Static suicide risk factors, by definition, are not modifiable.

A family history of mental illness, especially of suicide, is a significant suicide risk factor. Brent et al. (2002) found that a history of suicidal behavior in a parent raised sixfold the risks for suicidal behaviors in the offspring. A genetic component exists in the etiology of mood disorders, schizophrenia, alcoholism and substance abuse, and Cluster B personality disorders. These psychiatric disorders are associated with most suicides (Mann and Arango 1999). Genetic and familial transmission of suicide risk is independent of the transmission of psychiatric illnesses (Brent et al. 1996). Patients with intractable, malignant psychiatric disorders that end in suicide often have strong genetic and familial components to their illnesses. The Copenhagen Adoption Study revealed that adoptees who committed suicide had a sixfold increase in suicide in their biological relatives than in matched adoptees who had not committed suicide (Schulsinger et al. 1979). There were no suicides among the adopting relatives. This finding was independent of the transmission of a psychiatric disorder.

In the case example, the patient's suicide attempt is directed by command hallucinations. The earlier psychiatric literature indicated that command hallucinations accounted for relatively few suicides in schizophrenic patients (Breier and Astrachan 1984; Roy 1982). Nonetheless, an auditory hallucination that commands death is an important suicide risk factor requiring careful assessment. Command hallucinations can be the equivalent of intense suicidal ideation, intent, and plan. The patient needs to be asked, Are the auditory hallucinations that are commanding suicide acute or chronic, syntonic or dystonic, familiar or unfamiliar voices? Is the patient able to resist the hallucinatory commands, or has the patient attempted suicide in obedience to the voices?

Junginger (1990) reported that 39% of patients with command hallucinations obeyed them. Patients were more likely to comply with hallucinatory commands if they could identify the voices. Kasper et al. (1996) found that 84% of psychiatric inpatients with command hallucinations had obeyed them within the last 30 days. However, the resistance to command hallucinations that dictate dangerous acts appears to be greater than resistance to commands to perform nondangerous acts (Junginger 1995). This is not as true for patients who have obeyed command hallucinations dictating self-destructive behaviors. Hellerstein et al. (1987) reported the content of command hallucinations: 52% suicide, 5% homicide, 12% nonlethal injury of self or others, 14% nonviolent acts, and 17%

unspecified. Thus, 69% of command hallucinations dictated violence. Auditory hallucinations that command suicide require immediate psychiatric treatment and management.

In schizophrenia, the lifetime completed suicide rate is between 9% and 13%. The estimated number of suicides annually in the United States among patients with schizophrenia is 3,600 (12% of total suicides). The lifetime suicide attempt rate is between 20% and 40%. Suicide is the leading cause of death among persons with schizophrenia younger than 35. Suicide is a risk in schizophrenia throughout the individual's life cycle (Heila et al. 1997; Meltzer and Okaly 1995).

Harris and Barraclough (1997) abstracted 249 reports from the medical literature on the mortality of mental disorders. They compared the observed numbers of suicides with those expected. A standardized mortality ratio (SMR) was calculated for each disorder (see Table 2–6). The SMR is a determination of the relative risk of suicide for a particular disorder compared with the expected rate in the general population. It is calculated by dividing observed mortality by expected mortality. The authors concluded, "If these results can be generalized then virtually all mental disorders have an increased risk of suicide excepting mental retardation and dementia" (p. 205).

Harris and Barraclough also calculated the SMR for all psychiatric diagnoses by the treatment setting. The SMR for inpatients was 5.82; for outpatients it was 18.09. Prior suicide attempts by any method had the highest SMR, 38.36. In other words, the suicide risk for patients with prior suicide attempts is 38.36 times the expected rate in the general population. Risk was highest in the 2 years following the first attempt. The SMR for psychiatric, neurological, and medical disorders can be helpful to the psychiatrist in assessing the risk of suicide for a specific diagnosis in the assessment of suicide risk. Thus, gathering information from collateral sources and spending sufficient time with the patient to arrive at a correct diagnosis is essential in the treatment and safety management of the patient at risk for suicide. The presence of prior suicide attempts significantly raises the patient's risk for suicide.

The high SMR for prior suicide attempts is supported by other studies (Fawcett 2001). Between 7% and 12% of patients who make suicide attempts commit suicide within 10 years, making attempted

Table 2–6. Mental and physical disorders and mortality

Disorder	SMR[a]
Eating disorders	23.14
Major depression	20.35
Sedative abuse	20.34
Mixed drug abuse	19.23
Bipolar disorder	15.05
Opioid abuse	14.00
Dysthymia	12.12
Obsessive-compulsive disorder	11.54
Panic disorder	10.00
Schizophrenia	8.45
Personality disorders	7.08
AIDS	6.58
Alcohol abuse	5.86
Epilepsy	5.11
Child and adolescent disorders	4.73
Cannabis abuse	3.85
Spinal cord injury	3.82
Neuroses	3.72
Brain injury	3.50
Huntington's chorea	2.90
Multiple sclerosis	2.36
Malignant neoplasms	1.80
Mental retardation	0.88

[a]Standardized mortality ratio (SMR) is calculated by dividing observed mortality by expected mortality.
Source. Adapted from Harris and Barraclough (1997).

suicide a significant chronic risk factor for suicide. Oquendo et al. (2002) have shown that a history of suicide attempts is an important indicator of future attempts. For each suicide attempt, the risk of another suicide attempt occurring during a 2-year follow-up period increases by 30%. Malone et al. (1995) found that the best clinical indicator of a future suicide attempt is a prior suicide attempt. Near-lethal attempts are frequently followed within days by a completed suicide. However, most suicides occur in patients with no history of prior attempts. Mann et al. (1999) found that prior suicide attempts and hopelessness are the most powerful clinical predictors of completed suicide. It is estimated that 8–25 suicide attempts occur for every completed suicide (National Institute of Mental Health 2003).

No annual national data are available on attempted suicide. However, reliable research finds that the strongest factors for attempted suicide in adults are depression, alcohol abuse, cocaine use, and separation and divorce. In youths, the strongest factors associated with suicide attempts are depression, alcohol or other drug use disorder, and aggressive or disruptive behaviors (National Institute of Mental Health 2003). Assessing the lethality of suicide attempts is discussed in Chapter 6, "Inpatients."

Baldessarini et al. (2003) found that the overall SMR for bipolar disorder was 21.8. The SMR was 1.4 times higher for women than for men. Most suicide acts occurred within the first 5 years after the onset of illness. The SMR for bipolar II disorder was 24.1, compared with an SMR of 17.0 for bipolar I disorder and 11.8 for unipolar disorders.

Suicide risk factors vary among special populations. Practice parameters for the assessment and treatment of children and adolescents with suicidal behavior are available (American Academy of Child and Adolescent Psychiatry 2001). Risk factors for adolescents include prior attempts, mood disorder, substance abuse, living alone, male gender, age 16 years or older, and a history of physical or sexual abuse. Adverse childhood experiences—for example, emotional, physical, and sexual abuse—are associated with an increased risk of attempted suicide throughout the life span (Dube et al. 2001). Brodsky et al. (2001) found that a history of child abuse is associated with a higher rate of mood disorders and adult suicide behaviors, including a higher level of impulsivity. Suicidal women are more likely to have experienced childhood abuse than suicidal men (Kaplan et al. 1995). Brent (2001) provided a framework for the assessment of suicide risk in the adolescent that can be used to determine immediate disposition, intensity of treatment, and level of care.

In adults older than 65 years, important correlates of late-life suicide are depression, physical illnesses, functional impairment, personality traits of neuroticism, social isolation, and loss of important relationships (Conwell and Duberstein 2001). Mood disorder is the risk factor with the strongest correlation. Seventy percent of older adults saw their primary care physician within 30 days of committing suicide. Thus, primary care is an important point of suicide prevention for elders at high risk.

Personality disorders place a patient at increased risk for suicide (Linehan et al. 2000) (see Chapter 4, "Outpatients"). Patients with personality disorders have a risk for suicide seven times greater than that of the general population (Harris and Barraclough 1997). Of patients who commit suicide, 30%–40% have personality disorders (Bronisch 1996; Duberstein and Conwell 1997).

Cluster B personality disorders, particularly borderline and antisocial personality disorders, place patients at increased risk for suicide (Duberstein and Conwell 1997). In borderline personality disorder patients, impulsivity was associated with a high number of suicide attempts, after controlling for substance abuse and a lifetime diagnosis of depressive disorder (Brodsky et al. 1997). A combination of borderline personality disorder, major affective disorder, and alcoholism was found in a fatal subgroup in a longitudinal study of personality disorder (Stone 1993).

Personality disorder, negative recent life events, and Axis I comorbidity were identified in a large sample of suicides (Heikkinen et al. 1997). Recent stressful life events, including workplace difficulties, family problems, unemployment, and financial trouble, were highly represented among patients with personality disorders. Personality disorders and comorbidity, such as depressive symptoms and substance abuse disorders, are frequently found among patients who commit suicide (Isometsa et al. 1996; Suominen et al. 2000).

Suicide threats and gestures occur with much greater frequency than actual suicide attempts. Gunderson and Ridolfi (2002) estimate that suicide threats and gestures occur repeatedly in 90% of borderline patients. With the borderline patient, the clinician's suicide risk assessment should pay attention to comorbidity, especially mood disorder and substance abuse, prior suicide attempts or self-mutilating behaviors, impulsivity, and unpleasant recent life events.

Self-mutilating behaviors that commonly occur in borderline patients include cutting (80%), bruising (34%), burning (20%), head banging (15%), and biting (7%). Although self-mutilation is considered to be parasuicidal behavior (without lethal intent), the risk of suicide is doubled in its presence (Stone et al. 1987). Retrospectively, it may be difficult or impossible to distinguish a nonlethal suicide gesture from an actual suicide attempt. For example, the clinician must consider intent, not just behavior. A patient who takes 10 aspirin tablets with the belief that it will result in death is making a lethal suicidal attempt. A patient addicted to barbiturates who takes an overdose of 50 tablets may not have any intention to commit suicide and knows that death will not likely occur. An aborted attempt occurs when the intent to harm is interrupted and no physical harm results. O'Carroll et al. (1996) provided definitions for a variety of suicidal behaviors.

Impulsivity, usually a trait factor or a behavior associated with alcohol or substance abuse, is an important suicide risk factor requiring clinical assessment. Impulsivity also has been found in many suicide attempters with major depressive disorder, panic disorder, or aggressive behaviors linked to the serotonergic system (Pezawas et al. 2002). Patients who practice self-harm are more impulsive than members of the general population. Patients who repeat self-harm are found to be more impulsive than patients who perform self-harm for the first time (Evans et al. 1996). Impulsivity can be both acute and chronic. A history of chronic impulsivity can become acute when heightened by life stress, loss, and anxiety. Suicide attempts or violent suicide may result (Fawcett 2001). Mann et al. (1999) found that suicide attempters with major depressive disorder have higher levels of aggression and impulsivity than nonattempters.

"Shame suicides" may occur in individuals faced with intolerable humiliation (e.g., scandal, criminal charges). A "shame suicide" may be an impulsive act in a narcissistically vulnerable person. However, it may not be associated with a diagnosable mental disorder (Roy 1986).

A patient's suicide risk may be exacerbated by problems that arise from the treater. Some examples include physical or psychological impairment, incompetence, indifference, negative countertransference, fatigue ("burnout"), and deficient language skills (see Chapter 6, "Inpatients").

In order to perform an adequate suicide risk assessment, the clinician must be able to understand idiomatic phrases and slang expressions. In one instance, a severely depressed, suicidal patient with opioid dependence told the psychiatrist that she had "gone cold turkey." The psychiatrist, with limited English language skills, proceeded to ask the patient if she had an eating disorder.

SUICIDE RISK ASSESSMENT METHODOLOGY

A number of suicide risk assessment methods are available to the clinician (Clark and Fawcett 1999; Jacobs et al. 1999). Clinicians also may develop their own systematic risk assessment methods based on their training, their clinical experience, and their understanding and interpretation of the psychiatric literature. The example of suicide risk assessment used in Table 2–2 represents only one way of conceptualizing systematic assessment. No suicide risk assessment model has been empirically tested for reliability and validity (Busch et al. 1993). Table 2–2 is a teaching tool designed to encourage a systematic approach to suicide risk assessment. It is not presented as a form or a protocol to be applied in a mechanical fashion. The use of stand-alone suicide risk assessment forms is not recommended. Suicide risk factors vary in number and importance according to individual patients. The clinician's judgment is central in identifying and assigning clinical weight to risk and protective factors. It is important to assess protective factors against suicide to achieve a balanced assessment of suicide risk.

Malone et al. (2000) assessed inpatients with major depression for severity of depression, general psychopathology, suicide history, reasons for living, and hopelessness. The self-report Reasons for Living Inventory was used to measure beliefs that may act as preventive factors against suicide (Linehan et al. 1983). The total score for reasons for living was inversely correlated with the sum of scores for hopelessness, subjective depression, and suicidal ideation. The total scores on the Reason for Living Inventory differentiated between individuals who attempted suicide and nonattempters (Malone et al. 2000). The authors recommend including reasons for living in the clinical assessment and management of suicidal patients.

Protective factors against suicide may include family and social support, pregnancy, children, strong religious beliefs, and cultural sanctions against suicide (Institute of Medicine 2001). Protective factors, like risk factors, vary with the clinical presentation of individual patients at suicide risk. An ebb and flow exist between suicide risk and protective factors. The patient's protective factors can be overcome by the acuteness and severity of mental illness.

Table 2–2 divides assessment factors into five general categories: individual, clinical, interpersonal, situational, and statistical. The categories and the factors within them are not listed in any order of importance. The practitioner determines the order of importance based on the clinical presentation of the patient. Suicide risk and protective specific factors may be rated as facilitating or inhibiting (protective) the risk for suicide. A dimensional scale of low, moderate, high, or nonfactor reflecting the continuum of suicide risk is used. No bright line demarcates low, moderate, and high assessments from one another. The final risk rating is an informed clinical judgment call based on the overall assessment of the risk and protective factors. The purpose of Table 2–2 is to encourage systematic suicide risk assessment. Assessments can be made in a time-efficient manner, after thorough psychiatric examination and during continuing patient care. A concise, contemporaneous note that describes the clinician's suicide risk assessment and clinical decision-making process is adequate (see Table 2–7).

Table 2–7. Sample suicide risk assessment note: contents

- Suicide risk factors assessed and weighed (low, moderate, high)
- Protective factors assessed and weighed (low, moderate, high)
- Overall assessment rating (low, moderate, high, or range)
- Treatment and management intervention informed by the assessment
- Changes from prior suicide risk assessments, if any

Assessment factors may be rated according to a variety of clinical parameters in suicide risk assessment (see Table 2–8). For example, assessment factors may be rated as acute or chronic (present for a year or longer before assessment). Acute suicidal patients are at imminent, high risk for suicide (within days or weeks). Chronic suicidal patients are at low, moderate, or high risk but not at imminent risk for suicide. After initial psychiatric examination and systematic suicide risk assessment, the clinician can evaluate the course of acute suicide risk factors that brought the patient to treatment. Modifiable and treatable suicide risk factors should be identified early and treated aggressively. For example, anxiety, depression, insomnia, and psychotic symptoms usually respond to medications as well as psychosocial interventions.

Table 2–8. Dimensional parameters in suicide risk assessment

Risk—Protective

Acute—Chronic

Necessary—Sufficient

Individual—Situational

State (Axis I)—Trait (Axis II)

Impulsivity may be triggered by a stressful life event and substance abuse. It may respond to treatment with anticonvulsants (Hollander et al. 2002). Psychosocial interventions can help mitigate or resolve interpersonal issues at home, work, or school. At discharge, a final systematic suicide risk assessment allows comparison with the initial office visit or hospital admission assessment.

Suicide risk assessment is a process, not an event. Suicide risk exists along a continuum that can vary from minute to minute, hour to hour, and day to day. Thus, assessments may need to be performed at a number of clinical junctures—for example, change in safety status, removal from seclusion and/or restraint, ward changes, and passes. The suicide risk assessment process that follows the acute risk factors is illustrated in the case example. For outpatients, systematic suicide risk assessment is critical to clinical decision making regarding voluntary or involuntary hospitalization.

Patients with Axis I psychiatric disorders, such as schizophrenia, anxiety disorders, major affective disorders, and substance abuse disorders, often present with acute (state) suicide risk factors. Patients with Axis II disorders often display chronic (trait) suicide risk factors. Exacerbation of an Axis II disorder or comorbidity with an Axis I disorder (including substance abuse) may convert chronic suicide risk factors into acute risk factors. A family history of mental illness, especially in association with suicide, is an important chronic (static) risk factor to assess. The offspring of patients with mood disorders who attempt suicide are at a markedly increased risk for suicide (Brent et al. 2002). In the case example, the patient's aunt was diagnosed as a "chronic schizophrenic" and a "manic-depressive" uncle committed suicide. Comorbidity significantly increases the patient's risk for suicide (Kessler et al. 1999). As noted earlier, suicide risk increases with the total number of risk factors, providing a quasi-quantitative dimension to suicide risk factor assessment (Simon 1998).

Necessary (e.g., depression) and sufficient (e.g., situational) factors provide another assessment parameter. For example, the patient with major depression who also is experiencing a personal loss or work-related crisis may present with both necessary and sufficient suicide risk factors. Evaluating individual (e.g., unique or atypical suicide risk factors) and situational (e.g., loss) parameters can also be useful in suicide risk assessment. This is a variant of the necessary and sufficient analysis.

Mann et al. (1999) proposed a stress-diathesis model of suicide behavior. For suicide to occur, a trigger (stress) and a preexisting vulnerability to suicidal behaviors (diathesis) must be present. Maltsberger et al. (2003) identified a precipitating event in 25 or 26 patient suicides studied. In 19 of the cases, evidence linked the identified event to the suicide.

Systematic suicide risk assessment encourages the gathering of important clinical information. Malone et al. (1995) found that admission clinicians on routine clinical assessments failed to document a history of suicidal behavior in 12 of 50 patients who were identified by research assessment to be depressed and to have attempted suicide. Fewer total suicide attempts were clinically reported compared with data obtained by use of a comprehensive research assessment. Documentation of suicidal behavior was more accurate on hospital intake admission using a semistructured format than in discharge records by clinical assessment alone. The authors suggested that the use of semistructured screening instruments may improve documentation and the detection of lifetime suicidal behavior. Systematic assessment of the patient's suicide risk and protective factors is a clinical process that provides an improved means of gathering information and informing the identification, treatment, and management of patients at risk for suicide.

MANAGED-CARE SETTINGS

Before the managed-care era, the length of stay in psychiatric hospitals was generally dictated by the treatment and management needs of the patient. The length of hospitalization was considered a protective factor against suicide. Managed-care settings can become a significant suicide risk factor because of restrictions on insurance benefits that limit the frequency of outpatient visits and the hospital length of stay. In the case example, the patient with a diagnosis of acute schizophrenia was hospitalized for 7 days. He was discharged when the managed-care organization (MCO) denied additional hospital benefits. However, psychiatrists continue to owe a professional and legal duty to provide competent patient care, regardless of managed-care restrictions and protocols (Hall et al. 1999; Simon 1997). The clinician should not allow managed-care settings to become a risk factor for suicide.

MCOs, through utilization review, require that suicide risk assessment be a process. In inpatient settings, the hospital utilization reviewer is queried by MCOs regularly about the patient's level of suicide risk. Hospital length-of-stay certifications are based on the clinician's assessment of the patient's suicide risk. Some MCOs contact the utilization reviewer daily about the status of the suicidal patient. The absence of continuing suicide risk assessments leaves the utilization reviewer unable to respond to the MCO's questions. Premature termination of the patient's insurance benefits may result. Managed-care decisions can become risk factors for suicide if clinicians abrogate their duty of care to patients. The study by Mortensen and Juel (1993) suggests that the 56% increase in first-episode schizophrenic patients over a 10-year period was related to shorter hospitalizations and inadequate discharge planning.

In managed-care settings, much reliance is placed on "no-harm" or "suicide prevention" contracts as a substitute for adequate suicide risk assessment, often because of the high volume and rapid turnover of severely mentally ill patients. Identification of modifiable risk factors that can quickly lower suicide risk provides important data for patient care in all managed-care settings.

Depending on severity, a patient's depression may respond within a few days to a treatment relationship and therapeutic milieu. However, it is rare for patients with major depression who are responders to antidepressants to improve in a period of less than several weeks (Gelenberg and Chesen 2000). A full therapeutic response may require 8–12 weeks of treatment in responders. Some patients at risk for suicide may be energized by antidepressant treatment to attempt or commit suicide, if hopelessness continues unabated. Because of curtailed lengths of stay, patients with mood disorders are often discharged from the hospital before antidepressants and other medications have had a chance to work. Close postdischarge follow-up and monitoring of medications is necessary. Patients are at increased risk for suicide following discharge from the hospital (Roy 1982).

With shortened lengths of stay and rapid patient turnovers, the clinician must gather information about the suicidal patient quickly. Collateral sources, such as family members, partners, or friends, usually are able to provide important information. Merely listening to information provided by others does not violate patient confidentiality. Merely listening is not the same as disclosing, when the patient withholds authorization for release of information.

CLINICALLY BASED RISK MANAGEMENT

- Systematic suicide risk assessment informs treatment and management for patients at risk for suicide. It is secondarily a risk management technique.
- Treatable and modifiable suicide risk factors should be identified early and treated aggressively.
- Systematic suicide assessment identifies and weighs the clinical importance of both risk and preventive factors.
- Suicide risk assessment is a process, not an event. Psychiatric inpatients should have suicide risk assessments conducted at admission and discharge and at other important clinical junctures during treatment.
- Clinicians should assess impulsivity by asking the patient questions about violent rages, assaultive behavior, arrests, destruction of property, spending sprees, speeding tickets, sexual indiscretions, and other indicia of poor impulse control.
- Suicide prevention contracts must not take the place of conducting systematic suicide risk assessments.

- Contemporaneous documentation of suicide risk assessments is good clinical care and standard practice.
- Systematic suicide risk assessment performed at the time of discharge informs the patient's postdischarge plan.
- For inpatients at risk for suicide, information of clinical importance regarding prior or current suicide threats, ideation, plans, or attempts should be obtained from family members or others who know the patient. Whenever possible, this should be done with the patient's permission.
- During the treatment of outpatients at significant risk for suicide, it may become necessary to contact family members or others to facilitate hospitalization, to mobilize support, and to acquire information of clinical importance to the clinician. Whenever possible, this should be done with the patient's permission.
- Suicide risk assessments are the responsibility of the psychiatrist. They should not be delegated to others.
- Clinicians have a professional, ethical, and legal duty to provide adequate care to their patients, regardless of managed-care protocols and restrictions. Managed-care limitations on patient care must not be allowed to exacerbate a patient's risk for suicide.
- Clinicians should strive to be aware of personal factors that may adversely affect their care of the suicidal patient. This should include a realistic self-appraisal regarding the number of suicidal patients the clinician can competently treat at any one time.

REFERENCES

American Academy of Child and Adolescent Psychiatry: Summary of the practice parameters for the assessment and treatment of children and adolescents with suicidal behavior. J Am Acad Child Adolesc Psychiatry 40:495–499, 2001

American Psychiatric Association: The Principles of Medical Ethics With Annotations Especially Applicable to Psychiatry. Washington, DC, American Psychiatric Association, 2001

American Psychiatric Association: Practice guideline for the assessment and treatment of patients with suicidal behaviors. Am J Psychiatry 160 (suppl):1–60, 2003

Baldessarini RJ, Tondo L, Hennen J: Lithium treatment and suicide risk in major affective disorders: update and new findings. J Clin Psychiatry 64 (suppl 5):44–52, 2003

Beck AT, Brown G, Berchick RJ, et al: Relationship between hopelessness and ultimate suicide: a replication with psychiatric outpatients. Am J Psychiatry 147:190–195, 1990

Beck AT, Steer RA, Ranieri WF: Scale for suicide ideation: psychometric properties of a self-report version. J Clin Psychol 44:499–505, 1998

Black HC: Black's Law Dictionary, 7th Edition. St Paul, MN, West Group, 1999

Bongar B, Maris RW, Bertram AL, et al: Outpatient standards of care and the suicidal patient. Suicide Life Threat Behav 22:453–478, 1992

Breier A, Astrachan BM: Characterization of schizophrenic patients who commit suicide. Am J Psychiatry 141:206–209, 1984

Brent DA: Assessment and treatment of the youthful suicidal patient. Ann N Y Acad Sci 932:106–131, 2001

Brent DA, Bridge J, Johnson BA, et al: Suicidal behavior runs in families. Arch Gen Psychiatry 53:1145–1152, 1996

Brent DA, Oquendo M, Birmaher B, et al: Familial pathways to early-onset suicide attempt: risk for suicidal behavior in offspring of mood-disordered suicide attempters. Arch Gen Psychiatry 59:801–807, 2002

Brodsky BS, Malone KM, Ellis SP, et al: Characteristics of borderline personality disorder associated with suicidal behavior. Am J Psychiatry 154:1715–1719, 1997

Brodsky BS, Oquendo MA, Ellis SP, et al: The relationship of childhood abuse to impulsivity and suicidal behavior in adults with major depression. Am J Psychiatry 158:1871–1877, 2001

Bronisch T: The typology of personality disorders: diagnostic problems and their relevance for suicidal behavior. Crisis 17:55–58, 1996

Busch KA, Clark DC, Fawcett J, et al: Clinical features of inpatient suicide. Psychiatr Ann 23:256–262, 1993

Busch KA, Fawcett J, Jacobs DG: Clinical correlates of inpatient suicide. J Clin Psychiatry 64:14–19, 2003

Clark DC, Fawcett J: An empirically based model of suicide risk assessment of patients with affective disorders, in Suicide and Clinical Practice. Edited by Jacobs DJ. Washington, DC, American Psychiatric Association, 1999, pp 55–73

Conwell Y, Duberstein PR: Suicide in elders. Ann N Y Acad Sci 932:132–150, 2001

Coryell W, Leon A, Winokur G, et al: Importance of psychotic features to long-term course in major depressive disorder. Am J Psychiatry 153:483–489, 1996

Dube SR, Anda RF, Felitti VJ, et al: Childhood abuse, household dysfunction and the risk of attempted suicide throughout the lifespan: findings from the adverse childhood experiences study. JAMA 286:3089–3096, 2001

Duberstein P, Conwell Y: Personality disorders and completed suicide: a methodological and conceptual review. Clinical Psychology: Science and Practice 4:359–376, 1997

Evans J, Platts H, Liebenau A: Impulsiveness and deliberate self-harm: a comparison of "first-timers" and "repeaters." Acta Psychiatr Scand 93:378–380, 1996

Fawcett J: Treating impulsivity and anxiety in the suicidal patient. Ann N Y Acad Sci 932:94–105, 2001

Fawcett J, Scheftner WA, Clark DC, et al: Clinical predictors of suicide in patients with major affective disorders: a controlled prospective study. Am J Psychiatry 144:35–40, 1987

Fawcett J, Scheftner WA, Fogg L, et al: Time-related predictors of suicide in major affective disorder. Am J Psychiatry 147:1189–1194, 1990

Fawcett J, Clark DC, Busch KA: Assessing and treating the patient at risk for suicide. Psychiatr Ann 23:244–255, 1993

Gelenberg AJ, Chesen CL: How fast are antidepressants? J Clin Psychiatry 61:712–721, 2000

Gunderson JG, Ridolfi ME: Borderline personality disorder: suicide and self-mutilation. Ann N Y Acad Sci 932:61–77, 2002

Hairston v Alexander Tank and Equip. Co., 310 N.C. 227, 234, 311 S.E.2d 559, 565 (1984)

Hall RC, Platt DE, Hall RC: Suicide risk assessment: a review of risk factors for suicide in 100 patients who made severe suicide attempts: evaluation of suicide risk in a time of managed care. Psychosomatics 40:18–27, 1999

Harris EC, Barraclough B: Suicide as an outcome for mental disorders. A meta-analysis. Br J Psychiatry 170:205–228, 1997

Heikkinen ME, Henriksson MM, Isometsa ET, et al: Recent life events and suicide in personality disorders. J Nerv Ment Dis 185:373–381, 1997

Heila H, Isometsa ET, Henriksson MM, et al: Suicide and schizophrenia: a nationwide psychological autopsy study on age- and sex-specific clinical characteristics of 92 suicide victims with schizophrenia. Am J Psychiatry 154:1235–1242, 1997

Heila H, Heikkinen ME, Isometsa ET, et al: Life events and completed suicide in schizophrenia: a comparison of suicide victims with and without schizophrenia. Schizophr Bull 25:519–531, 1999

Hellerstein D, Frosch W, Koenigsbert HW: The clinical significance of command hallucinations. Am J Psychiatry 144:219–225, 1987

Hollander E, Posner N, Cherkasky S: Neuropsychiatric aspects of aggression and impulse control disorders, in American Psychiatric Press Textbook of Neuropsychiatry and Clinical Neurosciences, 4th Edition. Edited by Yudofsky SC, Hales RE. Washington, DC, American Psychiatric Press, 2002, pp 579–596

Institute of Medicine: Reducing Suicide: A National Imperative. Washington, DC, National Academy Press, 2001

Isometsa ET, Heikkinen ME, Martunen MJ, et al: The last appointment before suicide: is suicide intent communicated? Am J Psychiatry 152: 919–922, 1995

Isometsa ET, Henriksson MM, Heikkinen ME, et al: Suicide among subjects with personality disorders. Am J Psychiatry 153:667–673, 1996

Jacobs DG, Brewer M, Klein-Benheim M: Suicide assessment: an overview and recommended protocol, in The Harvard Medical School Guide to Suicide Assessment and Intervention. Edited by Jacobs DJ. San Francisco, CA, Jossey-Bass, 1999, pp 3–39

Junginger J: Predicting compliance with command hallucinations. Am J Psychiatry 147:245–247, 1990

Junginger J: Command hallucinations and the prediction of dangerousness. Psychiatr Serv 46:911–914, 1995

Kaplan M, Asnis GM, Lipschitz DS, et al: Suicidal behavior and abuse in psychiatric outpatients. Compr Psychiatry 36:229–235, 1995

Kasper ME, Rogers R, Adams PA: Dangerousness and command hallucinations: an investigation of psychotic inpatients. Bull Am Acad Psychiatry Law 24:219–224, 1996

Kessler RC, Borges G, Walters EE: Prevalence of and risk factors for lifetime suicide attempts in the National Comorbidity Survey. Arch Gen Psychiatry 56:617–626, 1999

Linehan MM, Goodstein JL, Nielsen SL, et al: Reasons for staying alive when you are thinking of killing yourself: the Reasons for Living Inventory. J Consult Clin Psychol 51:276–286, 1983

Linehan MM, Rizvi SL, Welch SS, et al: Psychiatric aspects of suicidal behaviour: personality disorders, in The International Handbook of Suicide and Attempted Suicide. Edited by Hawton K, Van Heeringen K. New York, Wiley, 2000, pp 147–178

Malone KM, Szanto K, Corbitt EM, et al: Clinical assessment versus research methods in the assessment of suicidal behavior. Am J Psychiatry 152:1601–1607, 1995

Malone KM, Oquendo MA, Hass GL, et al: Protective factors against suicidal acts in major depression: reasons for living. Am J Psychiatry 157:1084–1088, 2000

Maltsberger JT, Hendin H, Haas AP, et al: Determination of precipitating events in the suicide of psychiatric patients. Suicide Life Threat Behav 33:111–119, 2003

Mann JJ, Arango V: The neurobiology of suicidal behavior, in Guide to Suicide Assessment and Intervention. Edited by Jacobs D. San Francisco, CA, Jossey-Bass, 1999, pp 98–114

Mann JJ, Waternaux C, Haas GL, et al: Toward a clinical model of suicidal behavior in psychiatric patients. Am J Psychiatry 156:181–189, 1999

Meltzer HY: Treatment of suicidality in schizophrenia. Ann N Y Acad Sci 932:44–60, 2001

Meltzer HY, Okaly G: Reduction of suicidality during clozapine treatment of neuroleptic-resistant schizophrenia: impact of risk-benefit assessment. Am J Psychiatry 152:183–190, 1995

Meltzer HY, Alphs L, Green AI, et al: Clozapine treatment for suicidality in schizophrenia: International Suicide Prevention Trial (InterSePT). Arch Gen Psychiatry 60:82–91, 2003a

Meltzer HY, Conley RR, de Leo D, et al: Intervention strategies for suicidality. J Clin Psychiatry 6(2):1–18, 2003b

Monahan J, Steadman HJ: Violent storms and violent people: how meteorology can inform risk communication in mental health law. Am J Psychol 51:931–938, 1996

Mortensen PB, Juel K: Mortality and causes of death in first admitted schizophrenic patients. Br J Psychiatry 163:183–189, 1993

Murphy GE, Wetzel RD, Robins E, et al: Multiple risk factors predict suicide in alcoholism. Arch Gen Psychiatry 49:459–462, 1992

National Institute of Mental Health: Suicide facts. Available at: http://www.nimh.nih.gov/research/suifact.htm. Accessed January 3, 2003

O'Carroll PW, Berman AL, Maris RW, et al: Beyond the Tower of Babel: a nomenclature for suicidology. Suicide Life Threat Behav 26:237–252, 1996

Oquendo MA, Kamali M, Ellis SP, et al: Adequacy of antidepressant treatment after discharge and the occurrence of suicidal acts in major depression: a prospective study. Am J Psychiatry 159:1746–1751, 2002

Oquendo MA, Halberstam B, Mann JJ: Risk factors for suicidal behavior: the utility and limitation of research instruments, in Standardized Evaluation in Clinical Practice. Edited by First MB. Washington, DC, American Psychiatric Publishing, 2003, pp 103–130

Pezawas L, Stamenkovic M, Reinhold J, et al: A longitudinal view of triggers and thresholds of suicidal behavior in depression. J Clin Psychiatry 63:866–873, 2002

Pokorny AD: Predictions of suicide in psychiatric patients: report of a prospective study. Arch Gen Psychiatry 40:249–257, 1983

Pokorny AD: Suicide prediction revisited. Suicide Life Threat Behav 23:1–10, 1993

Resnick PJ: Recognizing that the suicidal patient views you as an adversary. Current Psychiatry 1:8, 2002

Roose SP, Glassman AH, Walsh BT, et al: Depression, delusions, and suicide. Am J Psychiatry 140:1159–1162, 1983

Roy A: Suicide in chronic schizophrenia. Br J Psychiatry 141:171–177, 1982

Roy A: Suicide. Baltimore, MD, Williams & Wilkins, 1986, pp 6, 93–94

Schulsinger F, Kety SS, Rosenthal D, et al: A family study of suicide, in Origins, Prevention and Treatment of Affective Disorders. Edited by Schou M, Stromgen F. London, Academic Press, 1979, pp 277–287

Shekelle PG, Ortiz E, Rhodes S, et al: Validity of the Agency for Healthcare Research and Quality clinical practice guidelines: how quickly do guidelines become outdated? JAMA 286:1461–1467, 2001

Silverman MM: Understanding suicide in the 21st century (editorial). Preventing Suicide: The National Journal 2(2), March/April 2003

Simon RI: Clinical Psychiatry and the Law, 2nd Edition. Washington, DC, American Psychiatric Press, 1992

Simon RI: Discharging sicker, potentially violent psychiatric inpatients in the managed care era: standard of care and risk management. Psychiatr Ann 27:726–733, 1997

Simon RI: The suicidal patient, in The Mental Health Practitioner and the Law: A Comprehensive Handbook. Edited by Lifson LE, Simon RI. Cambridge, MA, Harvard University Press, 1998, pp 166–186

Simon RI: Concise Guide to Psychiatry and Law for Clinicians, 3rd Edition. Washington, DC, American Psychiatric Publishing, 2001

Simon RI: Suicide risk assessment: what is the standard of care? J Am Acad Psychiatry Law 30:340–344, 2002

Stepakoff v Kantar, 473 N.E.2d 1131, 1134 (Mass. 1985)

Stone MH: Long-term outcome in personality disorders. Br J Psychiatry 162:299–313, 1993

Stone MH, Stone DK, Hurt SW: Natural history of borderline patients treated by intensive hospitalization. Br J Psychiatry 10:185–206, 1987

Suominen KH, Isometsa ET, Henriksson MM, et al: Suicide attempts and personality disorder. Acta Psychiatr Scand 102:118–125, 2000

Vythilingam M, Chen J, Bremmer JD, et al: Psychotic depression and mortality. Am J Psychiatry 160:574–576, 2003

Williamson v Liptzin, 353 N.C. 456, 548 S.E.2d 734 (N.C. 2001)

Zimmerman M, Chelminski I: Generalized anxiety disorder in patients with major depression: is DSM-IV's hierarchy correct? Am J Psychiatry 160:504–512, 2003

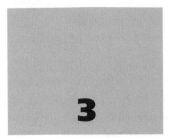

3

SUICIDE PREVENTION CONTRACTS

Contracts are made to be broken.
Legal aphorism

Before you trust a man, eat a peck of salt with him.
Proverb

INTRODUCTION

The suicide prevention contract has achieved wide acceptance, although no studies demonstrate that it is effective in preventing suicide (Stanford et al. 1994). The suicide prevention contract goes by a variety of names, such as the "no-harm contract," the "no-suicide contract," and the "contract for safety." It is used by psychiatrists and other mental health professionals in outpatient and inpatient settings and in hospital emergency departments. Suicide prevention contracts are now an integral part of nursing assessments (Egan 1997). In nursing, patient contracting is an established practice for chronic, life-threatening illnesses in which noncompliance with treatment is common (e.g., diabetes, kidney dialysis) (Egan 1997).

Drye et al. (1973) proposed the use of a specific suicide prevention contract in 1973. Twiname (1981) introduced the suicide prevention contract into the nursing literature in 1981. With the advent of the managed-care era, mental health professionals have come to rely on suicide prevention contracts to manage a patient's risk for suicide (Simon 1999). In both outpatient and inpatient settings, most patients are treated briefly. The average length of stay for patients in acute-care psychiatric units and hospitals is often 5 days or less. The most frequent admissions are severely mentally ill patients who are at risk for suicide. The admission requirements usually exceed the substantive criteria for involuntary hospitalization.

The therapeutic alliance may fail to develop in managed-care settings because of limitations on treatment sessions and an increased reliance on medications. Empathic interaction, pivotal to the development of a therapeutic alliance, is difficult to maintain in high-patient-volume managed-care settings. Suicide prevention contracts have little or no value in settings where mentally ill patients are rapidly treated, stabilized, and discharged. Yet these settings are precisely where such contracts are heavily relied on.

CASE EXAMPLE

Ms. Franklin, a 32-year-old single stockbroker, is admitted from the emergency department to the psychiatric unit of a local community hospital. She was coaxed off the roof of her 25-story apartment building after threatening to jump. Her therapist was present and assisted the police in Ms. Franklin's rescue and transport to the emergency department.

Dr. Raymond performs the psychiatric examination. She learns that Ms. Franklin is under criminal investigation for alleged "irregularities" in her clients' stock transactions. In addition, Ms. Franklin had learned that her outpatient therapist, whom she has been seeing once or twice a week for psychotherapy since age 22, would not be able to see her for an indeterminate period of time because of impending surgery. Arrangements were made for Ms. Franklin to be followed by the psychiatrist who had been managing her medications during the past year. The prospect of facing criminal charges without the support of her therapist made Ms. Franklin's life seem unbearable. She felt that suicide was the "only way out." Dr. Raymond makes the diagnosis of major depression, recurrent, severe without psychotic features.

Ms. Franklin has had three prior psychiatric hospitalizations at this community hospital following suicide attempts. Each admission occurred after the termination of a romantic relationship. Ms. Franklin slashed her wrist 3 years ago, which led to the last admission. Surgical repair of tendons in her left wrist was required. The first and second admissions occurred 5 and 8 years ago, following overdoses of sleep medication (benzodiazepine) and antidepressant medication (selective serotonin reuptake inhibitor [SSRI]). Diagnoses of major depressive disorder, moderate to severe without psychotic features, and borderline personality disorder were made at each prior admission.

As part of the psychiatric examination, Dr. Raymond conducts a systematic suicide risk assessment. In addition to Ms. Franklin's serious suicide threat, Dr. Raymond's high suicide risk rating is based on a number of other risk factors, including the diagnosis of severe major depression, the history of borderline personality disorder, and the prior suicide attempts leading to three hospitalizations.

It is the nursing staff's policy to engage patients in a negotiated suicide prevention plan. Ms. Franklin refuses to sign or verbally agree to the plan. Dr. Raymond does not rely on pro forma suicide prevention contracts. Instead, Dr. Raymond collaborates with the nursing staff and treatment team for safety management of the patient. The nursing staff inform Dr. Raymond of Ms. Franklin's rejection of the suicide prevention plan. In Dr. Raymond's experience, rejection of a suicide prevention plan is generally a more reliable indicator of a patient's suicide risk status than acceptance. On further inquiry by Dr. Raymond, the patient states, "It's no use, I want to die. It's hopeless."

It is Dr. Raymond's standard treatment and safety management practice to perform continuing systematic suicide risk assessments, with focus on the therapeutic alliance. Dr. Raymond feels that the presence of a therapeutic alliance with the patient can be a potent protective factor against suicide.

Dr. Raymond has not treated Ms. Franklin previously. She contacts Ms. Franklin's outpatient therapist to obtain additional history after Ms. Franklin provides a written authorization. An antidepressant medication is started. The most pressing clinical issue is Ms. Franklin's safety. Because she is a new patient at high suicide risk, Ms. Franklin initially is placed on a couch in front of the nurses' station for constant visual observation by the clinical staff. Because of new admissions of severely disturbed patients that have caused turmoil on the unit, Dr. Raymond orders one-to-one, arms-length suicide precautions for Ms. Franklin and moves her to a room adjacent to the nurses' station. Dr. Raymond explains to Ms. Franklin the reasons for close observation and the starting of antidepressant medication. Ms. Franklin takes the medication as prescribed. Dr. Raymond explains that she may experience transient nausea and diarrhea side effects from the antidepressant medication. Dr.

Raymond expresses the hope that they can work together to maintain her safety while she is hospitalized. Ms. Franklin does not answer.

On the second day of hospitalization, Dr. Raymond gathers additional information from the treatment team. She speaks with Ms. Franklin's supportive mother and two younger brothers during their visit. The treatment team members find Ms. Franklin to be cooperative with unit policy and procedures. Family members describe Ms. Franklin as very competent and highly intelligent but extremely sensitive to criticism and rejection. She is a successful stockbroker with many clients, some of whom are close friends. The ongoing criminal investigation has been devastating for Ms. Franklin. She adamantly denies any wrongdoing.

The nursing staff have received specialized training in negotiating suicide prevention plans with patients. The staff again approach Ms. Franklin with the suicide prevention plan. The nurse explains that a written contract is not necessary. Ms. Franklin is asked to choose a period of time during which she would feel reasonably safe from acting on suicidal intentions. Ms. Franklin decides on 12 hours. The nurse, after consultation with the treatment team, feels that it is too long a time. Following negotiations with Ms. Franklin, the suicide safety period is set at 6 hours. The time of expiration is noted in the patient's chart. The nursing staff make sure that a nurse will be present to renegotiate the next phase of the safety plan.

At the end of 6 hours, a nurse renegotiates the contract with Ms. Franklin. The nursing staff have learned that suicide prevention encounters and negotiations help build a therapeutic alliance. Suicide prevention becomes a process negotiated with the patient rather than a robotic event. It engages the patient in the overall treatment plan.

Dr. Raymond explains the multidisciplinary treatment plan and the need for continued one-to-one observation. Despite Ms. Franklin's severe depression, Dr. Raymond finds her mental capacity to be adequate for making health care decisions. Ms. Franklin bitterly complains that the constant safety observations by the staff are intrusive. She is embarrassed and humiliated by the constant presence of a "stranger" who observes her going to the bathroom and taking a shower.

Dr. Raymond balances the benefits and risks of continued one-to-one suicide precautions. Ms. Franklin states, "It makes me feel more hopeless and depressed." The nursing staff inform Dr. Raymond that Ms. Franklin is participating in a negotiated suicide safety process. As part of safety management, Ms. Franklin agrees to stay out of her room during scheduled ward activities. She is actively involved in the exercise group and other activities that were negotiated at the same time. Dr. Raymond considers the developing therapeutic alliance an important factor in her decision to decrease the level of suicide precautions. The observation level is decreased to 15-minute checks. Before changing the observation level, Dr. Raymond performs a suicide risk assessment, paying close attention to the acute suicide risk factors that led to Ms. Franklin's hospitalization. Ms. Franklin denies suicidal ideation, intent, or plan.

Dr. Raymond meets with Ms. Franklin each day of her hospitalization. A number of protective factors against suicide are weighed (family support, competency, cooperativeness, an emerging alliance, and favorable news about the investigation). Ms. Franklin's attorney called to inform her and Dr. Raymond that the criminal investigation was placed on hold and most likely will not go forward. Ms. Franklin is greatly relieved.

Dr. Raymond is unrushed, spending sufficient time with Ms. Franklin to gather a detailed history and to explore the events that led to her hospitalization. Ms. Franklin is appreciative of the time spent and the interest displayed by Dr. Raymond. However, a potential disruption in their relationship emerges over the issue of smoking.

Hospital policy does not permit patients to leave the ward for 24 hours following admission. Smoking is not allowed on the unit. Ms. Franklin is angry that she cannot smoke. This matter is successfully negotiated when Ms. Franklin grudgingly agrees to use a nicotine patch. After the third hospital day, Dr. Raymond discontinues the 15-minute suicide precautions. Ms. Franklin is permitted to leave the unit for 20 minutes four times a day with a supervised group of smokers. She attends all treatment groups and is a constructive participant. Dr. Raymond's suicide risk assessment indicates that Ms. Franklin's risk has decreased from high to moderate. The suicide prevention plan is now negotiated for 24 hours.

Ms. Franklin is sleeping better by the fifth day of hospitalization. Her depression is much improved. Ms. Franklin is reassured by her outpatient therapist that he will have time to see her after she is discharged from the hospital during the few weeks before his surgery.

On the sixth hospital day, the therapeutic alliance is tested again when Ms. Franklin requests a pass to go to her apartment alone before discharge. She wants to return to her job as soon as possible. Although Ms. Franklin is adamant about going alone, she reluctantly agrees with Dr. Raymond's suggestion that her mother accompany her on the first pass. The pass goes well. An unattended pass on the seventh hospital day is productive. Ms. Franklin feels comfortable being alone in her apartment.

The acute suicide risk factors that led to Ms. Franklin's suicide threat have diminished. Ms. Franklin maintains a working therapeutic alliance with Dr. Raymond and the treatment team. Ms. Franklin has friendly relations with other patients. She takes her medications as prescribed. The safety negotiations are discontinued. The process of negotiating safety has been very helpful in building a therapeutic alliance with the psychiatrist, the nursing staff, and the entire treatment team. It also supports Ms. Franklin's self-esteem and facilitates her sense of control and autonomous functioning. Dr. Raymond assesses that Ms. Franklin's risk for suicide is low.

The therapeutic passes "red-flag" the managed-care organization to deny insurance coverage beyond 8 hospital days. After doctor-to-doctor appeal, an additional hospital day is approved. At the discharge planning meeting with the treatment team, also attended by Dr. Raymond and Ms. Franklin, all team members agree that she is ready for discharge. Dr. Raymond feels that Ms. Franklin's serious suicide threat was situationally driven by the criminal investigation and the pending absence and suspension of the support of her therapist. However, she remains at chronic suicide risk because of the diagnoses of severe recurrent major depression, borderline personality disorder by history, and three prior hospitalizations following suicide attempts.

Systematic suicide risk assessments are used to monitor the course of Ms. Franklin's acute risk factors and the therapeutic alliance and to guide treatment and safety management decisions. Although Dr. Raymond does not rely on suicide prevention contracts, she pays close attention to the safety negotiations conducted by the nursing staff that help her assess the therapeutic alliance. The presence of a solid therapeutic alliance gives Dr. Raymond and the treatment team confidence in their decision making about the safety management of Ms. Franklin. Dr. Raymond places considerable weight on the therapeutic alliance as a crucial factor in the assessment of suicide risk.

On the ninth hospital day, Ms. Franklin is discharged. Family support is available to her. She is eager to return to work, which is a major source of self-esteem. Ms. Franklin will be seen by her regular outpatient therapist the day after discharge. The therapist will smooth the transition to the outpatient psychiatrist who will be covering for him while he recovers from surgery. The outpatient psychiatrist will see the patient regularly until the regular therapist returns. Ms. Franklin accepts a referral to the hospital's partial hospitalization program. She will attend the program on the day following discharge.

DISCUSSION

ALLIANCE VERSUS CONTRACT

The therapeutic alliance is a key factor in the assessment of suicide risk. In patients at risk for suicide, the absence of a therapeutic alliance between the clinician and the patient may increase suicide risk. The presence of a therapeutic alliance is a protective factor against suicide. In the case example, Dr. Raymond and the treatment team relied on systematic suicide risk assessment and the therapeutic alliance for safety management, and not on a "one-time" suicide prevention contract.

A suicide prevention contract without a therapeutic alliance is meaningless. Moreover, suicide prevention contracts, if used, should be part of an ongoing suicide risk assessment and a treatment plan. There is no objective evidence that obtaining a suicide prevention contract reduces the risk of suicide or that such a contract can be used as a factor in the assessment of suicide risk (Chiles and Strosahl 1995). Suicide prevention contracts can create the illusion of patient safety, reducing staff anxiety without achieving the intended purpose of providing effective safety management for the suicidal patient. The clinician's perception of risk of suicide is lowered, but the real risk of suicide may be unchanged or even heightened by the misperception of risk.

The effectiveness of the therapeutic alliance is measured by patient behaviors, not just words alone. In the case example, Dr. Raymond assessed the strength of the therapeutic alliance by Ms. Franklin's willingness to compromise on contentious issues, by her adherence to the treatment, and by her engagement in the process of safety management. Also, Ms. Franklin's cooperation with the safety management process helped solidify the therapeutic alliance.

The therapeutic alliance is a "two-way street." The patient's cooperation with the treatment plan forms the basis for the trust the clinician places in the patient. However, some patients at risk for suicide will cooperate fully so that they can be discharged as early as possible to commit suicide. There is nothing straightforward about the management of suicidal behavior in patients.

The therapeutic alliance is defined as the conscious, task-oriented collaboration between the clinician and the patient for the mutual exploration of the patient's problems (Simon 1992). A therapeutic alliance with the patient at risk for suicide represents the willingness of the healthy part of the patient's personality to work with the therapist, showing a life-affirming belief on the part of the patient that "I believe *you* can help *me* learn to cope and be happier." This belief is the antithesis of feeling hopeless, such as when the patient says, "There is no hope for the relief of my unendurable pain; I am going away" (Shneidman 1985). The therapeutic alliance also contains unconscious cognitive and affective elements. The case example illustrates a near-ideal clinical situation in which the clinician, in collaboration with the treatment team, is able to nurture and grow a therapeutic alliance with the patient that diminishes suicide risk.

The therapeutic alliance may not develop or may be attenuated for a variety of reasons. In high-volume, short-length-of-stay inpatient settings, patients often develop alliances with members of the treatment team with whom they spend much of their time. Severely mentally ill patients with moderate to high suicide risk are treated rapidly and discharged. The psychiatrist may not have time or may not take the time to assess the patient's capacity to enter into a therapeutic alliance. There is little or no basis for relying on a suicide prevention contract obtained from a severely mentally ill patient. For these reasons, suicide prevention contracts are of little or no utility in emergency settings.

A patient who is determined to commit suicide may agree to a no-harm contract to avoid the detection of suicide intent. The psychiatrist is seen as the adversary with whom there is no therapeutic alliance (Resnick 2002). Patients who have not been mentally ill or previously psychiatrically hospitalized may minimize their illness and superficially agree to a suicide prevention contract. These patients may be at high risk for suicide (Simon and Gutheil 2002). Patients lacking sufficient mental capacity may be unable to rationally engage the clinician for the purpose of establishing and adhering to a suicide prevention contract. Other patients may give ready assent to a suicide prevention contract in order to gain patient privileges, for example, to be able to leave the psychiatric unit to smoke.

The therapeutic alliance is a dynamic interaction between the patient and the clinician that is in constant flux and subject to rapid change. Unexpected changes in situational factors and in symptom severity related to psychosis, mood instability, intoxication, agitation, impulsiveness, and hopelessness can undermine the therapeutic alliance and increase suicide risk. Language and cultural barriers can cause misunderstandings that may increase the patient's risk of suicide. A therapist may be "stunned and surprised" when a patient with whom a solid therapeutic alliance presumably existed commits suicide between sessions. The severity of a patient's mental illness may intensify between treatment sessions, undermining the therapeutic alliance. It is understandable that suicide prevention contracts are overvalued as a safety risk management technique. They often are used in an attempt to control the inevitable anxiety and uncertainty associated with treating patients at risk for suicide.

The suicide prevention contract tends to be an event, a "stand-alone" intervention. Systematic suicide risk assessment is a process that considers a number of risk and protective factors. The therapeutic alliance is continually assessed along with other suicide risk and preventive factors (see Chapter 2, "Suicide Risk Assessment"). In the case example, Dr. Raymond focuses on monitoring acute suicide risk factors over the course of Ms. Franklin's hospitalization. Special attention is paid to the status of her therapeutic alliance as a key protective factor. The greatest danger posed by the suicide prevention contract is to use it as a substitute for systematic suicide risk assessment and the process of safety management. Adequate suicide risk assessment by psychiatrists is standard clinical practice. The standard of care does not require psychiatrists to obtain suicide prevention contracts from patients.

Some clinics and hospitals may require clinicians to obtain suicide prevention contracts from patients. For clinicians who do not use such contracts, mandatory requirements to do so expose them to legal liability. Documenting the rationale for not using suicide prevention contracts may help avoid malpractice liability in case of patient suicide.

Some clinicians gauge the patient's risk for suicide by the willingness to formalize the alliance with a written contract. The suicide prevention contract (including terms and time limit) that the patient signs should be included as part of the medical record. Oral contracts are usually more acceptable. No standard exists that requires a written contract. However, a written suicide prevention contract provides external structure that is internalized by some patients during episodes of confusion and regression. A written suicide prevention contract may help some patients feel the caring presence of the therapist during a crisis. The natural human tendency to be wary of signing contracts is often intensified by mental illness, especially in conditions involving paranoia.

The time limit and terms of the oral contract should be documented. Suicide prevention contracts without time limits are more likely to be singular events. Time limits remind the clinician or hospital staff to revisit the therapeutic alliance that underpins the viability of the contract. If appropriate, patients should be allowed to set comfortable time limits. The time limit should be brief—hours or a few days (Chiles and Strosahl 1995). As in the case example, when the contractual time expires, a member of the clinical staff should be available to reassess the need for further safety contracting. Involving the patient in the contracting process helps promote the therapeutic alliance. Safety management is a negotiated process that promotes patient control over self and cooperation with treatment. Negotiation, however, does not mean abrogating the clinician's duty of care to the patient. The negotiation process is collaborative but not necessarily democratic.

When the patient is presented with a suicide prevention contract, responses vary between genuine acceptance, ambivalent acceptance, perfunctory acceptance, suggestion of amendments, refusal, and nonresponse. The rejection of a suicide prevention contract places the clinician on notice that the patient may be at high risk for suicide and that further assessment is necessary. A higher level of safety checks should be considered. The patient may need to be placed in a room close to the nurses' station and be restricted to the unit. However, some patients may refuse such contracts to underscore that they are "suicidal," in order to gain entrance to or remain in a hospital.

In outpatient settings with established patients, "oral understandings" are usually reached in which the therapist is to be contacted if a suicide crisis arises. Less commonly, a brief, written agreement might read as follows:

> We [therapist and patient] agree that you [patient] will call me if you find that you are concerned about harming yourself. If necessary, I will arrange to see you as soon as possible. If you need immediate help and cannot reach me, you agree to go directly to the nearest hospital emergency department.

All of the caveats and recommendations regarding suicide prevention contracts discussed here apply equally to outpatients. Outpatients who are treated over time usually develop enduring, stable therapeutic alliances with their therapists. The therapeutic alliance is put to the test when the therapist finds it necessary to recommend psychiatric hospitalization to the patient at significant risk for suicide (see Chapter 4, "Outpatients").

OTHER VIEWPOINTS

Professional opinions differ on the use of suicide prevention contracts. Miller et al. (1998) have stated that the role of suicide prevention contracts in reducing the risk of suicide is overvalued. The authors noted that these contracts do not reduce suicide risk and may interfere with thorough suicide risk assessment. Their survey documented widespread use of the suicide prevention contract but a relative absence of formal training in its use. They recommend an alternative approach to suicide risk management based on the principles of informed consent and shared uncertainty and responsibility with the patient.

Stanford et al. (1994), after reviewing the literature, asserted that the no-harm contract lacks broad consensus regarding its value, despite its wide use. Their review revealed that such contracts can be used to assess the patient's suicide risk, uncover issues that precipitate thoughts of suicide, and evaluate the patient's competency to enter into such a contract. Therapeutically, the contract may help initiate the therapeutic alliance, establish psychotherapeutic boundaries, and reduce patient and clinician anxiety. They concluded that although the no-harm contract is used to provide diagnostic information and therapeutic assistance, it can also "short-circuit" comprehensive suicide risk assessment, leading to ill-conceived and "potentially dangerous decisions."

Kroll (2000), in a survey of psychiatrists practicing in Minnesota, found that no-suicide contracts were used by 57% of the psychiatrists who responded. Of this group, 41% had patients who committed suicide after agreeing to safety contracts. Drew (2001) reported an increased likelihood of self-harm in hospitalized patients with no-suicide contracts. Of 100 suicide attempters studied by Hall et al. (1999), 83% had agreed to no-harm contracts. The authors concluded that these contracts did not prevent suicide attempts.

In a study by Davis et al. (2002), 135 suicidal psychiatric inpatients were surveyed regarding their opinions on the benefits and limitations of written no-suicide agreements. Most patients rated written no-suicide agreements positively. The positive views were not substantially affected by age, social disability, gender, Axis II disorder, or suicide risk at admission. However, the number of prior suicide attempts negatively affected patients' ratings of the helpfulness of suicide prevention contracts. Patients who made multiple attempts regarded these agreements as less helpful than did patients who had made no prior attempts or who made only a single attempt. The authors noted methodological and generalizability issues inherent in their survey.

Other safety management techniques used by some clinicians include an impulsivity control log and a discharge safety contract. An impulsivity control log is a tool that the patient can use when destructive impulses threaten. The log allows the patient to document the date/time, location, situation, intention of the impulse, options for management, and outcome of the exercise. Logging threatening impulses gives the patient pause before reflexively acting. Words replace destructive actions.

A discharge safety contract attempts to minimize the suicidal patient's denial by focusing attention on treatment and safety issues. For example, a patient denies suicidal ideation or intent shortly after admission, pressing the clinician hard for an early discharge. The patient refuses to consider early discharge planning. By agreeing to complete the clinical focus items on the discharge safety contract, the patient may be more realistic about treatment needs, agreeing to work with the clinical staff toward a safe and timely discharge.

A general consensus exists in the professional literature that suicide prevention contracts should not replace comprehensive or systematic suicide risk assessment. The use of these contracts can create the illusion of securing safety for the patient and peace of mind for the clinician. However, the patient's real risk for suicide may be overlooked, and the opportunity to beneficially intervene may be lost.

CLINICAL-LEGAL ISSUES

The suicide prevention contract is a clinical, not a legal, contract. An oral or written contract against suicide does not protect the clinician from being sued after a patient commits suicide (Simon 1999). The suicide prevention contract is an example of an "exculpatory clause" (*Olson v. Molzea* [1977]; *Porubiansky v. Emory Univ.* [1981]). An individual cannot enforce the terms of a contract that would relieve her or him from liability for any harm caused by negligence. Thus, a suicide prevention contract would not protect a clinician from legal liability if the clinician's conduct was negligent and was the proximate cause of the patient's suicide. Negligence cannot be contracted away. Efforts to do so would violate public policy (*Roy v. Hartogs* [1975]).

In *Stepakoff v. Kantar* (1985), the psychiatrist thought that he had a "solid pact" with a patient with bipolar disorder to contact him if the patient felt suicidal. The patient did contact Dr. Kantar and the covering psychiatrist on several occasions. After a favorable telephone assessment of the patient's mental stability and psychological defense mechanisms, Dr. Kantar determined that the patient was unlikely to commit suicide. Unfortunately, the patient committed suicide.

The Massachusetts Supreme Judicial Court held that the psychiatrist's legal obligation to the patient was to treat him according to the standard of care and skill of the average psychiatrist. The court found that having a "solid pact" with the patient against suicide fell within such a standard. The court did not express an opinion about the use of suicide prevention contracts.

It is unlikely that courts will give much credence to a suicide prevention contract if a clinician's deviation from the standard of care leads to the patient's suicide. In *Stepakoff*, the psychiatrist demonstrated that he provided appropriate patient care through frequent contact and assessment. The psychiatrist documented his consideration of involuntary hospitalization of the patient. He also provided an "active" substitute psychiatrist to provide care to the patient while he was on vacation. The psychiatrist did not rely exclusively on a "solid pact" with the patient.

When the suicide prevention contract is not part of a comprehensive assessment and treatment plan, it will not be credible. Producing a "stand-alone" suicide prevention contract in court that was signed by a patient who then committed suicide will not provide a legal defense for the clinician. The reliance on "contracts for safety" in the place of careful assessment of the patient at risk for suicide creates a high risk of legal liability (Bergstresser 1998).

Obtaining a suicide prevention contract establishes that the patient is at risk for suicide. It does not establish that suicide risk has been assessed. Not to follow it up with an adequate suicide risk assessment exposes the clinician to a malpractice suit if the patient attempts or commits suicide. The clinician cannot shift accountability for negligence to the patient.

When a patient senses that a suicide prevention contract is used primarily for defensive purposes, it may adversely affect the therapeutic alliance and increase the risk of suicide. Moreover, confronting a new patient with a request to sign a contract may create an adversarial tone between the clinician and patient, inhibiting or dooming the therapeutic alliance from the start. The defensive use of suicide prevention contracts may falsely lower the clinician's vigilance without reducing the patient's risk for suicide. A pattern of defensive practices will not be lost on the court, which would likely conclude that the clinician was more interested in fending off a lawsuit than in providing good clinical care.

The assessment of a patient's "competency" to understand the terms of a suicide prevention contract is emphasized by some commentators (Miller et al. 1998). Competency is a confusing term because it is often equated with legal competence. Competency is not a scientifically determinable state. The legal test of competency occurs as a singular event. Competency tests tend to be applied in a procrustean fashion by predetermined rules and definitions: the patient either fits or does not fit the test. Mental capacity, on the other hand, is continuous but variable, especially when affected by physical or mental illness.

Mental capacity for health care decision making is required when the patient is presented with an oral or written suicide prevention contract. The question often becomes, does a patient who is severely mentally ill have the mental capacity to understand the terms of the contract and to make his or her decision voluntarily? The process of negotiating safety management with patients as described in the case example represents this author's opinion of "best practices." Implementing a negotiated safety plan can be time and labor intensive. In this era of rapid patient turnover and understaffing, it may be viewed as impractical. Nonetheless, the principle of negotiating an ongoing safety management plan with the patient should hold true for most treatment settings. The process avoids the "one time" suicide prevention contract that provides only the illusion of patient safety. The process of safety management permits an ongoing assessment of the patient's mental capacity for health care decisions.

CLINICALLY BASED RISK MANAGEMENT

- The suicide prevention contract, if used, should be an adjunct to comprehensive psychiatric evaluation, ongoing suicide risk assessment, and a safety management plan. Suicide prevention contracts cannot "stand alone."
- Suicide prevention contracts should not take the place of systematic suicide risk assessment. The contract does not establish that suicide risk has been assessed.
- Safety management is a process. Suicide prevention contracts are usually events. When suicide prevention contracts are used, they should be reevaluated regularly with the patient and documented.
- The suicide prevention contract is a clinical, not a legal, contract. It does not immunize the clinician against a lawsuit.
- Suicide prevention contracts should not be used merely as a defensive risk management technique.
- Indications for the use, risks, and benefits of the suicide prevention contract should be documented.
- Mental health professionals should be trained in the appropriate indications, applications, and limitations of suicide prevention contracts.
- The process of safety management is determined by the clinical needs of the patient, not by the anxieties of the therapist or of the clinical staff.
- Suicide prevention contracts have little or no utility in emergency settings.

- Suicide prevention contracts that are not based on a viable therapeutic alliance are unreliable.
- The therapeutic alliance is a dynamic, changeable interaction between the clinician and the patient that is influenced by a number of illness and situational factors. The status of the therapeutic alliance should be assessed regularly and documented.
- The status of the therapeutic alliance can be a key suicide risk or preventive factor. It is assessed along with a number of other suicide risk and preventive factors in systematic suicide risk assessment.
- Health care decision-making capacity, the foundation for the patient's ability to enter into a viable suicide prevention contract or plan, often varies over the patient's clinical course. Mental capacity should be assessed regularly and documented.
- The existence and terms of agreement (including time limit) of a suicide prevention contract or plan should be documented as part of the medical record. The terms and time limit of an oral contract or safety plan also should be documented.
- The patient should be allowed, if appropriate, to set a brief time limit—hours or a few days—for complying with the terms of a suicide prevention contract or plan. The psychiatrist or clinical staff should be present when the contractual time expires to renegotiate the contract or plan, if necessary.
- Time-limited suicide prevention contracts or plans are a reminder to the clinician to revisit the therapeutic alliance. The contract or plan is then incorporated into the process of suicide risk assessment.
- Whenever possible, the clinician's interventions should be directed at fostering and maintaining the therapeutic alliance. A solid, stable therapeutic alliance is one of the most important protective factors against suicide.
- The acceptance or rejection of a suicide prevention contract or plan by the patient usually involves a variety of motivations that should be assessed.

REFERENCES

Bergstresser CD: The perspective of the plaintiff's attorney, in The Mental Health Practitioner and the Law: A Comprehensive Handbook. Edited by Lifson LE, Simon RI. Cambridge, MA, Harvard University Press, 1998, pp 329–343

Chiles JA, Strosahl KD: The Suicidal Patient: Principles of Assessment, Treatment, and Case Management. Washington, DC, American Psychiatric Press, 1995

Davis SE, Williams IS, Hays LW: Psychiatric inpatients' perceptions of written no-suicide agreements: an exploratory study. Suicide Life Threat Behav 32:51–66, 2002

Drew BL: Self-harm behavior and no-suicide contracts in inpatient settings. Arch Psychiatr Nurs 15:99, 2001

Drye RC, Goulding RL, Goulding ME: No-suicide decisions: patient monitoring of suicidal risk. Am J Psychiatry 130:171–174, 1973

Egan MP: Contracting for safety: a concept analysis. Crisis 18:23, 1997

Hall RC, Platt DE, Hall RC: Suicide risk assessment: a review of risk factors for suicide in 100 patients who made severe suicide attempts: evaluation in a time of managed care. Psychosomatics 40:18–27, 1999

Kroll J: Use of no-suicide contracts by physicians in Minnesota. Am J Psychiatry 157:1684–1686, 2000

Miller MC, Jacobs DG, Gutheil TG: Talisman or taboo: the controversy of the suicide prevention contract. Harv Rev Psychiatry 6:78–87, 1998

Olson v Molzea, 558 S.W.3d 429 (Tenn. 1997)

Porubiansky v Emory Univ., 156 Ga. App. 602, 275 S.E.2d 163 (1981)

Resnick PJ: Recognizing that the suicidal patient views you as an adversary. Current Psychiatry 1:8, 2002

Roy v Hartogs, 81 Misc. 2d 350, 366 N.Y.S.2d 297, 301 (1975)

Shneidman ES: Definition of Suicide. New York, Wiley, 1985, p 126

Simon RI: Clinical Psychiatry and the Law, 2nd Edition. Washington, DC, American Psychiatric Press, 1992

Simon RI: The suicide prevention contract: clinical, legal and risk management issues. J Am Acad Psychiatry Law 27:445–450, 1999

Simon RI, Gutheil TG: A recurrent pattern of suicide risk factors observed in litigated cases: lessons in risk management. Psychiatr Ann 32:384–387, 2002

Stanford EJ, Goetz RR, Bloom JD: The no harm contract in the emergency assessment of suicide risk. J Clin Psychiatry 55:344–348, 1994

Stepakoff v Kantar, 473 N.E.2d 1131, 1134 (Mass. 1985)

Twiname BG: No-suicide contracts for nurses. J Psychiatr Nurs 19:11–12, 1981

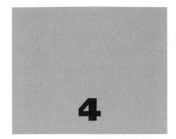

4

OUTPATIENTS

I am tired of tears and laughter,
And of men that laugh and weep;
Of what may come hereafter
For men that sow and reap:
I am weary of days and hours,
Blown buds of barren flowers,
Desires and dreams and powers
And everything but sleep.

> Algernon Charles Swinburne,
> *The Garden of Proserpine*

The thought of suicide is a great consolation:
by means of it one gets successfully through many a bad night.

> Friedrich Wilhelm Nietzsche, *Beyond Good and Evil*

INTRODUCTION

Most patients at low to moderate risk for suicide, and even some patients at high risk, are treated in outpatient settings. Many patients that were formerly treated as inpatients are now treated as outpatients, some after only a brief hospital stay. Heretofore, lawsuits against therapists for outpatient suicides have been relatively infrequent. Courts have reasoned that when an outpatient attempts or commits suicide, the therapist may not necessarily have breached a duty to protect the patient from self-harm because of difficulty in controlling the patient (*Speer v. United States* [1981/1982]; *Bellah v.*

79

Greenson [1978]). However, in *Kockelman v. Segals* (1998), the patient was treated for depression as an outpatient. He committed suicide by taking an overdose of medications. The psychiatrist's attorney moved to dismiss the case on the basis of a California law that did not impose a duty on a psychiatrist to prevent an outpatient from committing suicide. The appellate court held that a psychiatrist owes a duty of care to a patient who commits suicide, whether the patient is an outpatient or an inpatient.

In the managed-care era, insurance benefits for the treatment of outpatients are limited by managed-care organizations (MCOs). The more severely ill inpatients are discharged to outpatient treatment after a brief hospitalization, some at continued significant risk for suicide. Approved therapists receive patient referrals from MCOs for outpatient treatment. Some of these patients are at significant risk for suicide and require time-intensive psychotherapy. Only a few sessions may be authorized. If the therapist simply abandons the patient after insurance coverage ends, the liability risk is high should the patient attempt or commit suicide. The therapist's duty of care to the patient is not defined or limited by managed-care arrangements. Clinics or group practices should not have policies that call for the summary discharge of patients when insurance benefits end. Such policies are invitations for lawsuits alleging negligent treatment and abandonment, especially if the patient attempts or commits suicide. The therapist's professional responsibility to the patient exists independently of MCO payments for treatment (Simon 1998a).

Split-treatment arrangements, in which the psychiatrist manages the patient's medications while a nonmedical psychotherapist conducts the psychotherapy, are fraught with liability exposure for both treaters, especially when the patient is at risk for suicide (see Chapter 6, "Inpatients"). Partial hospitalization programs (PHPs) and intensive outpatient programs (IOPs) also treat patients who are at heightened risk for suicide. PHPs ordinarily treat patients who have recently been discharged from inpatient treatment but continue to require intensive transitional care to maintain stability, to ensure safety, and to prevent rehospitalization. However, some patients at high risk for suicide do not adhere to follow-up treatment programs, posing significant liability risk for therapists.

In the managed-care era, the outpatient therapist has increased malpractice liability exposure in the treatment of patients at risk for suicide (see Table 4–1). Currently, outpatient clinicians are just as likely to be sued for malpractice as the inpatient psychiatrist for alleged negligent treatment of a patient who attempts or commits suicide (Bongar et al. 1998).

Table 4–1. Malpractice liability for outpatient suicides: reducing the risk

Evaluation

Accurately diagnose the patient

Perform systematic suicide risk assessments

Obtain prior treatment records

Treatment

Formulate, document, and implement a comprehensive, rational treatment plan

Adequately assess the patient's suicide risk

Actively collaborate in split-treatment arrangements

Hospitalize, voluntarily or involuntarily, patients at imminent risk for suicide

Management

Provide safety management (e.g., ensure availability for emergencies, adjust frequency of visits)

Communicate and enlist support of family or significant others during a patient's suicide crisis

---

CASE EXAMPLE

Mr. Williams is 43 years old, is married with two young children, and seeks treatment for depression. Dr. Franks, a psychiatrist, sees Mr. Williams for a brief, initial evaluation. Mr. Williams provides a history of mood lability and recurrent major depressions since his early 20s. He currently is a tenured university professor in computer science. Mr. Williams experiences difficulty concentrating, early morning awakening, and loss of appetite and has undergone a 15-pound weight loss during the past month. "Fleeting suicide thoughts" are present. He ascribes his current depression to frequent arguments with his wife about her new job.

Dr. Franks obtains the following history. Mr. Williams is the oldest of three boys. His parents were divorced when he was 12 years

old. His relationship with his father and brothers has been rival-
rous. Mr. Williams was an excellent student. It was important for
him to "be always first and always right." He describes his marriage
as "rocky." However, his children appear to be "doing well."

Mr. Williams was psychiatrically hospitalized for a week at age
32, following a defeat in a local election. He has had an interest in
politics since his college days. In the local election, Mr. Williams
was "beaten in a landslide." He felt extreme embarrassment and
humiliation, refusing to leave his home. He told his wife that he was
very depressed and was harboring thoughts of killing himself with
a handgun that he owned.

Prior to this episode, he had experienced periods of energy and
productivity followed by periods of depression. During the hospitalization, he was placed on an antidepressant and lithium. Soon
after discharge, he stopped his medications because he felt "stigma-
tized." Mr. Williams married in his mid-20s. He has experienced ri-
valrous feelings toward his wife, who has risen rapidly to important
posts in the university administration. Mr. Williams recognizes that
her recent promotion to university provost threatens his "need to
be first."

It is Dr. Franks's practice to see prospective patients for a brief
period of evaluation. With proper authorization, he contacts the
psychiatrist who had previously hospitalized Mr. Williams. Mr.
Williams explicitly withholds authorization for any communication
with his wife.

Dr. Franks also obtains a faxed copy of Mr. Williams's hospital
discharge summary. Dr. Franks performs a multiaxial diagnostic assessment. The information in the discharge summary confirms his
diagnosis of bipolar II disorder and narcissistic personality disorder. The previous psychiatrist described Mr. Williams as a "very
difficult patient." For example, Mr. Williams was nonadherent to
the medication regimen and constantly pushed for discharge. It
was very difficult for Mr. Williams to acknowledge that he was a
patient in need of help. Dr. Franks assesses Mr. Williams's risk for
suicide to be low to moderate.

Dr. Franks agrees to treat Mr. Williams in twice-per-week psychotherapy. A liberal university health plan authorizes the psychotherapy visits. He formulates an individualized treatment plan. It is
Dr. Franks's practice to regularly review and adjust the treatment
plan as necessary. He starts Mr. Williams on antidepressant medication. The psychotherapeutic focus centers on Mr. Williams's omnip-
otent strivings, his manipulative behaviors, and other narcissistic
defenses. These defenses are erected against pervasive feelings of in-
adequacy that, when exposed, result in "shame attacks."

Approximately 6 weeks after beginning treatment, Mr. Williams faces a crisis in his department. Allegations of falsified research are made against two of his associate professors. Although he is not accused of wrongdoing himself, as chairman of the department he is responsible for oversight of all research conducted.

Mr. Williams is distraught. His depression worsens. Suicidal ideation becomes more persistent. Ongoing suicide risk assessment reveals moderate to high risk, based primarily on worsening of Mr. Williams's depression, withdrawal from his family, hopelessness, and difficulty leaving home to go to work. Mr. Williams denies suicide intent or plan. During a regular session, Dr. Franks notices what appear to be rope burns on Mr. Williams's neck. On direct inquiry, Mr. Williams admits that he tried to hang himself in his basement, "but the rope broke."

The fact that Mr. Williams did not volunteer this information and the seriousness of the attempt alarms Dr. Franks. He realizes that the therapeutic alliance is tenuous at best. There is little support from his wife. Dr. Franks recommends to Mr. Williams that he be hospitalized immediately. Mr. Williams refuses and becomes confrontational. He angrily tells Dr. Franks, "After my last hospitalization, I vowed I would never go into a loony bin again." Dr. Franks informs Mr. Williams that he is left with no choice but to initiate involuntary hospitalization. Mr. Williams jumps up to leave, shouting, "Lots of luck, doctor. You'd better have good malpractice insurance." He slams the door on his way out.

Dr. Franks calls Mr. Williams's wife, informing her of her husband's profound depression, suicide attempt, and refusal of voluntary hospitalization. He also informs her that Mr. Williams meets the criteria for involuntary hospitalization, which include the presence of a mental disorder, a need for inpatient care or treatment, a danger to the life of the individual or others, an unwillingness or inability to be admitted voluntarily, and the unavailability of a less restrictive form of treatment.

Ms. Williams is afraid to file for her husband's involuntary hospitalization. She fears the repercussion from her husband. She admits that Mr. Williams told her earlier that day that he had tried to hang himself. The state permits spousal application for a court order for involuntary hospitalization. Dr. Franks completes the medical certification papers and calls the sheriff's office. As he arrives home, Mr. Williams is apprehended by the community mobile crisis unit and transported to a community hospital that accepts involuntary admissions. Dr. Franks is relieved but regrets that Mr. Williams's outpatient treatment was suddenly interrupted. However, he recognizes the importance of appropriate involuntary hospitalization as an emergency psychiatric intervention. Dr. Franks was not intimidated by Mr. Williams's threat of a lawsuit.

DISCUSSION

EVALUATION

Gutheil (1992) identifies the "one-shot" evaluation, usually in the private office, clinic, or emergency department as high risk for both therapist and patient. The therapist does not have sufficient knowledge of the patient, and there is no therapeutic alliance for the therapist to martial. The one-shot evaluation frequently occurs in the emergency department of a general hospital or in a high-volume office practice, especially in a split-treatment arrangement. In the latter, collaborating treaters may each assume that the other has conducted a thorough evaluation (see Chapter 5, "Collaborative Treatment"). In the case example, Dr. Franks took sufficient time for the evaluation of Mr. Williams to diagnose bipolar II disorder and a narcissistic personality disorder. Both diagnoses were key to his understanding of the treatment and management necessary for his patient.

Currently, more than 450 types of psychotherapy are recognized (Simon 2001). Psychiatrists and other clinicians are usually identified by the type of therapy they provide (e.g., cognitive-behavioral therapist, family therapist, child or adolescent therapist, group therapist, psychoanalyst). Therapists, regardless of the type of therapy they provide, must be able to correctly diagnose the patient and to develop, document, and implement a comprehensive treatment plan. It is easy to become quickly focused on the crisis that brings the suicidal patient into treatment, while overlooking careful diagnosis that informs treatment and management planning.

An essential part of the psychiatric evaluation of the patient is the initial screening for suicide risk. Every patient should be asked if he or she has current suicidal ideation, intent, or plan; hopelessness; prior suicide attempts; or a family history of suicide. If the answer to any of these questions is positive, a systematic suicide risk assessment should be performed and documented (see Chapter 2, "Suicide Risk Assessment"). No standard of care exists that requires specific psychological tests or checklists to be used as part of the systematic assessment of suicide risk (Bongar et al. 1992).

The law judges therapists on the reasonableness of their suicide risk assessment process (Simon 1992). Courts also scrutinize a suicide case to determine whether the patient's suicide was foreseeable. Because therapists cannot predict who will commit suicide, only the risk of suicide is foreseeable. Thus, systematic suicide risk assessment that evaluates the balance between risk and protective factors in arriving at the patient's overall level of suicide risk should more than meet the foreseeability standard. The overall suicide risk assessment is a clinically informed judgment call.

Patients who have made prior suicide attempts or have had bouts of suicidal ideation usually present unique, individualized suicide risk factors that repeat during subsequent episodes of illness. The risk factor patterns are a function of individual psychodynamics, personality structure, developmental vulnerabilities, specific stresses, and other factors. Some patients display recurrent clinical "quirks" when they become suicidal. In the case example, Mr. Williams's prior suicidal ideation and plan at age 32 as well as the current suicide attempt were precipitated by "shame attacks." In another example, a patient who stuttered would begin to speak clearly when descending into a suicidal depression; the stuttering would return as the patient's depression improved. Another patient would begin to compulsively whistle in an irritating, atonal manner when becoming depressed and suicidal.

The mental status examination may reveal nonverbal indicators of suicide risk, such as agitation, severity of depression, psychomotor retardation, responses to auditory hallucinations, impulsivity, diminished mental capacity, hopelessness, and an inability to meaningfully relate to or cooperate with the therapist during the evaluation. In a prospective study of 6,891 psychiatric outpatients, a univariate survival analysis revealed that severity of depression, hopelessness, and suicidal ideation were significant risk factors for eventual suicide (Brown et al. 2000). In the same study, multivariate survival analyses found that significant modifiable and unique risk factors included suicidal ideation, major depressive disorder, bipolar disorder, and unemployment status. Dr. Franks assessed these risk factors, including Mr. Williams's inability to work, as moderate to high in his systematic suicide risk assessment.

Gathering information is essential to developing an individualized treatment plan. Time is of the essence in obtaining prior records of treatment. Patients usually will grant permission for the therapist to speak to former treaters and to obtain their records. As part of the evaluation process, the therapist should try to speak directly to the former therapist, after the patient has given proper authorization. Summaries of hospital records may be obtained by fax. Generally, it is sufficient for the clinician to read the discharge summary. The entire hospital record usually is not available for review in outpatient settings. However, outpatient clinics may have the entire patient record immediately available for review. The request for prior psychiatric records should be standard practice. If a prior treater or hospital facility fails to respond to a request for the patient's records, the failure should be documented. In the case example, Dr. Franks was able to contact his patient's previous inpatient psychiatrist by telephone and also obtain a faxed copy of Mr. Williams's prior hospitalization discharge summary within the evaluation period.

Other sources of important information include family members, partners, and friends. High-risk patients often communicate their suicide intent only to the most important persons in their lives, but not necessarily to the psychiatrist, even after direct questioning. Approximately 25% of suicidal patients do not admit to being suicidal (Fawcett et al. 1990). However, patients at mild to moderate risk for suicide usually communicate their intent to physicians or to other family members. The majority of patients who commit suicide do not communicate their suicide intent during their last therapeutic appointment (Isometsa et al. 1996). Practitioners should be alert for the clinical indicia of suicide risk, such as depression, prior suicide attempts, hopelessness, substance abuse, and recent loss. When a patient is at significant risk for suicide, the therapist should consider contacting the patient's significant others, with the patient's permission. If the patient refuses to grant permission, this should be documented. In the latter instance, the therapist is free to listen but not to divulge information. Listening does not breach confidentiality.

Most patients who are voluntarily hospitalized in managed-care settings must meet stringent admission criteria, often exceeding the criteria for involuntary hospitalization. The patient must be severely mentally ill and an imminent danger to self or others. Systematic suicide risk assessment can greatly assist in the therapist's decision of whether to hospitalize a patient. A patient at moderate to high risk may be continued in outpatient treatment if important protective factors are present (e.g., supportive family, solid therapeutic alliance). Another patient assessed at moderate risk may not possess sufficient protective factors against suicide and require psychiatric hospitalization. Clinical judgment informed by systematic suicide risk assessment should guide decisions about hospitalization. Consultation with a colleague may be appropriate in difficult cases.

A suicidal patient may choose to communicate with the therapist via e-mail. The subject line may read "I have overdosed," or the e-mail may contain a suicide note (Kassaw and Gabbard 2002). Evaluating, treating, or managing a patient at suicide risk by e-mail should be avoided. The American Medical Association (2000) guidelines state that e-mail communication is inappropriate for most mental health issues. Face-to-face interaction between psychiatrist and patient is essential in treating the patient at risk for suicide. Suicide risk assessment is difficult enough even with a direct examination of the patient.

TREATMENT

An extensive psychiatric literature exists on treatment and management issues for the suicidal patient. In this section, assessing and managing suicide risk is presented from the perspective of the clinician's personal reactions to the suicidal patient. For example, the identification of countertransference reactions in the therapist may endanger the patient, increase the risk of suicide, and expose the clinician to malpractice liability. The clinical-legal issues associated with split-treatment arrangements are discussed in Chapter 5, "Collaborative Treatment."

Psychotherapeutic interventions are very important in the treatment of patients at risk for suicide. Before clinical interventions can be effective, the therapist must establish an empathetic, supportive working alliance with the patient. The treatment and management process is multifaceted, rarely relying on medications alone. A psychodynamic understanding of the patient provides an important guide to treatment. Outpatient treatment of some patients at moderate to high risk for suicide may be practicable and effective in the presence of a strong therapeutic alliance, implementation of appropriate treatment modalities, and careful follow-up with continuing assessment of suicide risk. Among the more than 450 types of therapy currently used, there is no evidence that a specific therapy reduces patient suicides.

Maltsberger and Buie (1974) describe complex clinician reactions to suicidal patients, such as anger, despair, frustration, and hopelessness. Clinicians may experience countertransferential hate toward suicidal patients because the suicide of a patient is perceived as raising significant doubts as to their competence. Gabbard and Lester (1995) point out that the therapist may use the defense of reaction formation in an effort to deny hostile feelings toward the patient. Another commonly observed countertransference reaction occurs when the therapist assumes the role of the "good parent" rescuer. The therapist feels responsible for the patient's life rather than maintaining a concerned clinical focus on treatment and management. The patient must take responsibility for his or her life, making the decision to live or die. Therapists cannot stop patients who are determined to kill themselves. Inevitably, the "love and save" approach ends in futility and despair for the therapist, clouds clinical judgment, dooms the therapy, and can increase the patient's risk for suicide.

It sometimes happens that a desperate therapist at an impasse with a suicidal patient seeks legal solutions. The focus shifts from the clinical stalemate to a perhaps unavailable legal resolution. Although legal consultation may be useful in certain situations, consultation with a respected colleague is usually the best initial step in helping the therapist maintain clinical focus. Lawyers tend to be risk averse, providing competent legal opinions that may not necessarily square with appropriate clinical approaches to the patient at risk for suicide. All verbal consultations should be documented. It is preferable to receive a written report from the consultant that is added to the patient's record.

The treatment and management of suicide risk can be one of the most difficult clinical challenges encountered in the therapist's practice. Most therapists cannot handle more than a few suicidal patients. The strong emotional reactions usually evoked by the suicidal patient must be identified and managed (Roose 2001). The uncertainty of treatment outcome; the potential devastating personal, professional, and legal consequences for the therapist; the intense anguish of bereft, angry suicide survivors—these and other factors can all create anxiety that interferes with effective clinical care. Therapists should realistically gauge their ability to tolerate the inevitable anxieties and vicissitudes of treating patients at risk for suicide (Simon 1998b).

PERSONALITY DISORDERS

In today's managed-care environment, the therapist may not have sufficient time to evaluate patients for personality disorders. The diagnostic criteria for personality disorders are less well established than for Axis I disorders. It is more difficult for the therapist to achieve early diagnostic clarity when patients at risk for suicide present with complex comorbid Axis I (state) and Axis II (trait) disorders.

Patients with Axis II disorders, especially the Cluster B personality disorders (antisocial, borderline, histrionic, and narcissistic), often are erratic, impulsive, and difficult to engage in a therapeutic alliance. Patients with Cluster B personality disorders also tend to be nonadherent to their prescribed medication plans and to their schedule of appointments. Help seeking, help-rejecting patients who sorely try the patience of the therapist usually have one or more personality disorders. The suitability for individual psychotherapy of prospective patients who are at risk for suicide requires careful evaluation.

Patients with personality disorders are usually treated as outpatients. Personality disorders place a patient at increased risk for suicide (Linehan et al. 2000) (see Chapter 2, "Suicide Risk Assessment"). Patients with personality disorders are at seven times greater risk for suicide than the general population (Harris and Barraclough 1997). Of patients who commit suicide, 30%–40% have personality disorders (Bronisch 1996; Duberstein and Conwell 1997). Cluster B personality disorders, especially borderline narcissistic and antisocial personality disorders, place patients at increased risk for suicide (Duberstein and Conwell 1997). In borderline personality disorder patients, impulsivity is associated with a high number of suicide attempts, after controlling for substance abuse and a lifetime diagnosis of depressive disorder. In the case example, the patient has a history of shame-related suicide attempts. Patients with narcissistic personality disorder are vulnerable to acute deflations of their self-worth following adverse life events, resulting in impulsive "surprise or shame suicides" (Brodsky et al. 1997).

Personality disorder, adverse recent life events, and Axis I comorbidity were found in a large sample of suicides (Heikkinen et al. 1997). Unfavorable recent life events including work difficulties, family problems, unemployment, and financial trouble were highly represented among patients with personality disorders. Interpersonal difficulties were thought to be common among such recent life events. A combination of borderline personality disorder, major affective disorder, and alcoholism formed a fatal subgroup in a longitudinal study of personality (M.H. Stone 1993).

Suicide threats and gestures occur at a much greater frequency than actual suicide attempts. Gunderson and Ridolfi (2001) estimate that suicide threats and gestures occur repeatedly in 90% of borderline patients. Self-mutilating behaviors that commonly occur in borderline patients include cutting (80%), bruising (34%), burning (20%), head banging (15%), and biting (7%) (Shearer 1994). Although self-mutilation is considered to be parasuicidal behavior (without lethal intent), the risk of suicide is doubled in its presence (M.H. Stone 1987).

Personality disorders and comorbidity, such as depressive symptoms and substance abuse disorders, are highly represented among patients who commit suicide (Isometsa et al. 1996; Suominen et al. 2000). In the borderline patient, suicide risk assessment requires close attention to comorbidity, especially mood disorder and substance abuse, prior suicide attempts or self-mutilative behaviors, impulsivity, and adverse recent life events. In the case example, Mr. Williams is given a diagnosis of an Axis I disorder (bipolar II) and an Axis II personality disorder (narcissistic). This comorbidity places Mr. Williams at increased risk for suicide, especially when he undergoes a personal crisis.

MANAGEMENT

Whether to hospitalize a patient can be a trying decision for the therapist. As depicted in the case example, the decision is considerably more complicated when the need for hospitalization is clear but the patient refuses the recommendation. The decisions that the therapist makes at this point are critical from both a clinical and a risk management perspective.

Voluntary hospitalization can be a straightforward matter. The therapist, after systematic suicide risk assessment, determines that the patient is at a level of suicide risk that requires hospitalization. The risks and benefits of continuing outpatient treatment are weighed against the risks and benefits of hospitalization. If the patient agrees, arrangements for immediate hospitalization are made. The patient must go *directly* to the hospital, accompanied by a responsible person. The patient should not stop to do errands, get clothing, or make last-minute arrangements. A detour may provide the patient with the opportunity to attempt or commit suicide. If the patient is driven to the hospital, a safety locking mechanism under the sole control of the driver may prevent the patient from jumping out of the car. In some cases, psychiatrists have accompanied the patient to the hospital. However, psychiatrists have no legal duty to assume physical custody of the patient (*Farwell v. Un* [1990]).

If the patient disagrees with the therapist's recommendation for hospitalization, the matter is taken up initially as a treatment issue. However, the need for hospitalization usually is acute, not permitting a prolonged inquiry into the patient's unwillingness to accept the recommendation for hospitalization. The therapeutic alliance may become strained. It is this situation that tries the professional and personal mettle of the therapist. Consultation and referral are options for the clinician to consider, if time and the acuity of the patient's condition allow.

In the case example, Dr. Franks is certain that Mr. Williams intended to commit suicide during the failed attempt to hang himself. It is clear to Dr. Franks that Mr. Williams has to be hospitalized, either voluntarily or involuntarily. However, the factors that lead the therapist to consider hospitalizing a patient may not be as clear-cut as in the case example.

The therapist may decide not to hospitalize a patient who is assessed to be at moderate to high suicide risk. Protective factors may permit continuing outpatient treatment. For example, a strong therapeutic alliance may be present, the therapist may have worked with the patient for some time, family support may be present, or the patient's suicide risk may be manageable with more frequent visits and treatment adjustments. However, protective factors may be overwhelmed by a severe mental illness. In contrast, a patient assessed to be at moderate risk for suicide may need hospitalization when protective factors are few or are absent.

For the therapist, the decision to hospitalize the patient or continue outpatient treatment should be informed by systematic suicide risk assessment combined with a careful analysis that considers the risks and benefits of hospitalization versus the risks and benefits of continued outpatient treatment. Therapists can become paralyzed in their decision making when it is not based on a comprehensive assessment process.

The therapist may decide that the patient at risk for suicide who refuses hospitalization does not meet substantive criteria for involuntary hospitalization. The therapist's options are to continue to treat the patient and deal with the issue of hospitalization as a treatment matter, see the patient more frequently, adjust medications, obtain consultation, reexamine the therapeutic alliance, consider an adjunctive intensive outpatient program or PHP, refer the patient, or all of the above. The referral option may not be feasible until the patient's current suicide crisis has passed.

A patient at risk for suicide who is not committable may inform the therapist of his or her intention to terminate treatment. Again, the patient's decision should be addressed initially as a treatment issue, whenever possible. Some patients unilaterally terminate treatment simply by not keeping further appointments. In the latter instance, depending on the clinical situation, it may be appropriate to contact the patient. The purpose of the contact would be to determine the reasons for termination and to offer possible assistance to the patient. If it is determined that the patient has terminated treatment, a follow-up letter, certified with return receipt requested, should be sent acknowledging the patient's unilateral termination, stressing the need for continued treatment, and offering assistance in finding another therapist (Simon 2001). These steps also apply to patients at risk for suicide who are no-shows after an initial appointment. Roy (1982) found that 58% of outpatients who committed suicide had seen a psychiatrist the prior week. Thus, the identification of patients at high risk for suicide and of the imminence of suicide are poor.

When the suicide crisis persists or worsens, the patient may need to be involuntarily hospitalized. The therapist is not required to

Table 4–2.	Typical substantive and miscellaneous criteria for civil commitment

Substantive criteria

Mentally ill

Dangerous to self or others

Unable to provide for basic needs

Miscellaneous criteria (in conjunction with one or more of the above criteria)

Gravely disabled (unable to care for self to the point of likely self-harm)

Refusing hospitalization

Patient in need of hospitalization

Danger to property

Lacks capacity to make rational treatment decisions

Hospitalization represents least restrictive alternative

Note. Criteria are statutorily determined, varying from state to state.
Source. Reprinted from Simon RI: *Concise Guide to Psychiatry and Law for Clinicians,* 3rd Edition. Washington, DC, American Psychiatric Publishing, 2001. Used with permission.

provide useless treatment. However, the patient must not be abandoned during a suicide crisis (Simon 1992). Careful documentation of the therapist's decision-making process is essential. Consultation may be indicated.

Involuntary hospitalization should be utilized as an emergency clinical intervention, not a defensive tactic to avoid malpractice liability or to provide a legal defense against a malpractice claim. Unnecessary hospitalization may worsen a patient's psychiatric condition and damage trust for future treatment. Although state civil commitment statutes vary, the substantive legal criteria for involuntary hospitalization generally include severe mental illness, dangerousness to self or others or both, and the inability to provide for basic needs (see Table 4–2). Commitment statutes do not require involuntary hospitalization of patients but are permissive. Therapists usually have serious concerns about disrupting the patient's therapy by instituting involuntary hospitalization. Involuntary hospitalization also may jeopardize the patient's job and other relationships. Often, little or no therapeutic alliance exists when the acutely

mentally ill patient is at high risk for suicide and refuses hospitalization. In the case example, Dr. Franks does not have a viable therapeutic alliance with Mr. Williams to rely on in an emergency.
Discomfort or reluctance to involuntarily hospitalize a suicidal patient based on the therapist's belief that it is coercive may lead to
avoidance of a necessary hospitalization. Therapists often anguish,
"If I don't involuntarily hospitalize the patient, suicide may result.
If I do hospitalize the patient, my treatment relationship with the
patient will be destroyed." The compelling clinical issue for the
therapist should be patient safety. The therapist must be prepared
to take a firm stand if involuntary hospitalization is necessary.

In some localities, even if the patient requires involuntary hospitalization, meaningful psychiatric hospitalization does not exist.
The patient will likely be discharged within a few days from an
overcrowded institution that grudgingly must accept another involuntary suicidal patient. As a result, the patient's outpatient treatment may end without having achieved the goal of hospitalization.
The therapist may justifiably decide to continue to treat the patient
as an outpatient with appropriate adjustments made in the treatment plan. Consultation is advisable. The therapist should carefully
document the decision-making process.

The therapist should be familiar with state commitment laws and
the availability of community emergency mental health services. A
patient may be involuntarily hospitalized only when statutorily
mandated criteria are met. In the case example, Dr. Franks's aware-
ness of available emergency mental health resources enables him to
act decisively to call on the community's mobile crisis unit to assist
in the involuntary hospitalization of his patient.

Some therapists labor under the mistaken assumption that they
commit the patient when signing certification papers. Civil commitment (involuntary hospitalization) is a judicial decision. The court
or an administrative body may agree or disagree with the therapist's
recommendation to involuntarily hospitalize the patient.

The fear of being sued may also interfere with the therapist's clinical judgment concerning involuntary hospitalization. The most
common grounds for a lawsuit involving involuntary hospitalization is the claim of wrongful commitment, giving rise to a cause of
action for false imprisonment. Other theories of liability include assault and battery, malicious prosecution, abuse of process, and the

intentional inflection of emotional distress. To have a valid cause of action for false imprisonment or other torts, a plaintiff must prove that the defendant therapist failed to exercise reasonable care.

States have provisions in their commitment statutes granting psychiatrists and other mental health professionals immunity from liability when they use reasonable clinical judgment and act in good faith in petitioning for involuntary hospitalization (Simon 2001). Willful, blatant, or gross failure to follow statutory commitment procedures will not meet the good-faith provision. A malpractice suit for involuntary hospitalization of a patient is unlikely if an adequate examination is performed, statutory requirements are followed, and the certification is free of malice.

Statutory commitment laws do not require the therapist to involuntarily hospitalize a patient. These laws are permissive, leaving the decision to the discretion of the mental health professional (Appelbaum et al. 1989). However, malpractice suits have been filed against psychiatrists alleging failure to involuntarily hospitalize patients at risk for suicide. This type of suit is far more common than a lawsuit against a therapist for committing a patient. Carefully documented systematic suicide risk assessment, combined with the risk-benefit analyses for involuntary hospitalization, represents good clinical care as well as providing a solid legal defense.

In the case example, Dr. Franks tries to enlist Mr. Williams's wife's assistance in obtaining a certification for involuntary hospitalization. Ms. Williams is aware of her husband's suicide attempt. Communication of intent is present in 80% of suicides (Bongar et al. 1992). However, families are often the first and only ones to know about the patient's suicidal distress and are in a position to assist the therapist (Bongar et al. 1992). After Mr. Williams's wife refuses to obtain certification, Dr. Franks's knowledge of the statutory requirements and procedures for involuntary hospitalization facilitate Mr. Williams's hospitalization before he can attempt suicide again.

Circumstances may arise in which the therapist may feel uncertain as to whether involuntary hospitalization is the best clinical option for a patient at high risk for suicide. Involuntary hospitalization is justified if it appears likely that the patient will receive treatment and benefit from hospitalization (A.A. Stone 1976). Psychiatrists should rely on their training and clinical experience to determine the best treatment disposition for their patients. When involuntary hospitalization is sought, psychiatrists should leave it to the courts to temper any clinical biases through legal scrutiny and to make the final decision. The clinician's proper focus is the prevention of a patient's suicide.

A tension exists between patients' rights and clinicians' duty to treat. The medical model is outcome driven with a focus on patient and societal benefit. Civil libertarians express concern that the end of preventing suicide may not justify the means of involuntary hospitalization (Meltzer et al. 2003).

The risk of being sued for involuntary hospitalization is low. Any worries about a lawsuit should not affect clinical decision making. Once the decision to involuntarily hospitalize the patient is made, discussing the psychiatrist's reasons with the patient may help preserve trust for future treatment.

The therapist should not use the threat of involuntary hospitalization to coerce a suicidal patient into accepting treatments or procedures when there is no intention of petitioning for commitment. Persuasion engages the patient's reasoning ability to arrive at a desired goal. Coercion circumvents the patient's ability to reason and is undermined by manipulation (Malcolm 1992).

Involuntary hospitalization is a valid clinical intervention for appropriate patients. Looking back, most involuntarily hospitalized patients have understood the necessity for hospitalization, with some appreciative of the care they received (Gove and Fain 1977; Spensley et al. 1980).

SUICIDE WARNINGS

In the case example, Dr. Franks breaks confidentiality when he contacts the patient's wife about involuntarily hospitalizing her husband. *The Principles of Medical Ethics With Annotations Especially Applicable to Psychiatry* (American Psychiatric Association 2001) states, "Psychiatrists at times may find it necessary, in order to protect the patient or the community from imminent danger, to reveal confidential information disclosed by the patient" (Section 4, Annotation 8). Some states provide for statutory waiver of confidential information when a patient threatens self-harm (Simon 1992). The

Tarasoff duty to warn and protect endangered third parties, which exists in a number of jurisdictions, applies if the danger of physical harm is threatened toward others, not toward patients themselves (*Bellah v. Greenson* [1978]). However, in *Gross v. Allen,* a 1994 California appellate court case, the court held that if a patient has a history of dangerousness to self, the original caretaker is legally responsible for informing the new caretaker of this history. The court applied a *Tarasoff* analysis, extending the duty to warn and protect to threats of suicide.

Gross v. Allen does not appear to create a new duty for psychiatrists in the management of patients at risk for suicide. It is standard practice to take reasonable preventive measures to keep patients from harming themselves. Such measures may include communicating with family members about the patient's case, attempting to modify pathological interactions between the patient and family members, and mobilizing family support (e.g., removing lethal weapons, poisons, and drugs; administering and monitoring prescribed medications).

Suicide by firearms was the most common method for both men and women in 1999, accounting for 57% of all suicides (National Institute of Mental Health 2003). Other common methods of suicide include poisoning, hanging, stabbing and cutting, and carbon monoxide ingestion (Moscicki 1999). Since the introduction of selective serotonin reuptake inhibitors (SSRIs), suicide by overdose of antidepressants has become less common (Weber 2002). The greatest lethality by overdose is associated with over-the-counter and prescription analgesics, especially opioids. Some patients attempt or commit suicide by crashing their cars. If possible, car keys should be secured when the patient at risk for suicide has been warned not to drive. However, this may be a very difficult task when it is necessary for a patient to drive to work or other important functions. If the patient is agreeable, he or she may be dropped off and picked up by a family member or trusted friend. To adequately inform family members or significant others about safety management, it is important for the clinician to know the common methods of suicide. Patients who have made prior attempts have signaled their preferred method for committing suicide.

PARTIAL HOSPITALIZATION PROGRAMS AND INTENSIVE OUTPATIENT PROGRAMS

Managed care has facilitated the popularity of PHPs and IOPs as variations of outpatient psychotherapy. The legal liabilities associated with treating patients at risk for suicide in these venues are similar to those for the traditional private office outpatient setting. The main difference is that the level of suicide risk and the severity of mental illness are usually much greater in PHP and IOP settings. Liability exposure exists for failure to hospitalize a patient who is decompensating, who is at high risk for suicide, and whose symptoms that led to the initial hospitalization are recurring.

PHPs and IOPs provide short-term crisis stabilization services that usually are a step down from inpatient treatment. They also provide step-up treatment from outpatient therapy, when standard outpatient therapy alone is insufficient to maintain patient stabilization outside of the hospital.

The PHP treatment team typically consists of a psychiatrist, a nurse, a social worker, and counselors. The psychiatrist is the medical director. His or her primary role consists of evaluating patients on a regular basis and prescribing and monitoring medications. In some PHPs, the psychiatrist may provide medications only for patients who do not yet have a psychiatrist in their community. The outpatient psychiatrist usually is free to see and treat the patient on the PHP unit. Performing systematic suicide risk assessments is part of the continuing management of the patient by the psychiatrist and treatment team members.

Patients at significant risk for suicide can be treated in a PHP by conducting ongoing assessments. In addition, coverage should exist for after-hours emergencies. The patient should be instructed in how to contact help in an emergency. After-hours coverage is usually provided by the patient's outpatient therapist or psychiatrist or is made available through a local hospital emergency department.

The psychiatrist and other members of the treatment team should be able to reach the patient's outside therapist or psychiatrist if a crisis occurs. Worsening of a patient's condition requires the careful assessment of the patient's risk for suicide and for possible rehospitalization. Risk-benefit assessments regarding continued

PHP or IOP treatment versus hospitalization should be carefully documented. If it is determined that the patient needs to be hospitalized from the PHP or IOP, the patient should be accompanied by a staff member to the emergency department or psychiatric unit for admission.

CLINICALLY BASED RISK MANAGEMENT

- Before beginning outpatient treatment, the patient should undergo a brief period of evaluation. Comorbid Axis I and Axis II disorders are important factors that increase the risk of suicide.
- An initial screening for suicide risk should be conducted with new patients. The presence of suicide risk factors alerts the psychiatrist to conduct a systematic risk assessment.
- The practitioner should be alert to other clinical indicia of suicide risk in patients who deny suicidal ideation, intent, or plan after threatening suicide or making a suicide attempt.
- Clinicians should perform and document a differential diagnosis. An accurate diagnosis informs treatment and management of the suicidal patient.
- A comprehensive, rational treatment and management plan should be formulated before treatment is started. The initial treatment plan and any revisions should be documented in the patient's record.
- E-mail communication should be avoided in the evaluation, treatment, and management of the patient at risk for suicide.
- Suicide risk assessment is a process, not an event. Systematic suicide risk assessments should be conducted whenever there are significant changes in condition, treatment, or management of the suicidal patient. Documentation of suicide risk assessment is essential.
- For new patients, records of prior treatments should be obtained and direct contact with former treaters made, if possible. Records received require careful reading.
- Before speaking with family members, the therapist should obtain the patient's permission. If the patient withholds permission,

the refusal should be documented and addressed as a treatment issue. Merely listening to family members does not breach confidentiality.

- Countertransference reactions commonly occur in the treatment of patients at risk for suicide. The therapist needs to identify and constructively manage countertransference reactions so as not to interfere with the treatment of the patient.
- Limiting the number of suicidal patients in current treatment may help avoid or mitigate exhaustion and negative feelings toward the patient.
- Consultation with a colleague regarding assessment, treatment, and management in association with complex, difficult patients at risk for suicide should be considered. Consultation provides a "biopsy" of the standard of care. The clinician should never worry alone.
- The decision to hospitalize a patient at risk for suicide should be based on systematic suicide risk assessment combined with a risk-benefit analysis of factors favoring continued outpatient treatment versus hospitalization.
- Involuntary hospitalization should be used as an emergency clinical intervention, not to avoid malpractice liability or to provide a defense against malpractice suit. Clinically based risk management places the patient's treatment first. Unfounded fears of lawsuits may interfere with the therapist's clinical judgment.
- The therapist should be familiar with the state laws governing involuntary hospitalization. Knowledge of legal requirements and the availability of community emergency mental health services facilitates involuntary hospitalization.
- The therapist certifies the patient for involuntary hospitalization. A court or administrative body makes the judicial decision of whether to commit the patient.
- It is standard practice to take preventive measures to keep patients from harming themselves. Such measures may include enlisting family members and significant others to provide support during a time at which a patient is at heightened suicide risk (e.g., facilitating removal and safe disarming of guns and other means of suicide, instructing family members to administer and monitor the patient's medications).

- When the decision is made to hospitalize a patient, the patient must go directly to the hospital, accompanied by a responsible escort. A detour may provide an opportunity for the patient to attempt or commit suicide.
- Patients at risk for suicide who unilaterally terminate outpatient therapy should be sent a certified letter, return receipt requested, acknowledging the unilateral termination, the need for continued treatment, and the offer of assistance in finding another therapist. This procedure also applies to suicidal patients who are no-shows after the first appointment.

REFERENCES

American Medical Association: Guidelines for Patient-Physician Electronic Mail (H.478.997). Chicago, IL, American Medical Association, 2000

American Psychiatric Association: The Principles of Medical Ethics With Annotations Especially Applicable to Psychiatry. Washington, DC, American Psychiatric Association, 2001

Appelbaum PS, Zonana H, Bonnie R, et al: Statutory approaches to limiting psychiatrists' liability for their patients' violent acts. Am J Psychiatry 146:821–828, 1989

Bellah v Greenson, 81 Cal. App. 3d 614, 146 Cal. Rptr. 525 (1978)

Bongar B, Maris RW, Berman AL, et al: Outpatient standards of care and the suicidal patient. Suicide Life Threat Behav 22:453–478, 1992

Bongar B, Maris RW, Berman AL, et al: Outpatient standards of care and the suicidal patient, in Risk Management With Suicide Patients. Edited by Bongar B, Berman AL, Maris FW, et al. New York, Guilford, 1998, pp 4–43

Brodsky BS, Malone KM, Ellis SP, et al: Characteristics of borderline personality disorder associated with suicidal behavior. Am J Psychiatry 154:1715–1719, 1997

Bronisch T: The typology of personality disorders: diagnostic problems and their relevance for suicidal behavior. Crisis 17:55–58, 1996

Brown GK, Beck AT, Steer RA, et al: Risk factors for suicide in psychiatric outpatients: a 20-year prospective study. J Consult Clin Psychol 68:371–377, 2000

Duberstein P, Conwell Y: Personality disorders and completed suicide: a methodological and conceptual review. Clinical Psychology: Science and Practice 4:359–376, 1997

Farwell v Un, 902 F.2d 282 (4th Cir. 1990)

Fawcett J, Scheftner WA, Fogg L, et al: Time-related predictors of suicide in major affective disorder. Am J Psychiatry 147:1189–1194, 1990

Gabbard GO, Lester EF: Boundaries and Boundary Violations in Psychoanalysis. New York, Basic Books, 1995

Gove WR, Fain T: A comparison of voluntary and committed psychiatric patients. Arch Gen Psychiatry 34:669–676, 1977

Gross v Allen, 22 Cal. App. 4th 354, 27 Cal. Rptr. 2d 429 (1994)

Gunderson JG, Ridolfi ME: Borderline personality disorder: suicidality and self-mutilation. Ann N Y Acad Sci 932:61–77, 2001

Gutheil TG: Suicide and suit: liability after self-destruction, in Suicide and Clinical Practice. Edited by Jacobs D. Washington, DC, American Psychiatric Press, 1992, pp 147–167

Harris CE, Barraclough B: Suicide as an outcome for mental disorders. Br J Psychiatry 170:205–228, 1997

Heikkinen ME, Henriksson MM, Isometsa ET, et al: Recent life events and suicide in personality disorders. J Nerv Ment Dis 185:373–381, 1997

Isometsa ET, Henriksson MM, Heikkinen ME, et al: Suicide among subjects with personality disorders. Am J Psychiatry 153:667–673, 1996

Kassaw K, Gabbard GO: The ethics of email communication in psychiatric practice. Psychiatr Clin North Am 25:665–674, 2002

Kockelman v Segals, 61 Cal. App. 4th 491, 71 Cal. Rptr. 2d 552 (1998)

Linehan MM, Rizvi SL, Welch SS, et al: Psychiatric aspects of suicidal behaviour: personality disorders, in The International Handbook of Suicide and Attempted Suicide. Edited by Hawton K, Van Heeringen K. New York, Wiley, 2000, pp 147–178

Malcolm JG: Informed consent in the practice of psychiatry, in Review of Clinical Psychiatry and the Law, Vol 3. Edited by Simon RI. Washington, DC, American Psychiatric Press, 1992, pp 221–283

Maltsberger JT, Buie DH: Countertransference hate in the treatment of suicidal patients. Arch Gen Psychiatry 30:625–633, 1974

Meltzer HY, Conley RR, de Leo D, et al: Intervention strategies for suicidality. J Clin Psychiatry 6(2):1–18, 2003

Moscicki EK: Epidemiology of suicide, in The Harvard Medical School Guide to Suicide Assessment and Intervention. Edited by Jacobs DG. San Francisco, CA, Jossey-Bass, 1999, pp 40–51

National Institute of Mental Health: Suicide facts. Available at: http://www.nimh.nih.gov/research/suifact.htm. Accessed January 3, 2003

Roose SP: Suicide: what is in the clinician's mind? Ann N Y Acad Sci 932:151–157, 2001

Roy A: Risk factors for suicide in psychiatric patients. Arch Gen Psychiatry 39:1089–1096, 1982

Shearer SL: Phenomenology of self-injury among inpatient women with borderline personality disorder. J Nerv Ment Dis 182:524–526, 1994

Simon RI: Clinical Psychiatry and the Law, 2nd Edition. Washington, DC, American Psychiatric Press, 1992

Simon RI: Psychiatrists' duties in discharging sicker and potentially violent inpatients in the managed care era. Psychiatr Serv 49:62–67, 1998a

Simon RI: The suicidal patient, in The Mental Health Practitioner and the Law: A Comprehensive Handbook. Edited by Lifson LE, Simon RI. Cambridge, MA, Harvard University Press, 1998b, pp 166–186

Simon RI: Psychiatry and Law for Clinicians, 3rd Edition. Washington, DC, American Psychiatric Publishing, 2001

Speer v United States, 512 F. Supp. 670 (N.D. Tex. 1981), *aff'd*, 675 F.2d 100 (5th Cir. 1982)

Spensley J, Edwards D, White E: Patient satisfaction and involuntary treatment. Am J Orthopsychiatry 50:725–727, 1980

Stone AA: Mental health and law: a system in transition (Publ No ADM-6-176). Rockville, MD, National Institute of Mental Health, 1976

Stone MH: Psychotherapy of borderline patients in light of long-term follow-up. Bull Menninger Clin 51:231–247, 1987

Stone MH: Long-term outcome in personality disorders. Br J Psychiatry 162:299–313, 1993

Suominen KH, Isometsa ET, Henriksson MM, et al: Suicide attempts and personality disorder. Acta Psychiatr Scand 102:118–125, 2000

Weber J: Underusing overdose as a method of suicide: a trend analysis. American Association of Suicidology News Link 28:3, 8, 2002

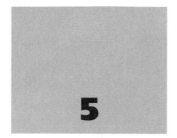

5

COLLABORATIVE TREATMENT

We must all hang together, or assuredly we shall all hang separately.

Benjamin Franklin, at the signing of the
Declaration of Independence, July 4, 1776

INTRODUCTION

Assessment and management for patients at risk for suicide is especially challenging in collaborative or split-treatment arrangements. The hospital length of stay is very short for most psychiatric patients. Patients referred to partial hospitalization programs are treated briefly. Consequently, many patients at moderate to high risk for suicide with severe psychiatric conditions receive split treatment. Patients are usually referred by managed behavioral health organizations (MBHOs) or primary care physicians to nonphysician mental health practitioners for psychotherapy and to psychiatrists for medication management.

MBHOs usually authorize patients to see psychotherapists for more frequent and longer sessions than psychiatrists who only prescribe medication. Referral to a psychiatrist for consultation or medication management may occur when the patient's clinical condition deteriorates. Frequently, the patient's deterioration is associated with an increased risk of suicide.

CASE EXAMPLE

Ms. Knowles, a 32-year-old divorced mother of a 3-year-old son, is referred by her MBHO to a psychotherapist for evaluation of depression. Her divorce became final 1 month ago. Ms. Knowles lives alone with her son. Her mother lives nearby and helps with the care of her son. The relationship with her mother is described as "close but stormy." Ms. Knowles has maintained friendships with co-workers. She tells the psychotherapist, Mr. Rogers, that she has problems with falling and staying asleep, loss of appetite, poor work performance, loss of interest in formerly pleasurable activities, and increased irritability, especially with her son.

Ms. Knowles's history reveals that her parents divorced when she was 15 years old. Her 17-year-old brother went to live with the father. Shortly after her parents divorced, she began having symptoms of bulimia. Ms. Knowles also superficially cut herself with a razor on both forearms. Within a year, she began to experience moderate to severe mood swings.

During college, Ms. Knowles had a series of unsatisfying romantic relationships associated with the use of alcohol, cocaine, and marijuana. Her relationships were intense, often ending after a perceived slight or actual rejection by the other person. Ms. Knowles experienced strong feelings of rage, abandonment, and depression. Her moods cycled from "deep depression" to "highs." She spent money imprudently, acted impulsively, and required little sleep. After the failure of a relationship with a man she "adored," Ms. Knowles took an overdose of aspirin. She was treated at a local community hospital emergency department and released. Ms. Knowles underwent psychotherapy briefly but terminated therapy when "I felt real good." She later saw a psychiatrist for 6 months for psychotherapy and received medications for "my mood swings." Suicidal ideation and superficial cutting of her forearms with a razor occurred twice while she was in treatment.

Ms. Knowles was married for 4 years, giving birth to her son during the first year of marriage. She experienced severe mood swings following the birth of her child. The marriage was chaotic, characterized by frequent verbal and physical fights. The fights would occur mainly when "I was running high." The couple separated more than a year ago. Her husband immediately filed for divorce. Ms. Knowles retained custody of her son.

Currently, Ms. Knowles states that she loves her son but has great difficulty taking care of his daily needs. Her job as a paralegal is in jeopardy. She is experiencing passive suicidal thoughts: "I would be better off dead. Maybe I'll get hit by a truck." Mr. Rogers makes the diagnosis of bipolar II depression, recurrent, moderate without psychotic features, and borderline personality disorder. The therapist obtains authorization for 10 psychotherapy sessions. Ms. Knowles begins once-a-week supportive psychotherapy.

Mr. Rogers recommends to the MBHO that the patient be referred to a psychiatrist for medication management. The psychiatrist, Dr. West, performs a complete psychiatric evaluation, determining that Ms. Knowles has a recurrent major depression as part of a bipolar II disorder. An Axis II diagnosis is deferred until Dr. West obtains additional clinical data. With the patient's permission and proper authorization, Dr. West calls her former psychiatrist. Ms. Knowles stopped seeing her former psychiatrist "because he was not a participating physician in my current insurance plan."

The patient's former psychiatrist informs Dr. West that he treated the patient with psychotherapy for symptoms and behaviors typical of borderline personality disorder. After many trials of different drugs, the combination of an atypical antipsychotic drug, lithium, and an anticonvulsant mood stabilizer proved to be the most effective regimen for controlling her mood lability. However, the patient complained about medication side effects. She stopped taking her medications and interrupted treatment. At the time of termination, suicide risk assessment revealed that Ms. Knowles remained at moderate risk.

Dr. West and Mr. Rogers have not worked together before. Dr. West calls Mr. Rogers to discuss her evaluation of Ms. Knowles and to establish their collaborative treatment relationship. Before calling Mr. Rogers, Dr. West obtains written authorization from Ms. Knowles.

Dr. West and Mr. Rogers share their clinical impressions. They discuss the overall treatment strategy and their plan for collaboration. Dr. West informs Mr. Rogers that no supervisory relationship is being established. Dr. West inquires about Mr. Rogers's training, experience, and malpractice coverage. Mr. Rogers is an independently licensed master's-level counselor with 10 years of clinical experience. He asks about Dr. West's training and experience. She has been in private practice for 21 years, with experience in treating outpatients and inpatients with a wide variety of psychiatric disorders. Dr. West believes that Ms. Knowles's level of risk for suicide could worsen quickly, given Mr. Rogers's impression that Ms. Knowles has both a bipolar II disorder and borderline personality disorder. Dr. West and Mr. Rogers discuss their individual approaches to suicide risk assessment. They agree to systematically assess both suicide risk and protective factors during Ms. Knowles's treatment. One will call the other if there is a change in her suicide risk level. They determine that she currently presents a moderate level of suicide risk.

Ms. Knowles accepts Dr. West's recommendation to restart the medications previously prescribed by her former psychiatrist that proved helpful. Dr. West adds a sleep medication. Side effects are discussed, and baseline laboratory studies are obtained. Ms. Knowles is prescribed 250 mg of divalproex four times a day, 300 mg of lithium four times a day, 5 mg of olanzapine once a day, and 10 mg of zolpidem at bedtime. Dr. West determines that close monitoring is necessary because of Ms. Knowles's current significant risk for suicide, nonadherence to medication regimens, and history of a suicide attempt by aspirin overdose.

Dr. West sees Ms. Knowles 3 weeks after her initial psychiatric evaluation. Mr. Rogers calls Dr. West a few days before the patient's appointment to share his concern that Ms. Knowles is more depressed, less functional, and more preoccupied with suicide. Ms. Knowles admits to Dr. West that she is having passive suicidal thoughts. She denies suicide intent or a plan. Dr. West's suicide risk assessment of Ms. Knowles indicates moderate to high risk. Dr. West adjusts Ms. Knowles's medications and gives her an appointment to be seen in 1 week. Only 1 week's supply of medications is provided. Ms. Knowles complains about the cost and inconvenience of weekly refills of her medications. She also complains about the medications' side effects, expressing her ambivalence about taking medication. Nonetheless, she agrees to continue taking her medications. Dr. West informs Mr. Rogers that the patient is at increased risk for suicide. Dr. West requests authorization from the MBHO to see Ms. Knowles for weekly appointments. The request is denied. Dr. West initiates a doctor-to-doctor appeal. Weekly visits are approved, based on the latest systematic suicide risk assessment, which indicates moderate to high risk.

Three days following her last visit with Dr. West, Mr. Rogers calls Dr. West to inform her that Ms. Knowles has a suicide plan, despite improvement in her depression. Ms. Knowles will not divulge the plan. The therapeutic alliance is strained. Ms. Knowles complains to Mr. Rogers that Dr. West is "only interested in pushing drugs." She complains of the medications' side effects. Ms. Knowles denies stopping or sporadically taking her medications when asked by Mr. Rogers. In their discussion, Dr. West and Mr. Rogers agree that Ms. Knowles is trying to split the psychiatrist and psychotherapist, which is a typical manifestation of her borderline personality disorder. Dr. West notes that Ms. Knowles complains to her that Mr. Rogers is "not attentive and does not listen."

Mr. Rogers and Dr. West discuss how to therapeutically manage Ms. Knowles's efforts to split their collaborative relationship. Each will reinforce to Ms. Knowles the importance of continuing to take her medications. They also discuss the possibility of referring Ms.

Knowles to an intensive outpatient program if her suicidal ideation intensifies. Dr. West gives Mr. Rogers her 24-hour emergency number to call if a crisis occurs that requires hospitalization of their patient. Mr. Rogers provides his office, home, and cell phone numbers. Ms. Knowles is encouraged to call Mr. Rogers if an emergency arises, because he is seeing her more frequently. If Mr. Rogers cannot be reached, Dr. West should be called. Questions about medications should be directed to Dr. West.

A few days after this conversation, Ms. Knowles has the impulse to take all of her medications. At the last moment, she changes her mind and calls Mr. Rogers. He reaches Dr. West at her emergency number. A mutual decision is made to hospitalize Ms. Knowles. She is immediately admitted to the psychiatric unit of a general hospital.

DISCUSSION

The case example illustrates an ideal collaboration and communication between psychiatrist and psychotherapist in assessing and managing the condition of a patient at risk for suicide. Nonetheless, the practice principles described in the case example apply to the real world of split treatment. The essence of collaborative treatment is effective communication. Communication in split treatment is essential, whether the psychiatrist and the psychotherapist have low-volume or high-volume practices.

Psychiatrists and psychotherapists with high-volume split-treatment practices may not take the time or have the time to adequately collaborate. For example, a psychiatrist who sees four patients for medication management every hour, 8 hours a day for 5 days a week, has 160 patient visits a week. Assuming that the psychiatrist receives 10 patient calls a day from this large patient base, the psychiatrist will receive 70 telephone calls a week. Such extremely busy, high-volume medication management practices are common. How will the psychiatrist find the time to collaborate? Collaboration takes time and effort. The psychiatrist and psychotherapist with high-volume practices may find the extent of the collaboration described in the case example to be impractical. However, adequate communication and collaboration between psychiatrist and psychotherapist is standard practice, especially for patients at risk for suicide.

Communication between psychiatrist and psychotherapist must occur to prevent the patient at risk for suicide from falling between the cracks of split treatment. In practices where psychiatrist and therapist work together in a clinic or some similar arrangement, communication about the patient is more easily accomplished. When the psychiatrist and psychotherapist are unknown to each other, failure to effectively communicate about the suicidal patient is more likely. Generally, communication between psychiatrist and psychotherapist is either minimal or nonexistent.

Split treatment presents unique clinical, ethical, legal, and administrative challenges for each clinician (Meyer and Simon 1999). For example, what is the specific duty of each clinician in assessing and managing suicide risk? The American Psychiatric Association (APA) "Guidelines for Psychiatrists in Consultative, Supervisory, or Collaborative Relationships With Nonmedical Therapists" define three classes of professional relationships: consultative, supervisory, and collaborative (American Psychiatric Association 1980).

In a consultative relationship, both clinicians are professionally autonomous. For example, the psychiatrist can render an opinion without assuming responsibility for the patient's continuing care. No doctor-patient relationship is created. The doctor requesting the consultation is under no obligation to accept the consultant's recommendations. Liability will arise only if the consultation is performed negligently. A doctor-patient relationship will be created, however, if the consultant acts as a treater (e.g., orders medication).

In a supervisory relationship, the psychiatrist is responsible for monitoring and directing *all* aspects of the patient's psychiatric treatment. The psychotherapist does not act autonomously. An example of this relationship is the psychiatrist's supervision of a dependently licensed counselor trainee in a licensed clinic or hospital.

Psychiatrists who employ others or supervise other professionals may be held liable for their negligence even though no direct contact occurred with the patient. Under the doctrine of *respondiat superior,* a supervising or employing psychiatrist is considered to be the *master* (legally speaking) of those under his or her direction and is *vicariously liable* for their acts. Vicarious liability occurs when the professional had the right or ability to control the subordinate (e.g., supervisee or employee). The subordinate's negligence must occur within the scope of his or her employment.

In the APA guidelines, the collaborative relationship applies directly to split-treatment arrangements (Meyer and Simon 1999). However, the definition of a collaborative relationship is general and lacks clarity when applied to split treatment: "Implicit in this (collaborative) relationship is a mutually shared responsibility (clinical duty) for the patient's care in accordance with the qualifications and limitations of each therapist's discipline and abilities" (p. 1490).

In a collaborative relationship, the psychiatrist and the nonmedical therapist meet professional qualifications for independent practice. In split treatment, they share responsibilities for the patient's treatment. Each clinician is independently licensed. Neither has the professional responsibility to direct the clinical conduct of the other, as in a supervisory relationship. As long as treatment continues under the psychiatrist's supervision, the psychiatrist is ethically and medically responsible for the patient's care. In the case example, the psychiatrist informs the psychotherapist that their relationship is not supervisory. The clarification between supervision and collaboration is important, especially in relation to treatment and management for patients at risk for suicide. In a supervisory relationship, the liability risk for the supervisor is the same as if he or she were the sole treater.

Sederer et al. (1998) point out that collaborative relationships hold the greatest potential ambiguity for clinical duties and responsibilities. Appelbaum (1991) recommends that the responsibilities of the patient, the psychiatrist, and the nonmedical therapist should be clearly specified, preferably in a written agreement. The sample letter in the Appendix at the end of the chapter can be used as a letter of mutual understanding or an issue outline for discussion with the therapist. The advantages and disadvantages of such a letter are discussed elsewhere (Meyer and Simon 1999).

COMPETENCE, LICENSURE, AND INSURANCE

It is very difficult, if not impossible, to judge the competence of a collaborating therapist whom the psychiatrist does not know professionally, and vice versa. This issue is especially important in the split treatment of patients at significant risk for suicide. For example, do the psychiatrist and therapist routinely conduct and document a systematic suicide risk assessment for patients at risk?

Discussing their approaches to suicide risk assessment can help prevent the situation in which each clinician assumes that the other is performing risk assessments. Comparing suicide risk assessments contemporaneously will allow discussion of significant disparities, if such exist. The APA ethical guidelines state,

> When the psychiatrist assumes a collaborative or supervisory role with another mental health worker, he/she must expend sufficient time to assure that proper care is given. It is contrary to the interests of the patient and to patient care if the psychiatrist allows himself/herself to be used as a figurehead. (American Psychiatric Association 2001, Section 5, Annotation 3)

The psychiatrist must have reason to believe that the therapist is able to conduct the indicated treatment, although the psychiatrist's role is medication management. As in the case example, the psychiatrist and therapist should inquire about each other's training, clinical experience, licensure, and insurance. If a patient attempts or commits suicide and a malpractice claim is filed, the plaintiff will seek monetary compensation for damages. In split treatment, the psychiatrist, who usually has the "deeper pockets," will almost always be sued, although his or her clinical role in the alleged malpractice may have been minimal or nonexistent. In most jurisdictions, the legal doctrine of "joint and several liability" applies to malpractice litigation (Macbeth 1999). For example, if two or more defendants are found to have contributed in any way to the harm suffered by a patient, the plaintiff may collect the entire judgment from any one or more defendants. If the therapist has inadequate malpractice insurance coverage, the psychiatrist may be liable for the psychotherapist's negligence, even in the absence of any wrongdoing by the psychiatrist.

CONFIDENTIALITY

For split treatment to be effective, the psychiatrist and therapist must be able to communicate freely as needed. This is especially important with patients who are at risk for suicide. The split-treatment arrangement should be explained to the patient and written permission obtained for a collaborative dialogue between psychiatrist and therapist. Patients who are paranoid, who are prone to splitting those in charge of their treatment, or who have realistic concerns about specific information in their history may be especially sensitive about confidentiality. The psychiatrist and psychotherapist should prospectively clarify and resolve confidentiality concerns with the patient. Patients who refuse to provide written authorization for psychiatrist-psychotherapist communication are not suitable for split treatment. Most patients in split treatment appreciate the importance of unencumbered communication between treaters and readily agree.

TREATMENT ROLES

Psychiatrists are trained in both psychotherapy and psychopharmacology. Thus, it is relatively easy to slip into an active psychotherapeutic role, especially with the patient at risk for suicide. Conversely, some nonmedical therapists may wander into the thicket of advising patients about medication management without contacting the psychiatrist.

Major sources of difficulty in split treatment are clinician role confusion and resulting misalignments between treaters and between treater and patient. Role confusion occurs when the psychiatrist performs psychotherapy and the psychotherapist acts as a psychopharmacologist. For example, the psychotherapist may wittingly or unwittingly encourage the patient to change or discontinue medication instead of discussing medication concerns with the psychiatrist. Conversely, the psychiatrist may feel that the patient's therapy is inadequate and take on the role of psychotherapist. Such role confusion will likely interfere with the patient's psychotherapy, possibly increasing the risk for suicide.

Misalignments may be facilitated by patients with good/bad splitting tendencies. For example, misalignments usually occur when the treater joins in the patient's idealization of or, more commonly, diminishment and marginalization of the other treater. In the case example, Ms. Knowles's attempt to split the psychiatrist and the psychotherapist was effectively managed by their continuing communication.

When role confusion and misalignment occur, the risk for patient regression and suicide may increase. For example, the patient may express to the therapist ambivalence about taking medication. The therapist then recommends to the patient that the medication be discontinued. The psychiatrist is not called until a suicide crisis occurs. This problem arises with unfortunate frequency. Transference and countertransference reactions to the patient or to the other clinician may contribute to role confusion and misalliance with patients (Busch and Gould 1993).

It bears repeating that the standard practice in the split treatment of the patient at risk for suicide is communication and collaboration. Each clinician should make clear what information about the patient's condition should be communicated immediately and what can wait (Macbeth 2001). For example, an increase in the patient's risk for suicide requires immediate communication between treaters. In the case example, communication between psychiatrist and therapist was essential to the continuing assessment and management of their patient's suicide risk.

Role responsibilities must be clearly articulated between clinicians and communicated to the patient (Meyer and Simon 1999). The clinical roles are demarcated by psychotherapy versus psychopharmacology management. For example, psychotherapy issues that the patient raises or that are of concern to the psychiatrist should be referred to the psychotherapist. Similarly, a patient's emotional, behavioral, or medical issues related to medication should be referred to the psychiatrist. The psychotherapist must not take on the role of psychopharmacologist and the psychiatrist the active role of psychotherapist. However, medication management and psychotherapy are inseparable. Their separation is a fiction created by managed care.

The administrative time spent in collaboration is not usually reimbursed, adding a financial disincentive to communication. If the psychiatrist sees the patient at risk for suicide infrequently, major changes may occur in the patient's clinical condition and suicide risk level that the psychiatrist is unaware of in the absence of communication. For example, in the presence of such changes, instead of contacting the psychiatrist, the psychotherapist may decide to obtain a suicide prevention contract from the patient or fail to make a change in the frequency of therapy visits. Similarly, the psychiatrist may fail to report the presence of a side effect to an antipsychotic drug, such as akathisia, that may increase a patient's risk for suicide. The sample letter in the Appendix at the end of the chapter clearly delineates the role responsibilities and appropriate therapeutic alignments for split treatment.

MEDICATION MANAGEMENT

The medication management of patients at risk for suicide in split treatment requires close monitoring. Psychiatrists owe a duty of care to their patients for the duration of their drug prescriptions. Psychiatrists are encouraged by insurers to prescribe medications in larger quantities. The patient may be given a 90-day prescription that can be mailed to a pharmacy. Such "mail-away" bulk prescriptions lower the cost of medication. In addition, the patient's copayment is reduced from once a month to once every 90 days. However, the prescription of large quantities of medications for patients at risk for suicide can be lethal. In the case example, the patient is prescribed per day 1,000 mg of a mood stabilizer, 1,200 mg of lithium, 5 mg of an atypical antipsychotic, and 10 mg of sleep medication. A 90-day prescription, or a 30-day prescription renewable three times, gives the patient 90,000 mg of a mood stabilizer, 108,000 mg of lithium, 450 mg of an atypical antipsychotic, and 900 mg of sleep medication. Even a 30-day supply of these medications would be lethal. The potential lethality of the medications prescribed for the patient should be conveyed to the psychotherapist (Silk 2001).

The case example is typical of patients in split treatment. Patients at risk for suicide commonly have more than one psychiatric diagnosis and are usually taking several medications. If the patient is scheduled for a 15-minute medication check once every 90 days, the risk of suicide may increase over this period. The psychiatrist must rely on the therapist's assessment and management of suicide risk during the 90-day period. The problem is not necessarily one of the competence of either clinician but one of collaboration. The "we are in this together" part of split treatment is negated unless frequent communication between psychiatrist and therapist is maintained according to the clinical needs of the patient. Close monitoring of patients at risk for suicide who are taking potentially lethal amounts of medication should be standard psychiatric practice. Failure to do so may lead to allegations of negligence and abandonment, if the patient attempts or commits suicide.

In the case example, Dr. West's request to see Ms. Knowles weekly is initially denied by the managed-care organization (MCO). However, Dr. West's latest systematic suicide risk assessment indicating moderate to high risk, combined with a doctor-to-doctor appeal, is successful in securing additional visits. Psychiatrists and other mental health professionals may be pressured by MCOs to restrict the frequency and duration of patient visits. The psychiatrist and the therapist have the responsibility to vigorously appeal the MCO's denial of benefits, especially when the denial places the patient's life in jeopardy. All appeals and denials should be documented. The psychiatrist and the therapist, not the MCO, bear the ultimate responsibility for the patient (Simon 1998a). According to one legal commentator, "A psychiatrist needs to follow every available road to attempt to obtain the care she believes is essential for her patient—regardless of how cumbersome and time-consuming such steps may be and how fruitless they may seem" (Macbeth 1999, p. 152).

The failure of clinicians in split treatment to communicate can occur from a variety of causes. For example, a patient at significant risk for suicide, who is taking a number of medications, drops out of psychotherapy, but the psychotherapist does not inform the psychiatrist. If the patient is seen by the psychiatrist every month, 6 weeks, 8 weeks, or 3 months, the suicidal patient goes for long periods of time without being monitored. Suicidal patients, who decompensate between medication appointments, may possess a lethal cache of medications. An understanding should exist between clinicians that the psychotherapist will call the psychiatrist in an emergency or if there is a change in the patient's status. The psychiatrist is not just a prescription writer.

Clinicians working together in the same clinic or other treatment setting have the opportunity to communicate regularly about patient care. However, different practice schedules may prevent face-to-face discussions. Interdisciplinary patient records contain treatment notes for ongoing review by collaborative treaters. The patient's chart should be read before each treatment session.

Psychiatrists who work in clinics or other group practice settings may experience considerable pressure to prescribe medication for unseen patients, whether the patient is or is not suicidal. Standard practice requires that patients be adequately evaluated before medications are prescribed. Signing treatment plans for unseen patients or without consultation with the treatment team presents liability risks.

Writing prescriptions for patients not personally examined by the psychiatrist is a violation of the medical code in a number of jurisdictions (Slovenko 2002). The practice occurs in large state hospitals where psychiatrists are unable to see all the patients or to see them regularly. Prescriptions for medications may be written for extended periods of time and are to be administered and monitored by nurses and other mental health personnel. Malpractice claims alleging negligent prescribing practices will likely assert that the state's statutory standard of care was breached, where such a statute exists.

High-functioning, stable patients with mild depression and low risk for suicide may be seen less frequently by psychiatrists for medication management. Patients with severe recurrent depression and moderate to high suicide risk will require more frequent visits and close monitoring by the psychiatrists and psychotherapists. Patients assessed to be at moderate to high risk for suicide may continue to be seen in split treatment if significant protective factors are present, such as a good therapeutic alliance, careful monitoring, and family support. As in the case example, the patient will need to be seen more frequently by both clinicians, maintaining close communication with each other. The frequency and duration of visits and the utilization of intensive outpatient treatment, a partial hospitalization program, or hospitalization are clinical judgments that are informed by systematic suicide risk assessment and the clinical needs of the patient.

Clinicians utilizing collaborative treatment should make provisions for the emergency treatment and management of patients in a suicidal crisis. Each clinician should ensure routine and emergency availability, as well as coverage during nights, weekends, and vacations. In the case example, Dr. West gives the psychotherapist her emergency number. The psychotherapist explains how he can be reached in an emergency. Although the psychiatrist's clinical contact with the patient may be limited, his or her liability exposure is not limited when emergencies arise. Failure of clinicians to discuss these contingencies may result in the psychiatrist being overused for emergencies, despite being disadvantaged by limited clinical information and contact with the patient (Meyer and Simon 1999). In an emergency, patients should be encouraged to contact the psychotherapist first. The psychotherapist, who works more frequently with the patient, usually has sufficient information to guide clinical responses to an emergency. Questions about medication can be addressed directly to the psychiatrist. If the therapist cannot be reached in an emergency, then the psychiatrist should be called.

PATIENT SUITABILITY

Is the patient who is at risk for suicide suitable for treatment and management in a split-treatment arrangement? The patient's diagnosis, severity of illness, and level of risk for suicide are all essential factors to consider for suitability when the patient is referred for split treatment. In the case example, a difficult patient at significant risk for suicide is accepted for split treatment only after careful evaluations are performed by the psychiatrist and the therapist and open communication and coordination are established between the clinicians.

The competence, level of training, and clinical experience of the therapist must be assessed in regard to a specific patient. For example, a patient with severe bipolar disorder who is paranoid, rapidly cycling, and at significant risk for suicide is not an appropriate patient for a bachelor's- or even a master's-level counselor. Integrated treatment by a psychiatrist is indicated, especially if psychiatric hospitalization may be necessary. However, the ability of the psychiatrist, based on training and experience, to treat a severely ill patient should not be assumed.

Suitability also applies to the relationship between psychiatrist and psychotherapist in split treatment. Some psychiatrists will not enter into a split-treatment arrangement unless they know the psychotherapist personally and have a good sense of his or her clinical competence. Some psychiatrists meet quarterly or semiannually with psychotherapists over breakfast or lunch.

A psychiatrist and psychotherapist who do not know each other personally or who are unfamiliar with each other's professional competency to conduct therapy should investigate their ability to treat the patient in split treatment. As mentioned earlier, the training and clinical experience of the therapist should be determined before initiation of a split-treatment relationship, especially with severely mentally ill patients at moderate to high risk for suicide. A therapist with limited training and experience may not be appropriate for such a patient.

It is the right of each clinician to terminate an unworkable split-treatment relationship. Despite the best efforts to collaborate, teamwork may fail. Problems causing incompatibility may include diagnostic differences, irreconcilable practice styles, and interfering transference and countertransference reactions to either the patient, the other clinician, or both. The clinician in an unworkable collaborative relationship should resign respectfully from treatment and give sufficient notice to allow the patient and the other clinician to make appropriate treatment arrangements. The patient's best interest must guide the explanations that are given about termination. Patients already at risk for suicide may have their risk increased by the perception of rejection and abandonment. Procedures for terminating treatment without abandoning the patient are discussed in Chapter 4, "Outpatients."

Split treatment artificially separates psychotherapy from medication management. Medication management is always accompanied by some psychotherapeutic interaction. The psychiatrist must not be just an impartial drug dispenser. Empathetic engagement of the patient as part of medication management encourages the development of a therapeutic alliance and increases the likelihood of medication adherence. The therapeutic alliance is an important protective factor against suicide (Simon 1998b).

CLINICALLY BASED RISK MANAGEMENT

- The psychiatrist should inquire about the psychotherapist's training, clinical experience, licensure, and malpractice insurance coverage. The psychiatrist should welcome the same questions from the psychotherapist.
- Unless the psychiatrist intends to provide supervision to a nonmedical therapist, it should be clearly understood by the therapist and by the patient that the split-treatment arrangement is not a supervisory relationship.

- Effective communication and coordination between clinicians is essential in collaborative treatment, minimizing the risk of divergent clinical goals.
- Potentially lethal amounts of medications must not be prescribed to patients at risk for suicide, despite managed-care policies that encourage bulk purchase of medications.
- Informed consent should be obtained from the patient for the psychiatrist and psychotherapist to communicate freely. Consent should also be obtained by the psychotherapist.
- Clinical role responsibilities should be clearly demarcated between the psychiatrist and psychotherapist to prevent harmful role confusion and misalignment between treaters and with the patient, possibly increasing the patient's risk for suicide.
- The psychiatrist should not assume an active psychotherapeutic role with the patient. The psychotherapist should refer questions and problems with medication to the psychiatrist. Neither should usurp the treatment role of the other clinician.
- Each clinician should be satisfied with the frequency and duration of treatment appointments with the patient and the frequency of contact between clinicians.
- Contacts between clinicians should be documented.
- Each clinician should provide for routine and emergency availability of coverage during nights, weekends, and vacations.
- Patients at risk for suicide must be informed about which clinician to contact for routine calls and emergencies. Emergency telephone numbers should be available to patients.
- In an emergency, the patient should be instructed to contact the psychotherapist first. Questions about medications should be directed to the psychiatrist.
- Psychotherapeutic interaction with the patient is an inseparable part of medication management. The therapeutic alliance is an important protective factor against suicide, also fostering patient adherence to prescribed medications.
- The psychiatrist should prescribe medication and sign treatment plans only for patients who have been personally examined or in consultation with the treatment team.
- Suicide prevention contracts must not take the place of systematic suicide risk assessment.

- Clinicians should not be bound to collaborative treatment that does not conform to their professional standard of care.
- When substantial disagreements arise between the psychiatrist and psychotherapist, a consultation should be considered.
- The psychiatrist and psychotherapist should be aware of their right and obligation to terminate participation in an unworkable split-treatment arrangement. Sufficient notice and treatment alternatives should be provided to the patient and to the other clinician.

REFERENCES

American Psychiatric Association: Guidelines for psychiatrists in consultative, supervisory, or collaborative relationships with nonmedical therapists. Am J Psychiatry 137:1489–1491, 1980

American Psychiatric Association: The Principles of Medical Ethics With Annotations Especially Applicable to Psychiatry. Washington, DC, American Psychiatric Association, 2001

Appelbaum PS: General guidelines for psychiatrists who prescribe medication for patients treated by nonmedical therapists. Hosp Community Psychiatry 42:281–282, 1991

Busch FN, Gould E: Treatment by a psychotherapist and a psychopharmacologist: transference and countertransference issues. Hosp Community Psychiatry 44:772–774, 1993

Macbeth JE: Divided treatment: legal implications and risks, in Psychopharmacology and Psychotherapy: A Collaborative Approach. Edited by Riba MB, Balon R. Washington, DC, American Psychiatric Press, 1999, pp 111–158

Macbeth JE: Legal aspects of split treatment: how to audit and manage risk. Psychiatr Ann 31:605–610, 2001

Meyer DJ, Simon RI: Split treatment: clarity between psychiatrists and psychotherapists. Psychiatr Ann 29:241–245, 327–332, 1999

Sederer LI, Ellison J, Keyes C: Guidelines for prescribing psychiatrists in consultative, collaborative and supervisory relationships. Psychiatr Serv 49:1197–1202, 1998

Silk KR: Split (collaborative) treatment for patients with personality disorders. Psychiatr Ann 31:615–622, 2001

Simon RI: Duties in discharging sicker and potentially violent inpatients in the managed care era. Psychiatr Serv 49:62–67, 1998a

Simon RI: Psychiatrists awake! Suicide risk assessments are all about a good night's sleep. Psychiatr Ann 38:479–485, 1998b

Slovenko R: Psychiatry in Law/Law in Psychiatry. New York, Brunner-Routledge, 2002

Appendix. Sample Letter From the Psychiatrist to a Psychotherapist

Dear Psychotherapist,

Thanks for your call regarding your patient _____, whom you want to refer for medication management. The evaluation may require more than one session. Because we have not worked together before and we are unfamiliar with each other's experience and clinical approach, I wanted to take this opportunity to outline several thoughts that I hope will facilitate our collaboration.

During my initial meetings with the patient, I will do a complete psychiatric evaluation in addition to inquiring about medication issues. This will allow us to share the same clinical foundation when we discuss the patient's treatment. It also will give me insight into the patient's overall psychology and the emotional experience of taking medication and of being a patient. I will be better able to make use of your knowledge and insight about _____ if I have had at least an initial patient contact. We should plan to talk after either the first or the second meeting to discuss our clinical impressions and a treatment plan. We should also each speak to the patient about our needing permission to confer in the future about the treatment so that the patient can sign the appropriate releases. Additionally, we should explain that although we are collaborating, neither of us is the supervisor of the other's work.

After the initial evaluation, if medication is indicated, I will focus my clinical interactions with the patient on the indications, anticipated response, and potential side effects of the medicine. At that point, I will also have an estimate of the immediate and more extended frequency of appointments for pharmacotherapy and a clearer sense of how often you and I may want to talk about the patient's care.

In any collaboration, clinical questions and concerns may arise. If during my regular follow-up meetings with the patient there are psychotherapy issues that the patient raises with me or that I have concerns about, I will first bring those concerns to you instead of exploring them therapeutically with the patient. Similarly, if you are aware of emotional, behavioral, or medical issues related to any medication I am prescribing, I would appreciate it if you would first talk to me about those concerns. Such issues could include the patient having side effects, having negative feelings about either the pharmacotherapy or me, being nonadherent with the medication, or using alcohol or drugs. Also, if you have questions about whether the patient might be ready for a change in dosage, continuance, or type of medication, I welcome this input. I would like you to raise those questions directly with me before exploring them with the patient.

Appendix.   Sample Letter From the Psychiatrist to a
Psychotherapist *(continued)*

*Because my follow-up meetings with the patient will be briefer and less
frequent than the patient's meetings with you, I rely on you to inform me of
significant changes in the patient's clinical status, including the progress of
the therapy. Anything that has a serious impact on the patient's or the
therapy's stability could also have significant consequences for the patient's
pharmacotherapy. I would prefer that you err on the side of providing more
rather than less information.*

*To reach me, you can leave a message at my office telephone, or if it is
outside of usual business hours, a second message can be left on my emergency
number. The emergency number has instructions for patients about access to
the emergency department. I will also be giving the patient those two
numbers. Would you please let me know what provisions you have made for
emergency coverage during and outside of your office hours? When I go on
vacation, I will make arrangements for a psychiatrist to cover my practice.
Would you let me know your customary arrangement for vacation coverage?*

*I am a licensed psychiatrist with malpractice insurance coverage. I can,
if you like, send copies of the actual certificates. I also want you to feel
comfortable asking me any additional questions about my training,
experience, and orientation. I will proceed on the assumption that you are a
clinical _____ [name of discipline] licensed in
_____ [psychiatrist's state], and that you have a malpractice
policy (_____ per occurrence). If these assumptions are not correct,
please let me know.*

*I thought it would be easier to identify those clinical issues that we should
clarify with each other in a letter before having a telephone conversation. If
these collaborative arrangements are agreeable, please just have your patient
call me for an appointment. I will plan to speak with you before or after the
patient's second meeting with me. If you have any questions or concerns,
please call me at _____. I look forward to our successful collaboration.*

Sincerely,

_____, *M.D.*

Source.   Adapted from Meyer and Simon (1999).

6

INPATIENTS

A suicidal depression is kind of a spiritual winter, frozen, sterile, unmoving. The richer, softer and more delectable nature becomes, the deeper that internal winter seems, and the wider and more intolerable the abyss which separates the inner world from the outer. Thus suicide becomes a natural reaction to an unnatural condition.

> Alfred Alvarez, *The Savage God: A Study of Suicide* (1971)

We know well enough that life is not so dear that it will not be readily sacrificed, when all that makes it worth retaining is taken away.

> Isaac Ray, M.D., *Treatise on the Medical Jurisprudence of Insanity* (1838)

INTRODUCTION

The inpatient treatment of psychiatric patients has changed dramatically since the advent of managed care. The goal of psychiatric hospitalization is the rapid stabilization of severely ill psychiatric patients through crisis intervention and safety management. Most psychiatric units are analogous to intensive care units in medical services, providing short-stay, acute care. Mainly psychiatric patients who are suicidal, homicidal, or gravely disabled pass the strict precertification criteria for admission. Many of these patients have comorbid disorders. A substantial number of patients have comorbid substance abuse disorders (Simon 1998a).

Sicker patients at high risk for suicide may be prematurely discharged because cost-cutting policies have shortened the hospital length of stay. The average length of stay may be as short as 3–4 inpatient days. Close scrutiny by utilization reviewers allows for only brief hospitalization (Wickizer et al. 1996). The hospital administration may push for early discharge to keep patient length-of-stay statistics within predetermined goals.

Premature discharge of severely ill patients at substantial suicide risk is a major clinical and liability problem for inpatient psychiatrists and hospitals. Early discharge planning begins at the patient's admission. Rapid diagnosis and treatment decisions are essential. The psychiatrist must be able to work collaboratively with other mental health professionals on the treatment team to develop and implement a rational treatment plan.

Inpatients come and go quickly. The psychiatrist has little time to develop a working alliance with patients. Some patients are too disturbed to provide a psychiatric history. Information should be obtained from other sources, such as family members or other individuals who know the patient. Current or previous therapists need to be contacted, with the patient's permission. Records of prior hospitalization should be obtained and read. A faxed copy of the discharge summary is typically the most information the psychiatrist is able to obtain quickly from other facilities.

In this hurly-burly inpatient environment, the systematic assessment of patients at risk for suicide is often neglected or overlooked. In its place, unfounded reliance is often placed on the suicide prevention contract (see Chapter 3, "Suicide Prevention Contracts"). Systematic suicide risk assessment is essential because it informs and updates treatment planning and safety management (see Chapter 2, "Suicide Risk Assessment").

There is no such thing as a suicide-proof psychiatric unit. Busch et al. (1993) reported that 5%–6% of the estimated 30,000 suicides a year in the United States occur in the hospital. Similar rates of inpatient suicides have been reported in the United Kingdom. Other studies have found that the suicide rate in the psychiatric hospital population is 1% of the total of 30,000 admissions a year (Simon 1992b).

In general, courts hold psychiatrists accountable more often for inpatient than outpatient suicides. A substantial number of inpatient suicides are litigated. The duty owed inpatients to prevent suicide attempts or suicide is higher than for outpatients (Macbeth et al. 1994). Courts reason that the opportunities to evaluate, observe, monitor, control, and anticipate a patient's risk for suicide are greater on the psychiatric unit than in the therapist's office. With the length of stay for patients in psychiatric hospitals drastically reduced, a greater percentage of suicides occur within a few days or months after discharge (Morgan and Stanton 1997). A malpractice suit filed against the psychiatrist claiming premature and negligent discharge of the patient is a distressingly common occurrence. Omissions or oversights in diagnostic evaluation, suicide risk assessment, treatment, and application of protective measures are other common claims in lawsuits filed against inpatient psychiatrists.

Between 1996 and 2001, the Joint Commission on Accreditation of Healthcare Organizations (JCAHO) analyzed hospital-based suicides (JCAHO 2003). The JCAHO identified the following environmental and practice deficiencies: nonbreakaway bars, rods, or safety rails; inadequate security; incomplete or inadequate suicide assessment methods; incomplete reassessment; incomplete orientation and training of staff or inadequate staffing levels; incomplete or infrequent patient observations; incomplete communication among caregivers or unavailable information; and inadequate care planning.

CASE EXAMPLE

Mr. Blake, a 48-year-old bank chief executive officer (CEO), is admitted to the psychiatric unit of an urban general hospital after brandishing a gun at home and threatening to kill himself. Mr. Blake is intoxicated on admission. His wife found a suicide note and called the police, who brought him to the hospital emergency department. Mr. Blake initially refuses to be hospitalized. He is confronted with the choice of voluntarily admitting himself or facing involuntary hospitalization. Mr. Blake accepts voluntary admission but denies current suicidal ideation, intent, or plan.

Dr. Green sees Mr. Blake within a few hours after admission. He appears sober. She takes time to obtain a complete psychiatric history. Mr. Blake has been married for 25 years. He describes the marriage as "rocky." The couple has two grown children, who live away from home and are well established in their careers. Mr.

Blake rose rapidly in his bank to the top position. His business acumen, affable manner, and strong drive to succeed propelled him into the position of CEO after 15 years with the bank. Mr. Blake states that he has "very good relationships at work." Dr. Green avoids the trap of providing "VIP" treatment for a CEO. She recognizes that "VIP" treatment is often inadequate treatment, sometimes facilitating an "executive suicide."

Mr. Blake reveals that he sought treatment for an episode of depression 5 years ago. The psychiatrist saw Mr. Blake for 5 months, treating him with psychodynamic psychotherapy and antidepressant medication. Mr. Blake does not recall the name of the antidepressant. Conflicts at work and in his marriage triggered the depression. "Fleeting" suicide thoughts were present that remitted with improvement of his depression. He denies any suicide attempts.

Approximately 6 months ago, his depression recurred. Suicidal thoughts were present, but he formed no intent or plan. Mr. Blake increased his intake of alcohol to "treat" his anxiety and depression. Decreasing business revenues, accounting irregularities at the bank, and continuing marital strife precipitated the second bout of depression. During the month prior to admission, Mr. Blake has been intoxicated most evenings. He experiences difficulty falling asleep and early morning awakening, anxiety, hopelessness, difficulty concentrating, loss of pleasure and interest, and an occasional panic attack. Mr. Blake has lost 25 pounds in the past 2 months. Appetite has been "nonexistent." It has become more and more difficult for Mr. Blake to go to work. During the week prior to admission, he arrived late for work each day, missing important meetings.

Mr. Blake was raised as an only child. His parents fought frequently, divorcing when he was 10 years old. Mr. Blake's father experienced recurrent depressions. His mother had an "alcohol problem." Mr. Blake was an excellent student, focusing his attention on academic and athletic activities at school. His main source of emotional support were his many friends and some of their parents. Episodes of alcohol intoxication occurred while he was in college.

After performing a complete psychiatric evaluation and differential diagnosis, Dr. Green makes the diagnoses of major depression, recurrent, severe without psychotic features, and alcohol abuse. A DSM-IV-TR (American Psychiatric Association 2000) multiaxial diagnosis is documented. A urine drug screen drawn in the emergency department tests positive for benzodiazepines. The blood alcohol level is 0.1%, a level sufficient to produce impaired judgment. Dr. Green formulates a comprehensive individualized treatment plan after performing a systematic suicide risk assessment. The risk for suicide is rated as high, despite Mr. Blake's denial of current suicidal ideation, intent, or plan. Mr. Blake is placed on 15-minute suicide safety checks based on his cooperativeness, visibility on the unit, and socializing with other patients. Mr. Blake is started on an alcohol withdrawal protocol. Dr. Green also obtains a medical consultation.

With Mr. Blake's permission, Dr. Green calls his former psychiatrist, obtaining the additional history information that suicidal ideation occurred during a period of marital strife. The outpatient psychiatrist confirms that there was no history of suicide attempts. The psychiatrist provides the name of the specific antidepressant that was effective in the outpatient treatment of Mr. Blake's depression. Dr. Green prescribes the same antidepressant. She informs Mr. Blake that antidepressant medications take time to become effective. She also prescribes trazodone 50 mg four times a day as needed to help ease Mr. Blake's anxiety and agitation. Benzodiazepines are avoided because of Mr. Blake's alcohol dependence. Within a few hours, he feels much more comfortable. A hypnotic medication is prescribed for his sleep disturbance. The central focus of Dr. Green's management plan is the aggressive treatment of Mr. Blake's acute suicide risk factors. Dr. Green also meets with Ms. Blake, the patient's wife. Mr. Blake is also present. Dr. Green's goal is to obtain any additional information that Ms. Blake may possess and to begin early discharge planning.

Ms. Blake reports that Mr. Blake is a good husband, except when he drinks. Then he becomes verbally abusive. He has been very depressed during the past month, talking about suicide even when he was not drinking. Ms. Blake gives Dr. Green her husband's suicide note that she found at home. It reads,

> Dear Flo: You know I have always loved you. I'm so sorry for the grief I have caused you and the kids. There are big problems at work, maybe a criminal investigation. I've done nothing wrong, but I can't take it any longer. I love you and the kids so much. Forgive me. Dan.

Ms. Blake states that her husband is a gun collector. He has guns both at home and at work. Dr. Green instructs Ms. Blake to have all the guns and ammunition removed immediately from the home and office and safely secured elsewhere. Dr. Green requests a call from Ms. Blake after the guns are safely secured. Ms. Blake complies. Ms. Blake thinks that her husband has been taking some of her "tranquilizers" prescribed by her primary care physician. Mr. Blake readily admits to taking the medication in combination with alcohol. He denies the illicit use of any other drugs.

Mr. Blake's suicide precautions are determined based on Dr. Green's daily systematic suicide risk assessments. Special attention is given to following the course of acute suicide risk factors and receiving continuous input from the treatment team. As Dr. Green sees the patient daily, she carefully reads the staff's entries in Mr. Blake's medical chart. The treatment plan is reviewed and updated. By the fifth hospital day, the acute suicide risk factors associated with depression, anxiety, and alcohol abuse diminish. Protective factors against suicide emerge, especially the presence of a therapeutic alliance, cooperation with treatment, and full participation in unit activities, including group therapies and social programs. Mr. Blake is placed on the unit's routine hourly suicide precautions. Suicide risk assessment reveals moderate risk.

On the basis of the utilization reviewer's report to the managed-care organization (MCO) of Dr. Green's current suicide risk assessment, the MCO approves only 1 more day of hospitalization. Dr. Green arranges a doctor-to-doctor appeal, based on her assessment that additional inpatient days are needed to adequately treat the patient's depression and moderate risk of suicide. Consultation with a colleague supports her appeal for additional treatment. The consultation is documented. The MCO approves 3 additional hospital days but will not approve any further hospital stay. Neither Mr. Blake's depression nor his suicide risk level is significantly improved at the end of the 3 additional hospital days. The hospital is supportive of Dr. Green's request for continuing Mr. Blake's hospitalization for 2 more days without insurance coverage. The antidepressant medication has not had sufficient time to take effect.

Final discharge planning for aftercare begins. Mr. Blake is less depressed. He looks forward to being discharged and returning to work. He calls his former outpatient psychiatrist and arranges for the first available appointment, which is 4 days after discharge. Dr. Green also speaks with the outpatient psychiatrist, apprising him of the patient's hospital course and treatment. She speaks with Mr. Blake and his wife together about the importance of marital counseling. They both agree to follow up on her recommendation. Mr. Blake makes an appointment with a marriage counselor. Despite their marital difficulties, Ms. Blake is caring and supportive of her husband. Dr. Green tells Ms. Blake to maintain careful control of her medications. Dr. Green again asks about the availability of guns. Ms. Blake reassures Dr. Green that all the guns have been moved from the home and the office to a secure place.

While hospitalized, Mr. Blake attends Alcoholics Anonymous (AA) meetings held at the hospital. He is accompanied by the hospital addiction counselor. Mr. Blake finds the AA meetings to be "very helpful in allowing me to understand the severity of my alcohol dependence." Mr. Blake makes plans to attend AA meetings held at a church near his home. With the assistance of the addiction counselor, he finds a sponsor. Mr. Blake will also be attending an outpatient alcohol rehabilitation program arranged by the psychiatric unit addiction counselor.

On the day of discharge, Dr. Green performs and documents her risk-benefit evaluation for continued hospitalization versus discharge. Dr. Green's systematic suicide risk assessment of Mr. Blake reveals continuing moderate risk. Mr. Blake's depression has improved but not remitted. A number of suicide risk and protective factors are assessed, including the severity of the depression; his likely adherence to follow-up care, including psychiatric treatment and AA, and an alcohol rehabilitation program; the ability to work productively; and the psychological stability to face a possible criminal investigation at his bank. Protective factors that may help mitigate suicide risk include Mr. Blake's clinical improvement, a supportive wife, marital counseling, his desire to resume work, his therapeutic alliance with Dr. Green, adherence to medication, and his promised cooperation with the aftercare planning. Dr. Green indicates that although the patient is still at moderate suicide risk, he is not an acute risk at the time of discharge. The risk-benefit assessment by Dr. Green is an informed clinical judgment that favors discharge.

Dr. Green also documents that the discharge suicide risk assessment is a "here and now" determination that is rapidly attenuated by time. She notes that acute suicide risk factors have abated but that chronic (long-term) suicide risk factors remain unchanged. Dr. Green documents the following: "The patient remains at chronic suicide risk. He could become acutely suicidal again, depending on the nature and course of his mental illness, the adequacy of future treatment, his adherence to treatment recommendations, and the exposure to unpredictable life stresses."

Dr. Green discusses the aftercare arrangements with Mr. Blake and answers his questions. He is informed by Dr. Green that it is the hospital's policy to have the social worker call to see if the patient at risk for suicide keeps the initial appointment. Mr. Blake does not feel that this is necessary in his case, but he understands that it may be helpful to others. He states, "I am fully committed to treatment and the follow-up program." He does agree with Dr. Green's request that his wife drive him to and from work until he has the first visit with the outpatient psychiatrist. If an emergency arises after discharge but before his first outpatient appointment, Dr. Green advises Mr. Blake to call his outpatient psychiatrist or to come back to the hospital's emergency department. He can also reach her by telephone. She gives Mr. Blake her office telephone number. Mr. Blake is discharged. His wife drives him home.

DISCUSSION

The case example illustrates many of the important points about assessing and managing suicide risk of psychiatric inpatients that are discussed below.

COMPLETE PSYCHIATRIC EXAMINATION

A complete inpatient psychiatric examination should be performed in a timely manner following the patient's admission and contemporaneously documented. A careful mental status examination provides information for the assessment of treatment and management of the suicidal patient. The mental status examination is the equivalent of the physical examination. It is the psychiatrist's stethoscope that auscultates the patient's mental functioning.

Patients often are admitted late in the evening or during early morning hours. In managed-care settings, inpatient admissions are usually emergency admissions. Many of the patients have severe psychiatric disorders associated with a heightened risk for suicide. Consulting with the nursing staff regarding the clinical status of the patient, including necessary suicide precautions, will help the psychiatrist determine whether the patient must be seen immediately. If the psychiatrist plans to see the patient sometime after admission, the staff should be instructed to call if they have any concerns about the patient's safety status. The clinical decision to psychiatrically hospitalize a patient is a useful indicator of increased suicide risk (Bostwick and Pankratz 2000).

Suicidal patients who are admitted late at night or during the early morning hours are often placed on standard 15-minute precautions until seen by the psychiatrist. However, standard 15-minute checks may not be appropriate for high-risk patients, especially following a serious suicide attempt. A patient may be imminently suicidal, requiring constant visual observation, one-to-one, arms-length supervision, or supervision at a distance reasonable for the patient's condition. Careful suicide risk assessment by the nursing staff may help the psychiatrist determine the patient's safety requirement before arriving to see the patient. A suicide prevention contract should not be relied on.

An essential part of the psychiatric evaluation is the physical examination. Psychiatric inpatients frequently have associated medical disorders or conditions that increase the risk for suicide. The risk for suicide is elevated in special medical populations (e.g., pancreatic and lung cancer, AIDS, chronic pain syndrome, lupus; Kelly et al. 1999). The Joint Commission on Accreditation of Healthcare Organizations (2002) requires that a history and physical examination and laboratory screening assessments be completed within 24 hours of the patient's admission. Given the advancements in medicine and the complex medical problems that some psychiatric inpatients present, consultation with a primary care physician or internist may be necessary. Self-inflicted wounds often require surgical attention. The physical examination and medical issues generally are managed by the medical consultant. However, some psychiatrists feel that they are qualified to perform the physical examination and manage the medical problems, including ordering appropriate laboratory studies.

An accurate diagnosis and development, documentation, and implementation of a rational multidisciplinary treatment plan is standard practice. It is also required for utilization review. A differential diagnosis should be performed and documented.

The rapid turnover of severely ill, suicidal inpatients presents assessment difficulties for the psychiatrist. Unless sufficient time is taken, the psychiatric examination may be compromised. The decreased length of stay entails concentrated, time-intensive evaluations for adequate treatment and management. In *Brandvain v. Ridgeview Inst.* (1988/1989), the psychiatrist was found negligent for the suicide of a second-year resident because of failure to inquire about the patient's history and life circumstances.

Harris and Barraclough (1997) abstracted 249 published reports on the mortality of mental, neurological, and medical disorders with follow-up of 2 years or more. They compared observed numbers of suicides with those expected. A standardized mortality ratio (SMR) was calculated for each disorder (see Chapter 2, "Suicide Risk Assessment"). The SMR is a determination of relative risk of suicide for a particular disorder compared with the expected rate in the general population. It is calculated by dividing observed mortality by expected mortality. The authors concluded, "If these results can be generalized then virtually all mental disorders have an increased risk of suicide excepting mental retardation and dementia" (p. 205).

Harris and Barraclough also calculated the SMR for all psychiatric diagnoses by treatment setting. The SMR for inpatients was 5.82. For outpatients it was 18.09. Prior suicide attempts by any method had the highest SMR, 38.36. Thus, the presence of prior suicide attempts significantly raises the patient's risk for suicide. The SMR for psychiatric, neurological, and medical disorders can be helpful to the psychiatrist in evaluating the suicide risk associated with a specific diagnosis. The psychiatrist should gather information from collateral sources and spend sufficient time with the patient to arrive at an accurate diagnosis that informs the assessment, treatment, and safety management of the patient at risk for suicide.

Utilization of the multidisciplinary team's input helps to determine the patient's diagnosis and suicide risk level. Records of prior admissions from the same hospital should be obtained immediately. Copies of psychiatric records from previous admissions to other psychiatric facilities are rarely available in a short amount of time. With a patient's written authorization, the psychiatrist or other staff member may be able to obtain a faxed discharge summary. Hospital discharge summaries usually contain sufficient information to assist the psychiatrist's evaluation of the patient. In malpractice cases, the failure to obtain prior records is easiest for experts to criticize.

Once obtained, the records must be read by the psychiatrist. Because of confidentiality issues or the time and effort required, some hospitals may not fax psychiatric records or discharge summaries, even after proper authorization by the patient. All efforts to obtain information from health care providers, successful or not, should be documented in the patient's chart.

In *Cohen v. State of New York* (1976/1977), negligent supervision and institutional policies governing patient management were addressed. A 23-year-old married medical student with a diagnosis of paranoid schizophrenia committed suicide on the day he was transferred from a restrictive to an open ward. The court found "many errors of judgment" by the resident and the supervisor, including the making of clinical decisions without reading the nonphysician treatment notes. Preferably before interviewing the patient, the psychiatrist should review the current psychiatric record for entries made by all members of the treatment team. The psychiatrist's interview with the patient, review of the patient's record, and discussion of the case with the treatment team or team member should be documented each time, in a format such as the following: "I saw the patient, reviewed patient's chart, and discussed the case with...(date and time)." In *Bell v. NYC Health and Hosp. Corp.* (1982), in finding liability, the court noted that the psychiatrist failed to inquire about important clinical symptoms documented in the patient's record before making treatment decisions. The patient, who was hallucinating and delusional, committed suicide after being released.

If an outpatient therapist has treated or is currently treating the patient, the psychiatrist or a treatment team member should attempt to call the therapist. However, some psychiatrists prefer to draw their own initial clinical impressions before requesting the patient's records or speaking with prior treaters. From both prior records and direct discussions with the patient's treaters, valuable information can be obtained regarding, for example, diagnosis; successful or unsuccessful treatments; prior suicidal ideation, intent, plan, or attempts; premature discharges; adherence to treatment and aftercare recommendations; and the adequacy of the patient's supporting environment. This information and its source should also be documented.

In the case example, Dr. Green learns important information by talking with the patient's former outpatient psychiatrist. The history of depression, marital strife, suicidal ideation but no suicide attempts, and the specific antidepressant that worked for Mr. Blake are important considerations in her diagnostic formulation and treatment plan. His wife's report of Mr. Blake's escalating suicidal ideation, and especially her provision of the actual suicide note, are critical data for the systematic suicide risk assessment and for safety management. Approximately 12%–15% of persons who commit suicide leave a note (Leenars 1988). The information provided by the patient's wife underscores the severity of the patient's depression, the severity of his alcohol abuse, and the seriousness of his suicidal ideation and intent.

SUICIDE RISK ASSESSMENT

Suicide risk assessment is an integral part of a comprehensive psychiatric examination (Simon 1992a) (see Chapter 2, "Suicide Risk

Assessment"). Observation of the patient during the psychiatric examination usually provides information about suicide risk factors that does not rely solely on subjective patient reporting. For example, slash marks on the arms or neck, burns, or other wounds may be apparent. The mental status examination may reveal diminished concentration, bizarre ideation, evidence of command hallucinations, incapacity to cooperate, restlessness, agitation, severe thought disorder, impulsivity, and alcohol or drug withdrawal symptoms.

Weisman and Worden (1972) devised a risk-rescue rating in suicide assessment as a descriptive and quantitative method of assessing the lethality of suicide attempts. For example, a patient who takes a few minor tranquilizers and immediately calls the physician is at low risk and high rescue. The patient who makes a few superficial slashes on the wrist with a razor while on the psychiatric unit but remains alone is at low risk and low rescue. A high-risk, high-rescue patient attempts a hanging in the presence of a friend. A high-risk, low-rescue situation occurs when the patient buys a hose to fit a car exhaust and waits for everyone to leave the house.

The hypothesis underlying the suicide risk rating is that the lethality of the method of suicide, defined as the probability of inflicting irreversible damage, may be expressed as a ratio of factors influencing risk and rescue. A risk-rescue rating correlates with the level of treatment recommended, the subject's sex, and whether the subject lived or died. By itself, the risk-rescue rating is not a predictive instrument. Considered along with other factors, such as explicit intention to die, history of mental illness, and availability of family and community support, the risk-rescue rating can be used to assist in suicide risk assessment.

Determining intent is essential to assessing the lethality of a patient's suicide attempt. For example, an individual who takes 5 aspirin tablets in the belief that he or she will die has made a lethal attempt. Conversely, a person addicted to barbiturates who ingests 40 butalbital tablets, but knows that death will not result, has made a nonlethal attempt.

Systematic suicide risk assessment is a process, not an event. Suicide risk exists on a continuum and can vary from minute to minute, hour to hour, and day to day. As the case example demonstrates, a suicide risk assessment should be conducted at admission, at discharge, and at significant clinical junctures (e.g., changes in safety observation levels, ward changes, off-ward privileges, passes). Systematic suicide risk assessment identifies and weighs risk and protective factors that inform treatment and safety management (Simon 2000). For patients who have difficulty speaking and understanding English, it may be necessary to perform the suicide risk assessment with the help of an interpreter. In the case example, Dr. Green performs systematic suicide risk assessments at admission and discharge. Following the admission assessment, the acute suicide risk factors that precipitated the patient's hospitalization are a focus of continued assessment throughout the patient's hospitalization. Also, when suicide risk assessment is a process, it assists the concurrent utilization review required by MCOs for determining the hospital length of stay.

In a prospective study of suicide in patients with major affective disorder, Fawcett et al. (1990) found short-term suicide risk factors that were statistically significant within 1 year of assessment. Anxiety-related risk factors included panic attacks, psychic anxiety, and depressive turmoil (agitation). Other short-term risk factors were loss of pleasure or interest, alcohol abuse, diminished concentration, and global insomnia. These findings were replicated in a review of 76 inpatient suicide cases (Fawcett et al. 2003). The combination of depression and anxiety (agitation) can become unbearable to the patient. Patients may become inured to depression, but the addition of anxiety or panic attacks may make life unbearable and an escape through suicide compelling. Clinical interventions should be aimed at aggressively treating anxiety and other modifiable short-term suicide risk factors in patients with major affective disorders and other psychiatric conditions. Anxiety symptoms usually respond rapidly to short-acting benzodiazepines alone or in combination with an atypical antipsychotic or divalproex. In some patients, however, benzodiazepines may promote dyscontrol of destructive behaviors. Given the short length of hospital stays, antipsychotic, antianxiety, and sleep medications may help to rapidly stabilize patients with anxiety-related suicide risk factors, providing an opportunity to treat depression, which takes longer.

Is an increased risk of suicide associated with psychotic depression? Roose et al. (1983) found that delusional depressed patients were five times more likely to commit suicide than depressed patients who were not delusional. Busch et al. (2003) also found that

54% of 76 inpatient suicides had an association between psychosis and suicide. In the Collaborative Study of Depression, however, no significant difference in suicide was found between depressed and delusionally depressed patients. But patients who had delusions of thought insertion, grandeur, and mind reading were significantly represented in the suicide group (Fawcett et al. 1987).

Simon and Gutheil (2002) reported a review of more than 100 suicide cases in litigation. A recurrent pattern of suicide risk factors emerged. Patients fitting this pattern committed suicide while inpatients or within a few days or weeks following discharge. Most of the suicides occurred in men between ages 30 and 50. The men were often described as middle-management, hard-working "family men" who were hospitalized for the first time (see Table 6–1). The central suicide risk factors were nonadherence to treatment, withdrawal and detachment from relationships, failure to form a therapeutic alliance, isolation on the inpatient unit, and avoidance of affect-laden treatment activities. However, litigation-derived cases represent a skewed sample that places limitations on the generalizability of the risk factors described here.

First-time hospitalized, high-achieving, high-functioning, ambitious patients who become depressed and are unable to work or to work productively are often at substantial risk for suicide. The reality of having a mental illness is not accepted. It is viewed as a personal failing and experienced as a devastating narcissistic injury. These patients are usually highly defined by their work. Before committing suicide, many of these previously high-functioning patients gradually withdraw from important relationships, much like patients who are terminally ill and preparing to die. A patient's first hospitalization usually indicates the onset of severe depression and significant suicide risk. The tendency of suicides to occur early during the course of a depressive illness is reported in the psychiatric literature (Fawcett et al. 1993).

Inpatients at significant risk for suicide who suddenly improve present the psychiatrist with a difficult clinical dilemma. Is the improvement genuine, feigned so that the patient can leave the hospital, or the result of relief based on the patient's final decision to commit suicide? For the determinedly suicidal patient who is feigning or is determined to commit suicide, nothing has really changed clinically. Eating and sleeping patterns usually remain the same. If

Table 6–1. Suicide risk factor patterns

- Male
- Age 30–50
- Major depression, single episode, severe
- First time psychiatric hospitalization
- Hopelessness, coupled with intolerance of dependency, regression, help, and revealing feelings
- Melancholic features
- Psychotic features (in some)
- Prominent anxiety or agitation
- Denial of psychiatric illness
- Nonadherence to treatment
- Press for discharge
- Withdrawn, detached from relationships
- No therapeutic alliance or pseudoalliance
- Avoids unit activities that focus on revealing feelings
- Denies current suicidal ideation, intent, or plan
- Recent history of suicidal ideation, intent, plan, or attempt
- Passively agrees to suicide prevention contract
- Stressful work or marital situation
- Unable to work or major conflict at work, or perceived threat to job
- Ready access to guns
- Financial constraints on care

Note. Not all factors are present in all patients.
Source. Reprinted from Simon RI, Gutheil TG: "A Recurrent Pattern of Suicide Risk Factors Observed in Litigated Cases: Lessons in Risk Management." *Psychiatric Annals* 32:384–387, 2002. Used with permission.

taken, medication has not had time to work or has energized the patient without decreasing hopelessness. The patient remains seclusive or has minimal or superficial contact with the staff and other patients. Little or no therapeutic alliance is present. Medication adherence is often poor. A near-lethal suicide attempt often precedes the hospitalization.

Systematic suicide risk assessment helps determine whether a substantial change has occurred in the patient's condition and behavior that supports the sudden improvement. For example, have the acute suicide risk factors that led to the inpatient admission ameliorated? Has anything changed from the time of admission in the patient's life circumstances? Patients at risk for suicide usually improve gradually. Sudden improvement may be based on an artificially revised risk assessment related to the MCO's denial of additional benefits or the patient's discovery that he or she has to pay out of pocket. The psychiatrist must be wary of "miraculous insurance cures."

TREATMENT

A comprehensive multidisciplinary treatment plan guides clinical interventions. It should be formulated and implemented in a timely manner according to departmental policies and procedures, and reviewed and updated regularly. In some jurisdictions, a completed multidisciplinary treatment plan is required by law (Md. Code. Ann., [Health-General] § 10-701 [2002]). The general goal of inpatient psychiatric treatment is crisis intervention, safety management, and stabilization of the patient. Because the length of stay for severely ill patients in most psychiatric units is often less than a week, a comprehensive treatment plan must be quickly formulated and implemented. Heavy reliance is placed on the multidisciplinary treatment approach to inpatient care. The treatment plan undergoes revision according to the clinical needs of the patient with contributions by all disciplines.

INTERVENTIONS

Suicide risk factors such as anxiety (agitation), impulsivity, and psychosis often respond rapidly to medications. In the case example, the patient's anxiety and agitation respond to trazodone, providing quick relief for the patient. Neuroleptic-induced akathisia has been related to patient suicide (Atbasoglu et al. 2002; Drake and Ehrlich 1985). It can be difficult to differentiate akathisia from psychic anxiety and agitation. The conditions may occur together, increasing the risk of suicide. Akathisia may also lead to medication nonadherence and indirectly affect suicide risk. Anticholinergic drugs and medication adjustments may reduce suicide risk in patients with severe, intolerable akathisia. However, a causal link between akathisia and suicide has not been subjected to empirical study.

Detoxification of suicidal patients with substance abuse disorders (including alcohol) may reduce this significant suicide risk factor, at least temporarily. Lithium significantly decreases suicide risk in patients with bipolar disorder (Baldessarini et al. 2001). The risk of suicide attempts in bipolar patients taking lithium is more than 8 times lower than among patients not taking the medication. Even with lithium, the completed suicide rate among bipolar patients is still 10 times higher than the suicide rate in the general population (Baldessarini et al. 2003). The potential for lethal overdose should guide the quantity of lithium prescribed for a patient at risk for suicide. In some responders, antidepressant medication can have a significant therapeutic benefit within several weeks. However, most responders require 8–12 weeks for maximum benefit following initiation of antidepressant treatment (Gelenberg and Chesen 2000). Patients should be informed that an antidepressant requires time to become effective. To combat hopelessness, the patient should be educated about the "ups and downs" in depressive symptoms that commonly occur in the course of improvement. According to some researchers, other than prior suicide attempts, hopelessness is the best indication of suicide risk (Beck et al. 1985; Malone et al. 1995a). During this "down time," the patient must be carefully monitored. Clozapine reduces the suicide attempt and completion rates in schizophrenia and schizoaffective disorder (Meltzer 2001; Meltzer et al. 2003). The U.S. Food and Drug Administration has approved clozapine for the treatment of recurrent suicidal behaviors in patients with schizophrenia or schizoaffective disorder.

Apart from the effects of medications, inpatients may improve quickly because of the intensive psychosocial interventions, the structure provided on the inpatient unit, and by peer interactions, which can be quite powerful. Although medications are very important in the treatment of psychiatric patients at risk for suicide, drug therapy must be accompanied by psychosocial interventions to be fully effective. Psychosocial interventions on the unit, especially group therapy, decreases anxiety, reduces isolation, improves reality testing, provides needed support, and shortens the hospital length of stay.

Suicidal ideation, intent, or plan in selected patients with mood and psychotic disorders is a main indication for electroconvulsive therapy (ECT), especially when alternative treatments are not appropriate or have not been effective (American Psychiatric Association 2001). ECT should be the treatment of choice when quick results are needed for the patient at high risk for suicide and delay would be life threatening. A rapid clinical response with reduction or resolution of suicidal behaviors often occurs with ECT, presumably by treatment of the underlying psychiatric disorder (Prudic and Sackheim 1999). As patients improve with ECT, they may remain at high risk for suicide because of increased energy. Careful monitoring is necessary.

There is little evidence that ECT has long-term effects on suicidal behaviors or suicide (Sharma 1999). Administration of inpatient ECT may be followed by outpatient maintenance ECT. The effectiveness ascribed to ECT may be difficult to differentiate from the co-administration of pharmacotherapy. As with any treatment, there are a certain percentage of patient nonresponders.

ECT is no longer a frequent source of malpractice claims against psychiatrists (Simon 1992b). ECT accounts for fewer than 1% of malpractice claims filed against psychiatrists. There is no increase in insurance premiums for psychiatrists who administer ECT.

The extensive use of antidepressant and antimanic treatments has not reduced the long-term rates of suicide or premature mortality from other causes of illness (Baldessarini et al. 2001). For example, the suicide rate for the United States between 1901 (11.8 per 100,000) and 2000 (10.6 per 100,000) dropped by only 1.2 per 100,000, despite the availability of antidepressants and other treatments since the 1950s (Silverman 2003). Because 90%–95% of individuals who commit suicide were mentally ill before their deaths, psychiatric interventions have not substantially reduced the suicide rate over 99 years (Barraclough et al. 1974). However, Isacsson (2000) examined the overall suicide rates in Sweden from 1978 to 1996, determining that suicide rates decreased with increased antidepressant use. In a 22-year prospective study of patients hospitalized with mood disorders, long-term medication (antidepressants, lithium, and neuroleptics alone or in combination) significantly lowered the suicide rates, despite the fact that more severely ill patients were treated (Angst et al. 2002). The antidepressant treatment of depressed patients at risk for suicide is often inadequate. Thus, the ability to measure the antisuicidal efficacy of antidepressants in naturalistic studies is undermined (Oquendo et al. 2002). Whether psychopharmacological agents reduce the long-term risk of suicide remains inconclusive. However, the day-to-day experience of clinicians is that improvement in the quality of life and the prevention of many patient deaths have resulted from treatment with antipsychotic, antimanic, and antidepressant drugs; ECT; and cognitive-behavioral and interpersonal therapies.

The psychiatrist's clinical focus must necessarily be on treating the patient's current condition. Treatment of the patient's current episode of psychiatric illness is frequently successful in decreasing or eliminating the associated acute risk of suicide. Factors unrelated to the efficacy of psychiatric treatment also affect suicide mortality rates in the long run. For example, Ostamo and Lonnqvist (2001), in a 5-year follow-up study of patients treated in hospital after suicide attempts, found an increase in mortality from suicide, homicide, and other causes. In the follow-up period, 16% of suicide attempters died, 40% of them by suicide. The nature of the patient, the efficacy of treatments, and the adherence and access to or availability of mental health resources were not considered.

The lifetime risk of suicide for patients with mood disorder is 4% (Bostwick and Pankratz 2000). Most depressed patients do not kill themselves. Suicide remains a low-base-rate event. For instance, the national suicide rate in the general population in the year 2000 was 10.6 per 100,000 (Silverman 2003). The suicide rate for individuals having bipolar disorder is estimated to be 193 per 100,000 (absolute risk), or 18 times higher (relative risk) than the rate for the general population (Baldessarini et al. 2003). Turning this statistic around, 99,807 patients with bipolar disorders will not commit suicide in a single year. Thus, on a statistical basis alone, the vast majority of patients with bipolar disorder will not commit suicide. The same statistical analysis can be applied to other psychiatric disorders. The clinical challenge is to identify those patients at significant risk for suicide at any given time (Jacobs et al. 1999). The preceding statistical analysis does not diminish the tragedy of a patient's suicide. Rather, it merely puts suicide mortality rates into a realistic perspective.

THE TREATMENT TEAM

Assessing and managing suicide risk in inpatient settings is clinically challenging. It requires collaboration with the treatment team. The treatment team usually consists of the psychiatrist, nurse, social worker, occupational therapist, and other mental health professionals. The psychiatrist cannot rely on the presence of a therapeutic alliance with severely ill suicidal inpatients, especially if they are seen briefly during the course of a short hospitalization. It is important for patients' care that the psychiatrist conduct case reviews with the clinical staff. The psychiatrist must be able to work closely with the treatment team. At some hospitals, patients attend the team's review and update of the treatment plan. A failed team approach may lead to fragmentation of the patient's care. The psychiatrist may be held legally accountable for the negligence of team members under a vicarious liability doctrine, if the patient is harmed.

The psychiatrist is leader of the treatment team, obtaining important clinical information about the patient and directing treatment interventions. The psychiatrist's relationship with the team is both supervisory and collaborative. Although team members have an independent role in assessing suicide risk, the psychiatrist should also conduct systematic suicide risk assessments and discuss them with team members. The psychiatrist cannot delegate to treatment team members his or her responsibility for performing suicide risk assessments. If the psychiatrist and team members do not collaborate in assessing and managing the patient's risk for suicide, the risk may be increased.

The psychiatrist's ability to coordinate and focus the team's continuing input on the assessment and documentation of the patient's risk for suicide constitutes good clinical care. The multidisciplinary treatment team functions 24 hours a day, 7 days a week. It has "a thousand eyes." Team members observe the patient's behaviors and mental functioning, share and integrate these data at team meetings, and document their findings in the patient's record. As previously noted, the time that psychiatrists usually spend with their patients is limited by comparison. However, the psychiatrist must spend sufficient time to psychotherapeutically engage the patient in order to provide adequate treatment and safety management. After performing an initial psychiatric examination, the psychiatrist cannot simply turn the patient over to the treatment team and walk away. The psychiatrist's role must be more than just one of prescribing medications.

It is essential that the psychiatrist thoroughly read the patient's medical record daily. A substantial difference in the team's perception of suicide risk compared with the psychiatrist's assessment of risk is cause for an immediate conference to explain the disparity and, if possible, reconcile the difference. It may be necessary to extend the patient's length of stay if differences persist and more time is required to resolve the problem (see Chapter 8, "Suicide Aftermath: Documentation, Confidentiality, and Survivor Care").

SAFETY MANAGEMENT

Inpatient suicides can occur at any time. However, they usually occur shortly after admission, during staff shift changes, and after discharge (a few hours, days, or weeks later). A newly admitted, severely mentally ill patient at significant risk for suicide, who is untreated and unknown to the clinical staff, should be placed immediately on suicide precautions. Nurses can exercise their discretion to place suicidal patients on suicide precautions or increase the precaution level if the psychiatrist cannot be reached or until the psychiatrist has an opportunity to call or examine the patient. If possible, the patient should be kept within view of the nurses' station. If suicidal precautions are imposed by the nursing staff, the psychiatrist should assess the patient prior to discontinuance of the precaution and document the reason or write an order to continue the precautions. Nurses cannot lower or discontinue suicide precautions.

Systematic suicide risk assessment of the patient at admission informs the level of suicide precautions. For example, does the patient require one-to-one, arms-length or close visual observation, are safety checks every 15 or 30 minutes or hourly called for, or is routine group observation sufficient? Standards for close observation usually differ for each hospital. Psychiatrists should know the definition of close observation when treating patients in different hospitals. Often, it is easier to place a patient on suicide safety precautions than it is to reduce or discontinue the precautions. Patients on one-to-one, arms-length, or close visual observation who require off-unit tests or procedures should be escorted by one or preferably two staff members. Patients who are still on individualized safety observations should not be discharged. A period of observation for the patient off individualized safety precautions usually should precede discharge. In the case example, Dr. Green carefully adjusts the patient's safety precautions based on ongoing systematic suicide risk assessment.

Automatic institution of 15-minute checks may not correspond to the patient's safety requirements. Patients can and do kill themselves in between 15-minute checks. A patient who has made a near-lethal suicide attempt just prior to admission will likely require one-to-one supervision initially. A patient who is determined to commit suicide will likely find a way to do it, even when the patient is on one-to-one safety precautions. Fawcett et al. (2003), in a review of 76 inpatient suicides, found that 42 of these patients were on 15-minute suicide checks. Nine percent of patients were on one-to-one observation or with a staff member at the time of suicide. They concluded that no specific suicide precautions are 100% effective.

Constant observation should be discontinued as soon as possible, consistent with the patient's safety requirement. The psychiatric unit is not a jail. Although safety is the primary concern, the decision to employ one-to-one close observation must be balanced against the psychological distress it causes the patient. Privacy in the performance of natural functions is lost. The patient cannot go to the bathroom or shower without the presence of an observer. Patients often experience acute embarrassment and humiliation that may increase hopelessness, depression, and suicide risk. Also, constant observation by a stranger is unnerving and intimidating, especially for a paranoid patient.

In *Topel v. Long Island Jewish Med. Ctr.* (1981), the malpractice suit claimed that the psychiatrist was negligent in ordering observation every 15 minutes instead of constant observation for a patient who had attempted suicide. The psychiatrist had documented his reasons for not ordering constant observation: the patient's negative reaction to constant observation, the possible aggravation of the patient's heart condition by constant surveillance, the judgment that the suicide attempt was a suicide gesture, and the expected benefits of treatment in the open ward. The court held that the psychiatrist's suicide observation was a matter of professional judgment for which the psychiatrist was not liable.

During periods of peak activity on the psychiatric unit, sufficient staff may not be available to provide one-to-one close observation. It may be necessary to "zone" the patient to a couch in front of the nurses' station, to a group of patients, or to a specific area of the psychiatric unit where the patient can be kept under constant visual observation. Moreover, the unit staff may not be able to provide safety precautions at 5- or 10-minute intervals. Usually, a number of other patients are also on suicide precautions. It is not possible for the staff to be running back and forth every 5–10 minutes to check on the patient. If 5- to 10-minute checks are required, it is usually better to place the patient on constant visual observation or on one-to-one, arms-length observation, monitored by either a staff member or a responsible "sitter." Some hospitals have two basic levels of suicide precautions. Level 1 is close observation (arms-length or visual). Level 2 is 15-minute, 30-minute, or hourly checks.

The patient at risk for suicide who attends group meetings, socializes with other patients, and is visible on the unit usually can be placed on 15-minute checks and be observed by the staff. Patients who are at high risk for suicide, are withdrawn, and are isolative may need one-to-one close observation. The observation level may need to be flexible. For example, a patient with melancholic depression may need closer supervision in the morning, when depressive symptoms are often worse. Patients usually are aware of peak periods of activity on the unit. A suicidal patient may take advantage of the staff's attention to other patients to attempt or commit suicide. The multidisciplinary team must be able to maintain safely vigilance, even though it is stretched. However, if the unit is understaffed or is overwhelmed by suicidal patients, it may need to be temporarily closed to new admissions. Just a few high-risk suicidal patients can exhaust the clinical staff.

There must be a rational nexus between patient autonomy in the hospital setting and the patient's diagnosis, treatment, and safety needs. Nonetheless, with patients at risk for suicide, standard precautions must be observed, such as removal of shoelaces, belts, sharps, and glass products. A thorough search for contraband on admission is standard procedure. Psychiatric units are usually fitted, at a minimum, with non–weight-bearing fixtures and shower curtain rods, very short cords for electrical beds (properly insulated), cordless telephones or telephones with safety nonremoval cords, jump-proof windows, barricade-proof doors, and closed-circuit video cameras. The most common and available method of committing suicide by inpatients is strangulation, usually accomplished by a bedsheet hooked up in the patient's bathroom. Patients may try unusual methods of attempting suicide, such as water intoxication. Once use of this method is recognized, the patient must be placed on a water intoxication prevention protocol.

Determining safety precautions is complicated by court directives that require highly disturbed patients to be treated by the least restrictive means (Simon 2000). In *Johnson v. United States* (1976/1978/1981), the court noted that an "open-door" policy creates a higher potential for danger. However, the court went on to say

> Modern psychiatry has recognized the importance of making every effort to return a patient to an active and productive life. Thus, the patient is encouraged to develop his self-confidence by adjusting to the demands of everyday existence. Particularly because the prediction of danger is difficult, undue reliance on hospitalization might lead to prolonged incarceration of potentially useful members of society.

The tension between promoting individual freedom and protecting a person from self-injury is inherent in the clinical, ethical, and legal aspects of managing suicide risk (Amchin et al. 1990). The individual facts of the case and the reasonableness of the staff's application of the open-door policy are determinative.

The patient admitted to an intensive care unit after a suicide attempt may be awaiting transfer to a psychiatric unit. "Sitters" may be required to constantly attend the patient. Nevertheless, a patient may seize an opportune moment and jump through an unsecured window of an intensive care unit or medical/surgical ward or walk off the unit. Medical/surgical units provide a number of opportunities for the patient to commit suicide through the presence of unsecured equipment and other safety hazards. They are not designed for the safety management of the psychiatric patient at risk for suicide. Transfer of the patient to the psychiatric unit should be a priority admission.

Hospital policies and procedures usually require the patient to be evaluated by the psychiatrist within a specified period of time following admission. Departures from policies and procedures by the psychiatrist deserve a documented explanation. Official policies and procedures are consensus statements that reflect the standard of care. If the psychiatrist departs from the policies and procedures and the patient is harmed, a malpractice suit filed against the psychiatrist will likely be difficult to defend (*Eaglin v. Cook County Hosp.* [1992]). In the absence of such policies, it is prudent not to issue off-ward privileges to new patients until their psychiatric evaluations are completed and safety needs determined. Emergency admissions of patients often occur late at night or in the early hours of the morning. Severely ill patients at high risk for suicide should be examined soon after admission. The nursing staff has a duty to contact the psychiatrist in a timely manner when a patient is admitted.

Psychiatrists should be careful about prescribing psychotropic medications for newly admitted inpatients whom they have not had an opportunity to examine. Patients who are emergency admissions often need to be medicated before being seen by the psychiatrist. Psychiatrists typically rely on the nursing assessment of the patient in this situation. Prescribing routine medications from an admission protocol usually does not pose a problem. In *Gaido v. Weiser* (1988/ 1989), the psychiatrist was found to be negligent for prescribing medication without examining the patient, who committed suicide 6 days after discharge from the hospital.

Some psychiatric units have policies that require new patients to stay on the psychiatric unit for a specified period of time. Smoking is prohibited on most psychiatric units, unless there is a designated, enclosed, properly ventilated area on the unit for smoking. Patients who smoke often exert considerable pressure on the psychiatrist and the clinical staff to allow them to go off the inpatient unit, usually with an escorted smokers' group. Off-ward privileges require discontinuing close observation for suicide. Patients should be informed of the reasons for the inpatient policy and offered the option of nicotine gum, patch, or inhaler. However, these smoking alternatives are often rejected by patients as unsatisfactory. Some patients, especially those with substance abuse problems, can become very angry and abusive toward the staff when prohibited from smoking. A number of these patients will threaten to leave or actually sign out against medical advice if they are not permitted to smoke.

In order to smoke, patients may deny suicidal ideation, but they remain at heightened risk for suicide. If the psychiatrist is not on the unit, he or she may be contacted by the nursing staff and informed of the patient's demand to smoke. The psychiatrist is told that the patient denies suicidal thoughts. It is a serious mistake, on the basis of a telephone discussion, to allow the patient at suicide risk to leave the unit to smoke. An "on-the-spot" suicide risk assessment performed by the nurse or members of the treatment team may help inform the decision to issue off-unit privileges. Obviously, the patient's safety, not his or her need to smoke, must determine the level of supervision. Telephone orders discontinuing suicide precautions can be made for known patients after consultation with the clinical staff. However, it is preferable that an evaluation of the patient be performed by the clinician before changes are made in a patient's safety requirements.

When safety precautions are prematurely discontinued, the MCO may determine that the patient is no longer a suicide risk and deny further benefits. A period of patient restriction is usually necessary for the evaluation and maintenance of the patient's safety before off-unit privileges or passes are issued. In a study by Anand et al. (2002), smokers were converted from voluntary status earlier than nonsmokers. The authors concluded that patients who smoke apply overt and covert pressure on clinicians to gain smoking privileges. An association exists between cigarette smoking and the presence and severity of suicidal behavior among patients with psychiatric disorders (Malone et al. 2003).

Contacting family members or significant others, after obtaining the patient's permission, is standard inpatient practice. Competent patients may not authorize the clinician or the staff to contact others. The patient's request should be honored unless an emergency exception to consent exists (see Chapter 7, "Emergency Psychiatric Services"). The patient's unwillingness to grant permission to speak with others should be documented. In the case example, Dr. Green meets with the patient's wife to enlist her help in removing her husband's guns from the home and from his office. Contact also may be made by telephone. The unit social worker usually makes the initial contact. It is preferable, if possible, for the clinician to meet with family members or significant others. When appropriate, the patient and family members should be seen together. The meeting usually provides the clinician with insight into the family's dynamics. Also, distortions and misunderstandings that exist between any or all of the parties can be addressed. The opportunity exists to educate the patient and family member about the patient's mental illness and its management. Fawcett et al. (1990) found that approximately 25% of suicidal patients deny suicidal ideation or intent. In most cases, the patient told family members about his or her suicide ideation or intent. Families or significant others often provide valuable information, especially if a history of impulsive or "surprise" suicide attempts have occurred (Jacobson 1999).

The psychiatrist should make a point of returning telephone calls from family members and significant others after obtaining the patient's permission. In addition to a call from a staff member, most families want to hear from the psychiatrist. The caller may have important information that can assist the psychiatrist and the clinical staff in treatment and management. The patient should be informed of the telephone calls and the ensuing discussion, if appropriate. If the patient does not want confidential information revealed to callers, the psychiatrist can explain this limitation to the caller and just listen. Listening but not disclosing does not constitute a breach of confidentiality. The telephone calls should be documented, including time and date. It is often necessary to appoint a spokesperson for the family to assist with timely communication. Otherwise, numerous calls from different family members overwhelm the psychiatrist's ability to respond. Family members then complain that their calls are not being returned. Some family members may not respond to requests for meetings with the staff. They may withdraw in order to recuperate from the stress and fatigue of caring for a severely mentally ill patient.

The psychiatrist must take reasonable steps to prevent patient access to lethal weapons, such as guns. Guns in the home have been shown to substantially increase the risk of suicide in psychiatric patients, as does the recent purchase of a firearm, especially for women (Brent 2001; Wintemute et al. 1999). Guns in the patient's home should be removed, disarmed, and safely secured before the patient is issued a pass or discharged. Some suicidal patients who have eloped from the hospital have gone straight home and committed suicide by firearm. Easy accessibility and the lethality of guns make them a weapon of choice for committing suicide. One study found that 92% of suicides with firearms result in fatality (Gessert 2003). Suicide by firearms was the most common method for both men and women in 1999 (National Institute of Mental Health 2003).

Halfway measures such as locking up or hiding a gun at home may have lethal consequences. Patients intent on killing themselves often find a way to gain access to a hidden or locked gun that is still in the home. Guns *must be removed* from the home by a *responsible* person, safely *disarmed,* and *secured* in a safe place. If the patient agrees, the clinician can meet with both the patient and the designated person who accepts responsibility for removal of the gun. More than one gun may be present in the patient's home or office. There may be an extra key to a lockbox that the patient possesses but does not reveal. Specific instructions for gun disarming and removal should be documented in the patient's records (i.e., requesting the responsible person to call the psychiatrist or a staff person after the gun is safely removed and secured). If a meeting cannot be arranged, the psychiatrist or a staff person may call the responsible family member or significant other with specific instructions for gun removal and request a call back after removal and safe securing of the gun(s). Whenever possible, gun removal arrangements should be made with an individual whom the psychiatrist or clinical associate has met with personally. Occasionally, the person who is asked to remove the gun may be more disturbed or less responsible than the patient.

The same safety precautions apply to knives, poisons, and lethal medications available in the home. Knives may need to be removed from the home. A family member may require instruction about administering and monitoring the patient's medications. The medications of family members may be taken by the patient to commit suicide. In the case example, the patient was abusing his wife's benzodiazepines. Other common methods for committing suicide include hanging, poisoning (including drug overdose), cutting, stabbing, jumping, and asphyxiation (e.g., carbon monoxide) (Moscicki 1999). Some patients commit suicide by crashing their cars. If possible, car keys should be kept from patients who have made threats of suicide by car. With the introduction of the safer selective serotonin reuptake inhibitors (SSRIs), suicide by overdose of antidepressants is less common (Weber 2002). The greatest lethality from overdose is associated with over-the-counter and prescription analgesics, especially opioids. Families may need guidance about observing the patient after discharge for signs and symptoms of regression, especially if the stressors that led to the patient's hospitalization remain. Returning home can be a difficult adjustment.

Some psychiatrists and other mental health professionals, especially nurses by protocol, rely on suicide prevention contracts in the management of patients at risk for suicide. However, suicide prevention contracts cannot substitute for systematic suicide risk assessments. Moreover, the "no-harm" contract is not a legal contract that will exculpate the psychiatrist from malpractice liability. There is no evidence that suicide prevention contracts diminish patients' risk for suicide. Patients who are determined to commit suicide view the psychiatrist and clinical staff as adversaries (Resnick 2002). A patient's refusal to agree to a suicide prevention contract may reveal an unwillingness or inability to participate in a therapeutic alliance.

Some clinicians erroneously believe that obtaining a no-harm contract from psychiatric inpatients is the standard of care. Although this may be true for nurses and other clinical staff, psychiatrists are not under a professional or legal obligation to obtain contracts from patients against self-injury or suicide. If the psychiatrist uses suicide prevention contracts in the safety management of inpatients, the rationale should be documented. The advantages and disadvantages of suicide prevention contracts are discussed in Chapter 3, "Suicide Prevention Contracts."

DISCHARGE AND AFTERCARE

EARLY PLANNING

Discharging mentally ill patients at significant risk for suicide is a complex and difficult decision, given their typically short length of stay. Patients at moderate or even moderate to high risk for suicide are routinely discharged to aftercare in today's managed-care environment. Early planning enables consideration of a wide variety of discharge options that can be narrowed as discharge approaches. It takes time to find and arrange for appropriate disposition of patients at risk for suicide; community mental health resources often are strained, minimal, or unavailable. Most patients are discharged at some level of risk for suicide, requiring thorough discharge planning and follow-up treatment.

The months following a patient's discharge are a period of increased risk for suicide (Roy 1982). Because of "quicker-sicker" discharges, the psychiatrist must work closely with the multidisciplinary treatment team (Simon 1998a). Early discharge planning begins at the time of the patient's admission. Social workers provide critical assistance in making early assessments of needed "environmental" interventions and in identifying community resources. Beneficial adjustments in a patient's life circumstance can provide important protective factors against suicide. A frequent omission of psychiatrists sued for alleged negligent release of patients is the failure of the psychiatrist and social worker to communicate with each other concerning interview information obtained from outside sources. Even more troublesome are cases in which no information is obtained from family members when it is readily available. Persons who are supportive to the patient should be brought into the patient's discharge planning. However, some families or other relationships may not be supportive or may even be "toxic" to the patient.

FAMILIES

Cooperative, supportive family members are essential participants in the patient's care. Families, however, may have certain limitations that should be considered in discharge planning. The confidence that the clinician places on information from family members is contingent. Information from family members or friends may be unreliable because of denial, shame, or ambivalence toward the patient or because of mental illness in family informants. Social workers and nurses are valuable members of the treatment team who can provide in-depth family evaluations and access collateral sources of information about the patient.

The interaction between the patient and the family may be impaired. Seriously mentally ill patients may come from families whose members have substantial psychological impairment. Moreover, some family members may be more disturbed than the patient. Releasing a patient at suicide risk to a troubled family could cause the patient to regress, increasing the risk of suicide. Family members have been known to dissuade the patient from taking necessary medications because of their denial of the patient's mental illness.

Family members are not trained to diagnose and manage suicidal patients. Asking family members to closely supervise the patient imposes a burden that they may not be able to manage. Specifically, asking family members to keep constant watch on the patient will likely fail. Family members cannot or will not follow the patient everywhere (e.g., the bathroom) or stay up all night to observe the patient. Moreover, family members may make exceptions, as a result of denial, fatigue, or the need to attend to other pressing matters. For example, one family that was told to keep the patient under constant watch allowed the patient to drive to work alone. Instead, the patient drove to a bridge and jumped to his death.

There is an important role for the family, but it is not as a substitute for the care provided by trained mental health professionals when such care is necessary. Family support and feedback about the patient's thoughts and behaviors is an appropriate, helpful role. Family members who have a reasonably good relationship with the patient are usually sensitive to reportable changes in the patient's mental condition.

PRECIPITOUS DISCHARGES

Patients may decide to leave against medical advice (AMA) for a variety of reasons. For example, patients with substance abuse disorders tend to sign out AMA, sometimes in the middle of the night. Informal (pure voluntary) and formal (conditional voluntary) admission policies determine whether the patient can be held for a period of evaluation. Both types of patient admissions may be found on one psychiatric unit. For example, patients admitted for substance detoxification may be informal admissions, whereas the psychiatric patients on the unit are formal admissions. Generally, substance-abusing patients without a comorbid psychiatric disorder cannot be held against their will. However, substance-using patients with comorbid psychiatric disorders can be held against their will. Only a few states continue to use informal admission procedures. Purely voluntary patients cannot be held against their will. Only moral suasion, not coercion, can be used to encourage continued hospitalization.

The psychiatrist may not have had the opportunity to examine the patient and perform a suicide risk assessment before the patient decides to leave AMA. Reliance must be placed on clinical staff members to conduct a suicide risk assessment and to inform the psychiatrist of their evaluation. Conditional voluntary patients at significant risk for suicide can be held for the period of time provided for further evaluation. During the holding period, some patients withdraw their requests to leave and decide to stay. Other patients may be allowed to leave AMA or may be involuntarily hospitalized.

An AMA form signed by the patient does not by itself provide immunity from legal liability. Patients intent on leaving the hospital usually just glance at the AMA form and sign without actually reading it. The patient's mental capacity (competence) to understand the risks of signing out AMA should be determined. Patients who lack the mental capacity to understand the serious ramifications of signing out AMA or who are at significant risk for suicide should not be permitted to leave without further evaluation (Gerbasi and Simon, in press).

MANAGED-CARE SETTINGS

Certain anomalous clinical practices may arise if clinicians attempt to "game" managed-care policies and procedures. For example, additional hospital days may be authorized by MCOs based on the clinician's inflated assessment of a patient's suicide risk. However, if the MCO determines that the patient can be treated in a partial hospitalization program or as an outpatient, authorization for additional hospital stay is denied. Faced with denial of the patient's insurance coverage, the clinician may declare the patient "improved" and ready for discharge.

Formal suicide risk assessment gives the clinician confidence that a realistic evaluation of a patient's suicide risk has been performed. "Gaming" the MCO becomes unnecessary. Exaggerating the severity of the patient's suicide risk to qualify for MCO approval exposes the psychiatrist to increased liability risk when the "miraculously cured" patient is discharged early or prematurely and then attempts or commits suicide (Simon 2002).

A related conundrum arises if a psychiatrist issues a therapeutic pass to assess the patient's ability to function outside the hospital (Simon 1997). Writing an order for any kind of pass usually raises a red flag for MCOs. MCOs have greatly restricted the use of this important assessment and treatment intervention. Once a therapeutic pass is issued, the MCO may deny further hospital benefits based on the presumption that the patient is demonstrably ready for discharge. Careful suicide risk assessment both before issuance of a pass and on the patient's return from the pass is essential in preventing a premature discharge. The patient may return from a pass in worse clinical condition than when he or she left the hospital. Because therapeutic passes are currently restricted, this opportunity for suicide is less available. Also, patients are hospitalized for only a brief time, making suicide more likely after discharge of the patient.

Conflicts with MCOs usually arise over quality of care due to limitation of services. When services are denied, the psychiatrist must be particularly diligent not to abandon the patient (Simon 1998b). The psychiatrist's duty of care to the patient is not determined by MCO payments (Ellison 2001). MCOs can limit or deny payment for services but not the actual services. The psychiatrist and patient may work out a lower fee arrangement, the patient may decide to pay the full fee for continued care out of pocket, or the psychiatrist may provide free care during emergency treatment. Psychiatrists should refer to their contracts concerning the permissibility of billing patients directly. Additional hospital costs will have to be negotiated by the patient. When insurance benefits run out, a patient who remains at significant risk for suicide may demand to leave the hospital. This presents the psychiatrist with a serious problem. Thorough suicide risk assessment should help inform the clinician's decision making regarding discharge options and aftercare planning.

Some manipulative individuals have learned to utter the magic words "I am suicidal" to gain hospital admission or to forestall discharge. Clinicians may feel helpless, manipulated, and frustrated by this declaration, but nevertheless resentfully acquiesce to admitting the individual or to deferring discharge. Some patients who admit suicidal intent when examined in the emergency department may vehemently deny it on admission to the psychiatric unit. Recanting of suicidal behaviors by the patient should not deter the psychiatrist and clinical staff from performing systematic suicide risk assessments. A study to ascertain the prevalence of malingering by inpatients who were admitted to an urban hospital for suicidal ideation or attempt demonstrated the difficulty in detecting malingering by clinical interview or by psychological tests (Rissmiller et al. 1998). Clinicians do not have to be held hostage by manipulative threats or sudden denials of suicide intent. A data-based, systematic suicide risk assessment should help to clarify the situation. Systematic suicide risk assessment can provide clinical confidence that replaces disturbing doubt.

ELOPEMENT

Some patients may require elopement precautions. Notice of elopement risk should be posted on both sides of entrances to the psychiatric unit. Patient elopements tend to occur shortly after admission, although they can happen at any time. Patients at high risk for suicide who elope often commit suicide within a short time after leaving (Morgan and Priest 1991). Patients usually exit the psychiatric unit's door when visitors enter or leave the unit. Some patients contrive ingenious methods of escape. A few have successfully exited the psychiatric unit hidden in a laundry or food cart. Other methods have involved crawling through ceiling spaces, donning a white coat and impersonating a doctor, and dressing in a coat and tie or a blouse and skirt and leaving with visitors. New construction on the unit or other patient areas may provide the occasion for patients to elope or commit suicide, despite safety precautions.

Assessing a patient's risk for eloping is part of the psychiatric examination. It is important to identify patients who are an elopement risk early and to institute elopement precautions. Patients who elope shortly after admission do so before rapport is established with the psychiatrist or treatment team. They tend to be noncompliant with rules, deny their illness, reject or "cheek" medications, remain isolated, and keep quiet. They may station themselves by the unit's door or hide in an adjacent room awaiting an opportunity to exit.

Many patients who elope are new patients who are unknown to the clinical staff. These patients usually express the belief that they do not belong on a "psych ward." If practicable, the new patient should not be given a room next to the unit's door. The patient who is preparing to elope in order to commit suicide may be fully cooperative, giving no warning of eloping. In managed-care settings, elopements are less frequent because of the short lengths of stay.

The best means of preventing elopement is to try to establish a relationship with the patient. If a patient does elope, the usual procedure is to notify hospital security and contact the treating psychiatrist to determine whether he or she wants to inform the police and notify the family. A patient who elopes from the psychiatric unit should be considered at high risk for suicide. If the patient is located and returned to the hospital, an assessment needs to be made regarding commitment.

CONSULTATION

The psychiatrist's liability will be determined by reference to professional standards. Consultation with other psychiatrists may provide additional protection when the discharge of a patient at suicide risk is problematic. Psychiatrists faced with complex, difficult decisions should not "worry alone." Consulting with a risk manager or an attorney may help clarify legal duties. Lawyers, however, tend to emphasize risk and to make conservative recommendations. Sound legal advice may not necessarily accord with the clinical realities of management for a specific patient. The psychiatrist's clinical judgment is paramount.

INVOLUNTARY HOSPITALIZATION

The usual candidate for involuntary hospitalization is the psychotic patient at high risk for suicide who adamantly refuses treatment and signs a formal request for discharge AMA. Involuntary hospitalization may be necessary if the patient meets civil commitment criteria for mental illness and dangerousness. If a less restrictive treatment setting is not available, involuntary hospitalization may be the only clinical option. Patients should not be involuntarily hospitalized simply because their insurance benefits run out.

Involuntary hospitalization should be a clinical intervention for patients at significant risk for suicide. It should not be used as a defensive tactic to avoid malpractice liability or to provide a legal defense against a malpractice claim (Simon 2001). Although it is relatively rare, psychiatrists may be sued for malicious prosecution, false imprisonment, assault and battery, and civil rights violations, especially when improperly initiating civil commitment proceedings (Simon 1992b). The psychiatrist is much more likely to be sued if a patient who should have been involuntarily hospitalized commits suicide. Psychiatrists may choose to err on the side of safeguarding a patient who is at high risk for suicide by seeking involuntary hospitalization, rather than be overly concerned about preserving civil liberties. Thorough documentation is essential to support the decision-making rationale of the psychiatrist. The clinician files a petition or medical certification that initiates the process of involuntary hospitalization. The clinician does not commit the patient. The final decision to involuntarily hospitalize the patient is judicially determined.

FINAL DISCHARGE PLANNING

Before the patient is discharged, a final postdischarge treatment and aftercare plan should be in place (see Table 6–2). Following discharge, suicide risk increases when the intensity of treatment is decreased (Appleby et al. 1999). However, a history of intensive treatment and prior suicide attempts increases the lifetime risk for suicide.

The patient's willingness to cooperate with discharge and aftercare planning is a critical determinant in establishing contact with follow-up treaters. A Veterans Administration (VA) study of outpatient referral found that of the 25% of inpatients referred to the VA mental health clinic, approximately 50% did not keep their first appointment (Zedlow and Taub 1981). The psychiatrist and the treatment team should structure the follow-up plan so as to encourage compliance. For example, psychotic patients at risk for suicide who have a history of stopping their medications immediately on discharge may be given a long-acting intramuscular neuroleptic until they reach aftercare. Patients with comorbid drug and alcohol abuse disorders should be referred to agencies equipped to manage dual diagnosis patients.

If not done earlier during the course of hospitalization, patients should be educated about their mental disorders. As noted above, family members should be similarly educated, when appropriate. One goal is to encourage patient adherence to treatment and aftercare recommendations. Patients and their families often complain that they were not told their diagnosis or educated about treatment by the psychiatrist or by any member of the multidisciplinary team. This may be a sequela of short hospitalization in a managed-care environment.

Limitations exist on the ability of psychiatrists to ensure follow-up treatment that must be acknowledged by both the psychiatric and the legal communities (Simon 1998b). Beyond stabilizing the patient, the psychiatrist's options in bringing about positive changes in the patient's environment may be limited or nonexistent. Also,

Table 6–2. Discharge considerations for suicidal patients

Analysis of risks and benefits of discharge

Determined by direct evaluation

Consultations with the treatment team

Review of patient's course of hospitalization: What is different about the patient's illness and life situation at the time of discharge?

Evidence of posthospitalization self-care ability

Can patient function without significant affective and cognitive impairment?

Support

Is patient physically and emotionally able to employ others for support?

Are appropriate mental health services available?

Is there support from family members or significant others? Are they stabilizing or destabilizing?

Remission of illness

What remains unchanged and can be dealt with as an outpatient?

Control by medication

Can side effects be tolerated and managed outside hospital?

Will patient comply with treatment?

Timing of proposed release

Does the staff have an adequate clinical understanding of the patient?

Has the patient adequately acclimated to the therapeutic milieu with sufficient time allowed to develop meaningful relationships?

Has sufficient time elapsed to evaluate the effect of treatment (e.g., medications)?

Therapeutic alliance

Will the patient continue to work with the psychiatrist or other mental health professionals after discharge?

Source. Adapted from Simon RI: *Concise Guide to Psychiatry and Law for Clinicians,* 3rd Edition. Washington, DC, American Psychiatric Publishing, 2001. Used with permission.

the patient's failure to adhere to postdischarge plans and treatment often results in rehospitalizations, hopelessness, and increased suicide risk. Most discharged patients retain the right to refuse treatment. Acutely ill psychiatric patients at risk for suicide are increasingly treated in outpatient settings. It is the psychiatrist's responsibility to competently "hand off" the patient to appropriate outpatient aftercare. The American Medical Association Council on Scientific Affairs has created evidence-based criteria for safe discharge from the hospital (American Medical Association 1996).

With the patient's permission, the psychiatrist or social worker should call the follow-up agency or therapist before discharge to provide information about the patient's diagnosis, treatment, and hospital course. In *Jablonski v. United States* (1983/1984), the Ninth Circuit upheld liability after a patient killed his common-law wife because, among other things, the defendant psychiatrist failed to record and pass on information that the patient was dangerous to the evaluating psychiatrist and failed to warn the spouse that her husband was dangerous. He also failed to obtain a prior record that indicated violent behavior. A year later, the Ninth Circuit overruled the decision on other grounds. Nonetheless, the court's reasoning is valid.

Follow-up appointments should be made as close to the time of discharge as possible. Most MCOs require that the patient have an outpatient appointment within a few days of discharge. The patient should have an actual appointment in hand, or the attending psychiatrist or hospital clinician may need to provide an interim follow-up appointment. Encouraging patients to make their own appointments while still in the hospital fosters independent functioning. However, some patients are too disorganized to make their own appointments. The patient should know whom to call or where to go if an emergency arises before the first outpatient appointment. Homeless patients at risk for suicide should be placed in aftercare programs where follow-up is maximized. However, consistent follow-up may not be possible for transient homeless patients. This limitation should be documented in the discharge note.

In the case example, Dr. Green informs the patient that it is hospital policy to make a follow-up call to determine whether he has kept his initial outpatient appointment. Dr. Green gauges the therapeutic alliance and the likelihood that Mr. Blake will follow the aftercare plan by his response to this policy. However, once a patient is discharged from the hospital, the psychiatrist's intervention options are limited or nonexistent.

If the patient is being transferred to another facility, the assessment of the patient's current condition, including the patient's risk for suicide, should be communicated to the staff at the new facility and to the persons transporting the patient. Written communications may be necessary; however, direct telephone conversations (duly documented) with the new treaters may be more effective in communicating information about the patient. Questions can be asked and explanations given. The failure to provide relevant information to treaters who may be unaware of the suicide risk of a transferred patient may create liability problems for the psychiatrist. Abstracts from the psychiatric record and discharge summary should be forwarded to the postdischarge treater in a timely manner.

Most discharges involve a complex process that should be tailored to the patient's individual treatment needs and circumstances. The decision to discharge a patient is often more difficult than the decision to admit the patient. A risk-benefit assessment should be documented that evaluates the risks and benefits of continued hospitalization versus the risks and benefits of discharge. A number of factors need to be considered and weighed in the risk-benefit assessment, such as the discharge suicide risk assessment, the severity of illness, the likelihood of compliance with follow-up care, the availability of family or other support, the presence of a substance abuse disorder, and comorbid conditions. The critical questions are as follows: Has the patient improved sufficiently to function outside the hospital, or is this discharge doomed to fail? What is different about the patient's condition or life situation at the time of discharge? In a study of inpatient suicide by Fawcett et al. (2003), the authors state that "78% of the patients denied suicidal ideation or intent as their last communication" (p. 18). When a patient denies suicidal ideation or intent, systematic suicide risk assessment can help identify other clinical correlates of suicide risk.

Legal defenses are available to psychiatrists who are sued for a patient's suicide (see Table 6–3 and Chapter 1, "Suicide and Malpractice Litigation"). A well-reasoned, clearly documented risk-benefit note that explains the psychiatrist's decision making at the time of discharge will help preempt second-guessing by a court if the patient commits suicide and a lawsuit is filed. Assessing the risk of suicide is a "here and now" determination. Patients who are no longer at acute risk for suicide often remain at chronic risk for suicide. The discharge note should indicate, as in the case example, the acute suicide risk factors that have abated or remitted and the chronic (long-term) suicide risk factors that remain. The discharge note should also address the patient's chronic vulnerability to suicide. For example, the patient may become acutely suicidal again, depending on a number of factors, including the nature and cause of the psychiatric illness, the adequacy of future treatment, the extent of adherence to treatment recommendations, and unforeseeable life vicissitudes. Suicidal behaviors are the result of dynamic, complex interaction among a variety of clinical, personality, social, and environmental factors whose relative importance varies across time and situations (Simon 1998a).

Table 6–3. Frequently used legal defenses in malpractice cases

• Exercise of reasonable professional judgment
• Compliance with the standard of care
• Patient's suicide not foreseeable
• Patient's suicide not preventable
• Justified allowance of movement ("open-door" policy)
• Superseding, intervening acts
• Governmental immunity

DOCUMENTATION

Careful documentation is fundamental to clinically supportive risk management (see Chapter 8, "Suicide Aftermath: Documentation, Confidentiality, and Survivor Care"). For example, the completeness of the medical record will aid the utilization review process in facilitating the provision of competent clinical care. Documentation should be clear, concise, complete, careful, contemporaneous, and readable. All documentation requires a date and a time. If the psychiatrist is sued a year after the patient's discharge, he or she may not remember the patient or the details of the patient's hospitalization. Complete records are invaluable in providing the necessary information for a sound legal defense. Errors have been made when members of the multidisciplinary team have been unable to decipher the psychiatrist's handwriting.

As discussed earlier, documentation of thorough risk-benefit analysis for both continued hospitalization and discharge is necessary. A risk-benefit note minimizes legal liability exposure when the decision to discharge turns out to be wrong. Errors alone are not legally actionable where reasonable skill and care were utilized and documented in making a discharge decision. Suicide risk assessments should be recorded in their entirety as opposed to a mere statement that a risk assessment was done. All contact with utilization reviewers concerning discharge of the patient also should be documented. Care that is not recorded is likely to be considered by the court not to have been done, if a malpractice claim arises.

The discharge summary should be completed at the time of discharge or shortly thereafter. Patients at risk for suicide may be readmitted to a hospital soon after discharge. A completed and available discharge summary will assist subsequent treaters in the assessment of the patient. In a malpractice suit, discharge summaries that are completed after a patient's suicide are viewed with suspicion by plaintiff's attorneys as self-serving, self-exculpatory documents.

Malone et al. (1995b) studied clinicians, including psychiatrists, who performed routine intake and discharge assessments of 50 patients identified by systematic research evaluations as having attempted suicide and having a current major depressive episode. They found that the clinicians failed to document adequately the presence of a lifetime history of a suicide attempt in 24% of cases on admission and in 28% of cases in the discharge summary. In 38% of the patients, the physician's discharge summary did not document the presence of recent suicidal ideation or planning behavior. The authors concluded that a significant degree of past suicidal behavior is not recorded during routine clinical assessment. They recommended the use of semistructured screening instruments to detect lifetime suicidal behavior. At the time of discharge, adequate documentation identified a high-risk population for appropriate outpatient care. The study underscores the importance of a documented, systematic approach to suicide risk assessment.

CLINICALLY BASED RISK MANAGEMENT

- The assessment, treatment, and management of the suicidal patient requires a full commitment of time and effort from the psychiatrist.

- Perform a timely, complete psychiatric examination, including a careful mental status evaluation.
- Formulate, document, and implement a comprehensive, rational treatment plan on admission. Review and update it as needed.
- Conduct systematic suicide risk assessments at the patient's admission and discharge and at other important clinical decision junctures.
- Monitor and aggressively treat the patient's acute suicide risk factors.
- When patients have threatened or attempted suicide, their denial of suicidal ideation, intent, or plan must not be accepted without further assessment. The clinician should be alert for other clinical correlates of suicide risk.
- Adjust the patient's safety precautions according to ongoing systematic suicide risk assessment.
- Obtain prior records of treatment and/or speak with current or prior treaters.
- Early discharge planning begins at the time of the patient's admission.
- Interview family members or significant others, with the patient's permission. If the patient refuses permission, listen but do not disclose patient information.
- Work closely with the multidisciplinary team in assessing suicide risk, in conducting treatment, and in providing safety management.
- Designate a responsible family member or other person to remove and safely disarm guns, which could be used by the patient to commit suicide. Request a telephone call from the responsible individual to confirm that guns were removed from the home and are safely secured elsewhere.
- Other lethal means for attempting or committing suicide should be secured. These may include knives, poisons, over-the-counter and prescription medications (e.g., analgesics), and car keys. A family member may need to dispense and monitor the patient's medications.
- Abide by hospital and psychiatric unit policy and procedures regarding the management of patients at risk for suicide. The standard of care is often reflected in official policies and procedures.
- Contemporaneously document assessment, treatment, and safety management decisions.

- If the patient attempts or commits suicide and litigation ensues, what is not documented may be considered by a court not to have been done.
- All documentation should have a time and date and should be legible.
- Patients should be allowed autonomy and freedom of movement consistent with their treatment and safety needs.
- At time of contemplated discharge, the risks and benefits of discharge versus the risks and benefits of continued hospitalization should be carefully assessed and documented.
- What remains unchanged from the time of admission to the time of discharge regarding the patient's mental condition and life situation? Can the patient be managed as an outpatient?
- Structure aftercare planning for maximal compliance by the patient.
- Patients who are on individualized suicide safety precautions should not be discharged. A period of observation of the patient who is off safety precautions should precede discharge.
- Are family members or significant others supportive or destabilizing to the patient? In the latter instance, are psychosocial interventions available that could make a difference?
- Exaggerating the severity of the patient's condition to qualify for MCO approval exposes the psychiatrist to increased liability risk when the patient is discharged early or prematurely.
- Educate patients and, if feasible, their families about their mental disorders.
- Patients should not be discharged from the hospital solely for financial reasons. Although the delivery of medical care has changed dramatically under managed care, psychiatrists must still provide competent care within this system.
- Prior to discharge, the psychiatrist should discuss with the patient whom to contact or where to go if an emergency arises after discharge. Telephone numbers should be provided.
- Inpatients should be seen each day of their hospitalization, including the day of discharge. A patient's clinical condition can deteriorate rapidly as discharge approaches.

REFERENCES

Amchin J, Wettstein RM, Roth LH: Suicide, ethics, and the law, in Suicide Over the Life Cycle. Edited by Blumenthal SJ, Kupfer DJ. Washington, DC, American Psychiatric Press, 1990, pp 637–663

American Medical Association: Report of the Council on Scientific Affairs: Evidence-Based Principles of Discharge and Discharge Criteria (CSA Report 4-A-96). Chicago, IL, American Medical Association, 1996

American Psychiatric Association: Diagnostic and Statistical Manual of Mental Disorders, 4th Edition, Text Revision. Washington, DC, American Psychiatric Association, 2000

American Psychiatric Association: The Practice of Electroconvulsive Therapy: Recommendations for Treatment, Training, and Privileging: A Task Force Report of the American Psychiatric Association, 2nd Edition. Edited by Weiner RD. Washington, DC, American Psychiatric Association, 2001

Anand VS, Ciccone JR, Kashtan I, et al: Factors predictive of changes in the legal status of psychiatric inpatients. J Forensic Sci 47:1365–1369, 2002

Angst F, Stassen HH, Clayton PJ, et al: Mortality of patients with mood disorders: follow up over 34–38 years. J Affect Disord 68:167–181, 2002

Appleby L, Dennehy JA, Thomas CS, et al: Aftercare and clinical characteristics of people with mental illness who commit suicide: a case-control study. Lancet 353:1397–1400, 1999

Atbasoglu EM, Schultz SK, Andreasen NC: The relationship of akathisia with suicidality and depersonalization among patients with schizophrenia. J Neuropsychiatry Clin Neurosci 13:336–341, 2002

Baldessarini RJ, Tondo L, Hennen J: Treating the suicidal patient with bipolar disorder: reducing suicide risks with lithium. Ann N Y Acad Sci 932:24–38, 2001

Baldessarini RJ, Tondo L, Hennen J: Lithium treatment and suicide risk in major affective disorders: update and new findings. J Clin Psychiatry 64 (suppl 5):44–52, 2003

Barraclough B, Bunch J, Nelson B, et al: A hundred cases of suicide: clinical aspects. Br J Psychiatry 125:355–373, 1974

Beck AT, Steer RA, Kovacs M, et al: Hopelessness and eventual suicide: a 10-year prospective study of patients hospitalized with suicidal ideation. Am J Psychiatry 142:559–563, 1985

Bell v NYC Health and Hosp. Corp., 90 A.D.2d 270, 456 N.Y.S.2d 787 (1982)

Bostwick JM, Pankratz VS: Affective disorders and suicide risk: a reexamination. Am J Psychiatry 157:1925–1932, 2000

Brandvain v Ridgeview Inst., 188 Ga. App.106, 372 S.E.2d 265 (1988), aff'd, 259 Ga. 376, 382 S.E.2d 597 (1989)

Brent DA: Firearms and suicide. Ann N Y Acad Sci 932:225–240, 2001

Busch KA, Clark DC, Fawcett J, et al: Clinical features in inpatient suicide. Psychiatr Ann 23:256–262, 1993

Busch KA, Fawcett J, Jacobs DG: Clinical correlates of inpatient suicide. J Clin Psychiatry 64:14–19, 2003

Cohen v State of New York, 51 A.D.2d 494, 382 N.Y.S.2d 128 (N.Y. App. Div. 1976), aff'd, 41 N.Y.2d 1086, 364 N.E.2d 1134, 396 N.Y.S.2d 363 (1977)

Drake RE, Ehrlich J: Suicide attempts associated with akathisia. Am J Psychiatry 142:499–501, 1985

Eaglin v Cook County Hosp., 227 Ill. App. 3d 724, 592 N.E.2d 205 (1992)

Ellison JM (ed): Treatment of Suicidal Patients in Managed Care. Washington, DC, American Psychiatric Publishing, 2001

Fawcett J, Scheftner WA, Clark DC, et al: Clinical predictors of suicide in patients with major affective disorders: a controlled prospective study. Am J Psychiatry 144:35–40, 1987

Fawcett J, Scheftner WA, Fogg L, et al: Time-related predictors of suicide in major affective disorder. Am J Psychiatry 147:1189–1194, 1990

Fawcett J, Clark DC, Busch KA: Assessing and treating the patient at risk for suicide. Psychiatr Ann 23:244–255, 1993

Fawcett J, Busch KA, Jacobs DG: Clinical correlates of inpatient suicide. J Clin Psychiatry 64:14–19, 2003

Gaido v Weiser, 227 N.J. Super. 175, 545 A.2d 1350 (1988), aff'd, 115 N.J. 310, 558 A.2d 845 (1989)

Gelenberg AJ, Chesen CL: How fast are antidepressants? J Clin Psychiatry 61:712–721, 2000

Gerbasi JB, Simon RI: Patients' rights and psychiatrists' duties: discharges against medical advice. Harv Rev Psychiatry (in press)

Gessert CE: Rurality and suicide. Am J Public Health 93:698, 2003

Harris EC, Barraclough B: Suicide as an outcome for mental disorders. A meta-analysis. Br J Psychiatry 170:205–228, 1997

Isacsson G: Suicide prevention: a medical breakthrough? Acta Psychiatr Scand 102:113–117, 2000

Jablonski v United States, 712 F.2d 391 (9th Cir. 1983), overruled by In re Complaint of McLinn, 739 F.2d 1395 (9th Cir. 1984)

Jacobs DG, Brewer M, Klein-Benheim M: Suicide assessment: an overview and recommended protocol, in The Harvard Medical School Guide to Suicide Assessment and Intervention. Edited by Jacobs DJ. San Francisco, CA, Jossey-Bass, 1999, pp 3–39

Jacobson G: The inpatient management of suicidality, in The Harvard Medical School Guide to Suicide Assessment and Intervention. Edited by Jacobs DJ. San Francisco, CA, Jossey-Bass, 1999, pp 383–405

Johnson v United States, 409 F. Supp. 1283 (M.D. Fla. 1976), *rev'd,* 576 F.2d 606 (5th Cir. 1978), *cert. denied,* 451 U.S. 1019 (1981)

Joint Commission on Accreditation of Healthcare Organizations: Hospital Accreditation Standards. Chicago, IL, Joint Commission on Accreditation of Healthcare Organizations, 2002, PE 1.7.1

Joint Commission on Accreditation of Healthcare Organizations: Sentinel Event Statistics: Root causes of inpatient suicide, 1995–2002. Available at: http://www.jcaho.org/accredited+organizations/ambulatory+care/sentinel+events/rc+inpatient+suicides.htm. Accessed July 21, 2003

Kelly MJ, Mufson MJ, Rogers MP: Medical settings and suicide, in The Harvard Medical School Guide to Suicide Assessment and Intervention. Edited by Jacobs DG. San Francisco, CA, Jossey-Bass, 1999, pp 491–519

Leenars AA: Suicide Notes. New York, Human Science Press, 1988

Macbeth JE, Wheeler AM, Sithers W, et al: Legal and Risk Management Issues in the Practice of Psychiatry. Washington, DC, Psychiatrists' Purchasing Group, 1994

Malone KM, Haas GL, Sweeney JA, et al: Major depression and the risk of attempted suicide. J Affect Disord 34:173–185, 1995a

Malone KM, Szanto K, Corbitt EM, et al: Clinical assessment versus research methods in the assessment of suicidal behavior. Am J Psychiatry 152:1601–1607, 1995b

Malone KM, Waternaux C, Haas GL, et al: Cigarette smoking, suicidal behavior, and serotonin function in major psychiatric disorder. Am J Psychiatry 160:773–779, 2003

Meltzer HY: Treatment of suicidality in schizophrenia. Ann N Y Acad Sci 932:44–58, 2001

Meltzer HY, Alphs L, Green AI, et al: Clozapine treatment for suicidality in schizophrenia: International Suicide Prevention Trial (InterSePT). Arch Gen Psychiatry 60:82–91, 2003

Morgan HG, Priest P: Suicide and other unexpected deaths among psychiatric inpatients. Br J Psychiatry 158:368–374, 1991

Morgan HG, Stanton R: Suicide among psychiatric inpatients in a changing clinical scene. Br J Psychiatry 171:561–563, 1997

Moscicki EK: Epidemiology of suicide, in The Harvard Medical School Guide to Suicide Assessment and Intervention. Edited by Jacobs DG. San Francisco, CA, Jossey-Bass, 1999, pp 40–51

National Institute of Mental Health: Suicide facts. Available at: http://www.nimh.nih.gov/research/suifact.htm. Accessed January 3, 2003

Oquendo MA, Kamali M, Ellis SP, et al: Adequacy of antidepressant treatment after discharge and the occurrence of suicidal acts in major depression: a prospective study. Am J Psychiatry 159:1746–1751, 2002

Ostamo A, Lonnqvist J: Excess mortality in suicide attempters. Soc Psychiatry Psychiatr Epidemiol 36:29–35, 2001

Prudic J, Sackheim H: Electroconvulsive therapy and suicide risk. J Clin Psychiatry 60 (suppl 2):104–110, 1999

Resnick PJ: Recognizing that the suicidal patient views you as an adversary. Current Psychiatry 1:8, 2002

Rissmiller DJ, Wayslow A, Madison H, et al: Prevalence of malingering in inpatient suicide ideators and attempters. Crisis 19:62–66, 1998

Roose SP, Glassman AH, Walsh BT, et al: Depression delusion and suicide. Am J Psychiatry 140:1159–1162, 1983

Roy A: Risk factors for suicide in psychiatric patients. Arch Gen Psychiatry 39:1089–1095, 1982

Sharma V: Retrospective study of inpatient ECT: does it prevent suicide? J Affect Disord 56:183–187, 1999

Silverman MM: Understanding suicide in the 21st century (editorial). Preventing Suicide: The National Journal 2(2), March/April 2003

Simon RI: Clinical management of suicidal patients, in Review of Clinical Psychiatry and the Law. Edited by Simon RI. Washington, DC, American Psychiatric Press, 1992a, pp 3–63

Simon RI: Clinical Psychiatry and the Law, 2nd Edition. Washington, DC, American Psychiatric Press, 1992b

Simon RI: Discharging sicker, potentially violent psychiatric patients in the managed care era: standard of care and risk management. Psychiatr Ann 27:726–733, 1997

Simon RI: Psychiatrists awake! Suicide risk assessments are all about a good night's sleep. Psychiatr Ann 28:479–485, 1998a

Simon RI: Psychiatrists' duties in discharging sicker and potentially violent inpatients in the managed care era. Psychiatr Serv 49:62–67, 1998b

Simon RI: Taking the "sue" out of suicide: a forensic psychiatrist's perspective. Psychiatr Ann 30:399–407, 2000

Simon RI: Psychiatry and Law for Clinicians, 3rd Edition. Washington, DC, American Psychiatric Publishing, 2001

Simon RI: Suicide risk assessment in managed care settings. Primary Psychiatry 9:42–43, 46–49, 2002

Simon RI, Gutheil TG: A recurrent pattern of suicide risk factors observed in litigated cases: lessons in risk management. Psychiatr Ann 32:384–387, 2002

Topel v Long Island Jewish Med. Ctr., 55 N.Y.2d 682; 431 N.E.2d 293; 446 N.Y.S.2d 932 (1981)

Weber J: Underusing overdose as a method of suicide: a trend analysis. American Association of Suicidology News Link 28:3, 8, 2002

Weisman AD, Worden JW: Risk-rescue rating in suicide assessment. Arch Gen Psychiatry 26:553–560, 1972

Wickizer TM, Lessler D, Travis KM: Controlling inpatient psychiatric utilization through managed care. Am J Psychiatry 153:339–345, 1996

Wintemute GJ, Parham CA, Beaumont JJ, et al: Mortality among recent purchasers of handguns. N Engl J Med 341:1583–1589, 1999

Zedlow PB, Taub HA: Evaluating psychiatric discharge and aftercare in a VA medical center. Hosp Community Psychiatry 32:57–58, 1981

EMERGENCY PSYCHIATRIC SERVICES

In a real dark night of the soul it is always three o'clock in the morning.

F. Scott Fitzgerald, *The Crack-Up*

The mass of men lead lives of quiet desperation.

Henry David Thoreau, *Walden*

INTRODUCTION

Patients at risk for suicide are frequently assessed and managed in emergency psychiatric services. Wingerson et al. (2001), in a study of 2,319 consecutive patients who visited a crisis triage unit, found that 30% had unipolar depression, 26% psychosis, 20% substance use disorder, 14% bipolar disorder, 4% adjustment disorder, 3% anxiety disorder, and 2% dementia. Dhossche (2000) found that 38% of psychiatric emergencies involved suicidal ideation or behavior. Ostamo and Lonnqvist (2001), in a 5-year follow-up study of patients treated in hospitals after suicide attempts, found an increase in mortality from suicide, homicide, and other causes. In the follow-up period, 16% of suicide attempters died, 40% by suicide.

Many psychiatric patients who are evaluated in the emergency department (ED) of a hospital have more than one psychiatric disorder, substantially increasing their risk for suicide (Kessler et al.

1999). Standardized mortality ratios (SMRs) establish that virtually all psychiatric disorders have an associated risk for suicide (see Chapter 2, "Suicide Risk Assessment"). Patients seen in emergency psychiatric services not only have an increased risk for suicide associated with their psychiatric disorders (necessary factors) but also experience stressful life circumstances (sufficient factors) that impart additional risk. The importance of stress factors in precipitating suicides is noted in a number of studies (Heikkinen et al. 1994; Maltsberger et al. 2003). Suicide attempts or completed suicides are invariably caused by the confluence of necessary and sufficient factors.

Important goals of emergency psychiatric services include provision of emergency assessments to determine the appropriate setting for treatment and to provide stabilization and safety for patients. The basic types of emergency psychiatric services are the consultation model and the specialized psychiatric emergency service (PES) (Breslow 2002). In the consultation model, the psychiatrist consults with the ED. Some EDs have crisis counselors who evaluate psychiatric patients after they have been "medically cleared" by ED physicians. The psychiatric consultant is contacted. The evaluation and proposed disposition of the patient are discussed with the psychiatrist. The psychiatrist may agree, disagree, or request additional information before making a final decision. When either the ED physician, crisis counselor, or psychiatrist disagrees with the evaluation or disposition, the psychiatrist is usually required to come to the ED and examine the patient. The same situation applies when the ED physician calls the "on call" psychiatrist, in the absence of a crisis counselor arrangement.

The PES provides comprehensive emergency psychiatric services that are hospital based, usually at large medical centers or medical school and residency teaching programs. The PES model corrects many of the deficiencies of the consultation model. Breslow (2002) discusses the advantages and disadvantages of each model.

CASE EXAMPLE

A 42-year-old physician, Dr. Allen, is brought by his wife to the ED of an urban general hospital after becoming inebriated and threatening suicide. He is medically evaluated. A blood alcohol level of 160 mg/dL is obtained, consistent with intoxication. The drug screen is negative. Dr. Allen's wife stays with her husband in a cubicle. Within a few hours, Dr. Allen's sensorium clears. He becomes more coherent and communicative. The ED physician "medically clears" Dr. Allen and calls the crisis counselor to have him evaluated.

The counselor conducts a systematic suicide risk assessment. Dr. Allen vehemently denies any suicidal ideation, intent, or plan. He states, "I just got drunk and said some stupid things." He admits to being depressed for the past month because of "difficulties" with his practice partners and heavy financial losses in the stock market. Dr. Allen denies any history of psychiatric disorder, substance abuse, or family history of suicide or mental disorder. He is outraged that his wife brought him to the ED, especially since he is a physician practicing in the community. Dr. Allen admits that he saw a psychiatrist during the past month for "depression" but refuses to give the crisis counselor the psychiatrist's name or telephone number because "it is unnecessary." He does admit to a loss of appetite and difficulty falling asleep associated with early morning waking but refuses to cooperate further. The counselor observes that Dr. Allen is easily agitated. The mental status examination reveals that he is fully oriented. His mood is depressed. There is no evidence of a psychosis.

The crisis counselor needs more information to complete the suicide risk assessment. Dr. Allen's wife is interviewed in an adjoining room. In the ED, patients at risk for suicide are placed in a room that is monitored by video camera. Mrs. Allen informs the counselor that her husband has been depressed and drinking excessively for months. During the past month, he has canceled his appointments with patients, staying in bed and drinking. Dr. Allen has been making repeated threats of killing himself, even when he is not drinking. He is a gun collector. Her husband did see a psychiatrist for one visit a month ago but did not keep his next appointment. The psychiatrist recommended antidepressant medication and psychotherapy, which Dr. Allen refused.

Dr. Allen's wife relates that her husband's depression began after a serious disagreement developed between him and his practice partners over the direction of their medical practice. The disagreement has grown bitter. Her husband does not speak to his colleagues. Moreover, alcohol has been detected on his breath and reported by the nursing staff at the hospital where he practices. His admitting privileges are in jeopardy.

During the past week, Dr. Allen has been extremely agitated, constantly pacing except when he is intoxicated. She describes his depression as "profound," with frequent expressions of hopelessness. This visit to the ED was precipitated by his wife's discovery of a loaded revolver under her husband's pillow. She requested help from a neighbor. Together, they were able to drive Dr. Allen to the ED, although he resisted.

Dr. Allen's wife provides the name and telephone number of the psychiatrist whom her husband saw for the single visit. After some friendly persuasion by the crisis counselor, Dr. Allen reluctantly authorizes her to call the outpatient psychiatrist. The crisis counselor is unable to reach the psychiatrist. The counselor's systematic suicide risk assessment indicates that Dr. Allen is at high risk for suicide. Because the crisis counselor has performed a systematic suicide risk assessment, she has confidence in her evaluation and recommendation. The psychiatrist on call for the ED is paged. She is an active attending physician on the psychiatric staff of the hospital. The psychiatrist returns her call within a few minutes. The counselor's evaluation of Dr. Allen is major depression, single episode, severe, and alcohol abuse. The risk for suicide is assessed as high. She recommends admission to the hospital psychiatric unit. The psychiatrist agrees.

Dr. Allen refuses voluntary admission. He states, "I will go back to the psychiatrist. I want to resume my practice and mend my relations with my partners." Dr. Allen gathers his belongings and prepares to leave. The crisis counselor alerts hospital security that Dr. Allen is attempting to leave the ED and should be prevented. The ED physician, whom Dr. Allen knows superficially, tries to persuade Dr. Allen to voluntarily admit himself to the psychiatric unit. Dr. Allen responds, "You are a physician. You know how being admitted to a psychiatric unit can ruin a doctor's reputation. I will get outpatient treatment." The patient's wife feels strongly that her husband should be admitted. The ED physician curbs his impulse to do a colleague a "favor." He also does not fall prey to the tendency of some physicians to minimize or deny the severity of mental illness with associated suicide risk in their medical colleagues.

As Dr. Allen tries to exit the ED, he is subdued and brought back by security personnel. He threatens to sue for "false imprisonment." A security officer remains by his side. Dr. Allen is informed that if he tries to escape again, he will be placed in the ED seclusion room. The crisis counselor again pages the psychiatrist, who decides to come to the ED and examine Dr. Allen. The consulting psychiatrist agrees with the counselor's diagnosis, suicide risk assessment, and recommendations for hospitalization. The patient again refuses the psychiatrist's recommendation for voluntary hospitalization. Persuasion fails. A certification for involuntary hospitalization is signed by the psychiatrist and the ED physician. Confronted with the prospect of involuntary hospitalization, Dr. Allen agrees to voluntary hospitalization. He is admitted to the psychiatric unit.

Discussion

The case example illustrates the importance of systematic suicide risk assessment, enhanced by critical collateral information, in a physician patient who vehemently denies suicidal ideation, intent, or plan. Even in the absence of collateral sources of information, systematic suicide risk assessment can help the clinician identify important risk factors that do not rely on the patient's reporting (see Chapter 2, "Suicide Risk Assessment").

Assessment

During the psychiatric evaluation, the safety of the suicidal patient must be secured. The ED physician, psychiatrist, or crisis counselor may be called out of the examining room or cubicle during the evaluation of the patient to attend to other emergent matters. Closed-circuit television or direct monitoring by ED staff is often required to ensure patient safety. Patients who are accompanied by supportive family members or friends are less likely to decompensate and attempt suicide in the ED. The patient's personal belongings should be secured. Dangerous items such as guns, knives, cigarette lighters, matches, and medications must be removed. Some hospital EDs search or scan patients by the use of metal detectors. In addition, police officers who accompany patients may be required to leave their guns outside the ED. A suicidal or homicidal patient might attempt to snatch the police officer's gun.

Patients must be thoroughly searched before being sent from the ED to the psychiatric unit. Patients have devised ingenious ways to hide contraband (e.g., in hollowed-out book, in pockets of the inside of belts, in stuffed animals, and even razors in sanitary napkins and tampons). Once on the unit, the suicidal patient may hide the contraband to attempt or commit suicide.

Before the crisis counselor or psychiatrist evaluates the patient, he or she must be "medically cleared." The federal Emergency Medical Treatment and Active Labor Act of 1986, as Amended (EMTALA 1995) requires that all patients who come for emergency treatment must be given an adequate medical screening examination (Quinn et al. 2002). Patients with head trauma or toxicity from substance abuse must be monitored carefully for changes in their level of consciousness. Dhossche (2000) found that 23%–46% of emergency patients were simultaneously intoxicated and suicidal. Drug screens should search for alcohol, barbiturates, opiates, cocaine, amphetamines, tetrahydrocannabinol, phencyclidine, hallucinogens, and some over-the-counter medications, such as antihistamines and anticholinergics (Reid and Balis 1987). EMTALA was enacted by Congress in 1986 to prevent "patient dumping," that is, refusing to provide emergency medical treatment to patients who do not have insurance. It applies to all Medicare and Medicaid participating hospitals.

Patients who have high tolerance for alcohol may not exhibit an unsteady gait or slurred speech. They may not appear to be intoxicated when expressing suicidal ideation or intent. Patients may be admitted to the hospital, or a petition may be filed for emergency commitment for suicidal threats or behaviors that are not present when the individual is sober (Simon and Goetz 1999). However, in the case example, the patient was also making suicidal threats while sober.

Blood alcohol levels or Breathalyzer measurements should be performed on patients deemed to be at risk for suicide. Many intoxicated patients are discharged from the ED once the alcohol level falls below the legal limit. Careful assessment should be conducted to determine whether the level of risk for suicide has diminished substantially or is no longer present. However, the patient can become intoxicated and suicidal again. Referral to alcohol rehabilitation program is essential.

Suicide risk assessment is central to patient safety and disposition. Systematic suicide risk assessment should be performed on all psychiatric patients evaluated in the ED. EMTALA provisions for adequate screening examinations apply to the assessment of suicidal and homicidal ideation (Quinn et al. 2002). Assessing the lethality of a suicide attempt is discussed in Chapter 6, "Inpatients."

The mental health clinician in the medical ED may have only one shot at suicide risk assessment. Systematic suicide risk assessment provides the best shot. Suicide prevention contracts have little if any utility with unknown, psychotic, agitated, or intoxicated patients. Challenging clinical decisions must be made quickly. The decision to hospitalize or discharge the patient to outpatient sources of treatment is dependent on the patient's level of risk for suicide.

Patients at high risk for suicide are usually hospitalized. However, outpatient treatment may be feasible for the patient at moderate to high risk who has substantial protective factors such as strong family support and a therapeutic alliance with an outpatient therapist who feels comfortable treating the patient outside of the hospital. Clinical judgment based on thorough assessment of both suicide risk and protective factors will help guide the clinician's decision. Forster and Wu (2002) believe that a treatment perspective regarding the decision not to hospitalize a patient, when outpatient treatment appears to be the most effective intervention, involves taking a risk that "can sometimes be the best decision" (p. 80).

In the case example, Dr. Allen's wife was able to provide vital clinical information. Fawcett et al. (1990) found that approximately 25% of depressed patients with short-term, anxiety-driven suicide risk factors tell family members of their suicidal ideation or intent but deny it to examining clinicians. The case example demonstrates this important point. Dr. Allen vehemently denies any suicidal ideation, intent, or plan. The patient's permission should be obtained to speak with significant others. However, the patient may refuse to grant permission. Merely listening does not violate confidentiality. The patient's mental capacity for health care decision making should be determined.

Although clinicians have a duty to evaluate and treat ED patients, patients also have a right to refuse treatment, provided they are competent (*Schloendorff v. Society of New York Hosp.* [1914]). Courts have recognized that denial of illness can render a patient incompetent to make medical treatment decisions (Mishkin 1989). If the patient lacks sufficient mental capacity, substitute health care decision makers are required to provide consent for treatment (*Mills v. Rogers* [1979/1980/1982/1984]; *Rennie v. Klein* [1979/1980/1982/1983]). However, in an increasing number of states, the proxy consent by next of kin for psychiatric patients is not available (Simon and Goetz 1999).

When the patient is competent and withholds consent to contact a third party, a number of options are available. As in the example, the clinician may try to persuade, but not coerce, the patient. Persuasion engages the patient's reasoning capacity. Coercion circumvents it. Ethically, it is permissible to break patient confidentiality in order to protect the patient at risk for suicide (American Psychiatric Association 2001). The emergency exception to obtaining consent is another available option. Collateral information is an important part of the evaluation process.

In an emergency situation, consent for treatment is implied (Simon 2001). In acute, life-threatening situations that require immediate psychiatric intervention and treatment, the law assumes that every rational person would consent under these circumstances. Consent is implied when the patient cannot receive or understand information provided or give competent consent, and a substitute decision maker is not present. The emergency must be severe and imminent.

Federal and state statutes and the courts define the term *medical emergency* either narrowly or expansively (Swartz 1987). Slovenko (2002) states that the term *emergency* is not self-defining. For example, at one extreme, an emergency may be considered to exist when the patient is injured, unconscious, and in need of immediate treatment. At the other extreme, an emergency is determined to exist when the need to alleviate pain and suffering is present. EMTALA regulations define an emergency medical condition as one that presents with acute symptoms of sufficient severity (including psychiatric and substance abuse symptoms) that place the health of the patient in serious jeopardy and cause serious impairment or dysfunction to bodily functions (Currier et al. 2002; Quinn et al. 2002).

Commitment statutes in most states permit police officers to obtain emergency evaluation petitions for individuals who may require emergency intervention. The police who accompany the patient should be asked who, what, where, when, and why questions. Whenever possible, collateral sources of information must be sought from significant others, from the records of prior admission to the same facility, and from outpatient treaters.

Most psychiatric patient visits to the ED occur during the evening, when other mental health agencies and therapists' offices are closed. Collateral sources of information usually are not available at 3:00 A.M. In the case example, the patient's psychiatrist could not be reached. Family members or partners may not accompany the patient to the ED or may be unreachable. An important source of guidance is systematic assessment of suicide risk that informs clinical decision making. To function effectively in the ED, psychiatrists and other clinicians must be able to *trust* their suicide risk assessments. The situation is analogous to that of airplane pilots, who must trust their instruments in an emergency.

Vexing situations often arise in the ED that test clinicians' confidence in their suicide risk assessments. During the winter, some individuals visit the ED uttering, "I am suicidal," an "open sesame" that gains them admission to the psychiatric unit for food and shelter. Some of these individuals may be well known to the ED. It is easy for ED clinicians to become cynical when dealing with individuals who falsely assert that they are suicidal. Clinicians often experience helplessness and anger when they feel manipulated by individuals they strongly suspect are malingering. Bias against psychiatric patients in general and anger at specific individuals who abuse the system may interfere with clinical judgment, possibly causing suicide risk to be missed in some individuals. Also, frequent patient readmissions (sometimes pejoratively dubbed "frequent flyers"), often due to incomplete treatment and brief hospital stays, add to the frustration of clinicians working in the ED. Systematic suicide risk assessment should help the clinician differentiate the patient at real risk for suicide from the individual faking suicide. In the malingerer, many of the significant suicide risk factors and their associated affects are missing. Obviously, reflexive hospital admissions must be avoided.

One study found that patients who threatened suicide or exaggerated suicide symptoms to gain hospital admission were more likely to be substance dependent, antisocial, homeless, unmarried, or in legal difficulty. Subsequent suicides were uncommon (Bonner and Bonner 1996). Yates et al. (1996) obtained completed questionnaires by psychiatrists on 227 patients seen for emergency services at an urban general hospital. Thirteen percent of the patients were strongly or definitely suspected of feigning symptoms. None received a primary diagnosis, and fewer than half were confronted. Motives for feigning psychiatric disorders or conditions included the desire for food and shelter, financial gains, and avoidance of jail, work, or family responsibilities.

The opposite situation arises when a suicidal individual, usually brought to the ED by the family or by the police, denies suicidal ideation, intent, or plan. Again, systematic suicide risk assessment will often uncover the presence of other clinical indicia of suicide risk and associated affects (e.g., depression, anxiety), despite the patient's denial. The clinician may determine that a patient is at significant risk for suicide, even though the patient denies suicide intent.

Patients with dementia and psychosis or patients with chronic, severe mental illnesses such as chronic schizophrenia often come to the ED and require emergency hospitalization. Psychiatric patients who make multiple visits to the ED may be at high risk for suicide (Hillard et al. 1983). Zealberg and Santos (1996) recommend that certain psychiatric patients always be admitted for inpatient care. These include patients whose suicide attempts involve highly lethal methods; patients with the intent, means, and a specific plan to commit suicide; patients who express the continued desire to die after a suicide attempt; and patients who make suicide attempts in the absence of protective factors such as family or other social supports. In the case example, the patient repeatedly expresses suicide intent while sober, is depressed, has an alcohol abuse problem, had a loaded gun found under his pillow, and is experiencing an acrimonious work situation—a combination of factors leading to an assessment of high risk for suicide and the need for immediate psychiatric hospitalization.

Managed-care organizations (MCOs) usually do not authorize precertification for hospitalization of psychiatric patients who deny suicide intent. Clinicians sometimes may feel the need to "manufacture" a finding of suicide intent to obtain precertification for inpatient admission. Another option is to conduct a systematic suicide risk assessment to determine the patient's level of risk. Quantitative data from the National Comorbidity Survey (Kessler et al. 1999) can be of assistance in assessing risk levels for suicide attempts. The survey found that 34% of individuals made the transition from suicidal ideation to plan; 72% from plan to an attempt, and 26% from suicidal ideation to an unplanned suicide attempt.

Suicide risk assessment may reveal the presence of significant suicide risk factors in patients who deny suicidal ideation, intent, or plan. Reporting the level of suicide risk along with other crucial clinical information may secure MCO approval to hospitalize the patient. However, the issue is not insurance but the patient's clinical needs. The decision to discharge or admit a patient from the ED should be informed by a risk-benefit assessment that considers the risks and benefits of hospitalization versus those of outpatient treatment (Simon and Goetz 1999). All assessments should be documented in the patient's ED records.

The covering psychiatrist for the medical ED consults with an ED physician or crisis counselor. The psychiatrist may not know the physicians or crisis counselors well enough to evaluate their clinical skills in systematically assessing suicide risk. When informed by the nonpsychiatrist clinician that a patient is "suicidal" and requires hospital admission, the psychiatrist should tactfully inquire about the thoroughness of the suicide risk assessment. If the nonpsychiatrist clinician's assessment of "no risk" relies solely on the patient's denial of suicidal ideation, intent, or plan, the assessment is insufficient (Simon 2000). All too often the notation in the ED record states, "No SI, HI, CFS" (no suicidal ideation, homicidal ideation, contracts for safety). Moreover, suicide prevention contracts should not be used in the ED. There is no basis for relying on them in an emergency (see Chapter 3, "Suicide Prevention Contracts").

MANAGEMENT

Management of psychiatric patients in the ED who are at risk for suicide involves treatment, safety, and disposition. For patients who have attempted suicide, stabilization (or transfer to the intensive care unit) is the immediate goal of treatment. Medications that decrease anxiety, agitation, and psychotic symptoms may also diminish the patient's immediate risk for suicide.

A major safety concern is the elopement of patients from the ED who are at high risk for suicide. In the case example, Dr. Allen attempts to leave the ED against medical advice. Once it is determined that Dr. Allen is at high risk for suicide, he is deemed a psychiatric emergency and is prevented from leaving. As discussed earlier, clinicians have implied consent in an acute psychiatric emergency to evaluate and treat the patient. This situation arises with the severely agitated patient at high suicide risk who refuses treatment and attempts to leave. It may be necessary to prevent the patient from leaving the ED or place the patient in the ED seclusion room until the evaluation can be completed. It is essential to follow ED policies and procedures for restraint and seclusion. When a patient at high risk for suicide elopes, the police should be immediately notified and a petition filed for involuntary hospitalization.

The basic dispositional decision regarding psychiatric patients in the ED is hospitalization versus discharge. The decision to hospitalize a patient at risk for suicide is often easier than the decision to discharge the patient from the ED. Patients at high risk for suicide who refuse voluntary admission may require involuntary hospitalization. In the case example, a physician-patient at high risk for suicide vehemently refuses voluntary admission. When mentally ill professionals and other "VIPs" are treated as "special" at the cost of receiving necessary treatment, the risk for an "executive" suicide is likely increased. The ED physician, in the case example, wisely resists the impulse to do a medical colleague a "favor" by discharging him to outpatient care. He does not fall prey to the "VIP syndrome" by allowing a person in a prominent position to influence medical decision making. Some clinicians feel personally threatened by the discovery of mental illness in their colleagues. The examining clinician may react by denying or by minimizing the patient's suicide risk, with possible lethal consequences.

Involuntary hospitalization is an emergency psychiatric intervention when less restrictive treatments are not clinically appropriate. The substantive criteria for involuntary hospitalization in all states are mental illness and danger to self or others. Associated criteria may include a violent act against oneself or others within a specified period of time, least restrictive criteria, grave disability, and a danger to property. State commitment statutes have provisions that grant psychiatrists and psychologists immunity from liability when certifying for involuntary hospitalization, if they use reasonable professional judgment and act in good faith (Simon 2001).

As in the case example, a patient confronted with the prospect of involuntary hospitalization may choose to be admitted voluntarily. However, shortly after admission to the psychiatric unit, the patient may sign out against medical advice. Admission to hospital psychiatric units is either informal (pure voluntary) or formal (conditional voluntary). The exact statutory language governing voluntary admissions differs from state to state. Only a few states permit informal voluntary admissions. In informal admissions, the patient is free to sign out against medical advice and leave at any time. Only moral suasion can be used to convince the patient not to prematurely leave the hospital.

In states with informal admission procedures, the ED clinician is often confronted with the challenging task of determining whether the patient at high risk for suicide will stay as a voluntary inpatient or is merely "gaming" the system to avoid involuntary hospitalization. In the latter instance, the decision to involuntarily hospitalize the patient at high risk for suicide is appropriate. In the majority of states, formal admission procedures permit the inpatient psychiatrist to hold a suicidal or violent patient for a specified period of time, once the patient provides in writing his or her intention to leave. This restriction may not apply to patients who are strictly substance users.

The psychiatrist who consults with the ED should have a working knowledge of the available mental health resources in the community. Crisis counselors can be of great assistance in making appropriate discharge decisions. In a study by Appleby et al. (1999a), 24% of the total number of patients who committed suicide did so within 3 months of hospital discharge. The study also found an association between elevated risk and a decreased intensity of treatment, especially following hospital discharge. Those patients who committed suicide were four times more likely to have had their care reduced at the last appointment before their death, compared with a matched group of patients discharged from the inpatient unit who did not commit suicide (Appleby et al. 1999b). However, a history of intensive treatment and past suicide attempts also increase the lifetime risk for suicide.

Patients at low to moderate risk for suicide are usually discharged from the ED. These patients should be informed about the available evaluation and treatment resources in the community. A number of these patients do not adhere to follow-up treatment recommendations. Whenever possible, the patient should be provided with an appointment for follow-up care as soon as possible following discharge from the ED. Before the patient is discharged, it should be ascertained from the patient or significant others whether guns and other lethal means (including knives, drugs, and poisons) are available to the patient in the home. Since the introduction of selective serotonin reuptake inhibitors (SSRIs), suicide by overdose of antidepressants has become less common (Weber 2002). The greatest lethality from overdose is associated with over-the-counter and prescription analgesics, especially opioids. Gun management at the time of discharge is discussed in Chapter 6, "Inpatients."

Patients at risk for suicide should be accompanied by emergency department staff when laboratory or other studies are required else-where in the hospital. The patient also must be accompanied by a staff person when being admitted to the psychiatric unit from the ED. At some facilities, a security guard is required to accompany the staff person and patient. At other times, additional personnel are optional according to the safety needs of the patient. The patient should not be sent with a family member, unaccompanied by hos-pital staff. If the hospital does not have a psychiatric unit or the unit is full, transfer arrangements must be made for hospitalizing the patient at an appropriate psychiatric facility. Patient "dumping" occurs when unwanted patients are transferred, such as those who are suicidal, violent, indigent, homeless, or medically ill. The facil-ities to which these patients are transferred often do not have the equipment or staff to provide proper care (Elliott 1993). Further-more, the patient must not be simply discharged and told to go to the psychiatric facility. The patient should be held until safe trans-portation can be provided for transfer (*Underwood v. United States* [1966]).

EMTALA regulations were enacted to protect patients from dan-gerous transfers by requiring that they be stabilized first (Quinn et al. 2002). A suicidal patient would likely be considered stable for discharge or transfer when he or she is no longer assessed to be an imminent threat to self or others. ED clinicians (including psychia-trists and crisis counselors) should be familiar with EMTALA requirements for appropriate transfer of patients generally, but especially for patients at risk for suicide.

EMTALA does not permit private legal claims against individual physicians, only against the hospital accused of an illegal discharge. However, under the statute, a physician responsible for the screen-ing examination, treatment, or transfer of a patient that violates EMTALA is subject, like the hospital, to a penalty of up to $50,000 for each violation (Wheeler 2001). On-call physicians who fail or refuse to appear within a reasonable time after being contacted by the ED are subject to similar penalties. Hospital policies and proce-dures usually specify the required time within which on-call psychi-atrists must respond to calls from the ED. The physician can be sued individually for malpractice, if the physician is negligent and the patient is harmed.

CLINICALLY BASED RISK MANAGEMENT

- Systematic suicide risk assessment should be performed on all psychiatric patients evaluated in the ED.
- Suicide prevention contracts have little or no utility in emergency settings.
- Individuals who come to the ED because of suspected suicidal behaviors may deny suicidal ideation, intent, or plan. However, the individual may have revealed to family members or significant others the full extent of suicidal intent or a plan. The clinician also should look for and assess other clinical correlates of suicide risk that do not rely on patient reporting.
- Patient information should be obtained from collateral sources (e.g., family, partners, police, ED records of previous visits, current and former treaters). Obtaining collateral information is an important part of the suicide risk assessment process.
- Drug and alcohol screening should be performed routinely on patients at risk for suicide.
- Some patients at moderate to high risk for suicide may be managed as outpatients, if sufficient protective factors against suicide are present.
- The risks and benefits of hospitalization versus the risks and benefits of discharge should be part of the dispositional decision-making process.
- Reflexive inpatient admissions or discharges from the ED must be avoided. Careful evaluation and systematic assessment of the patient at risk for suicide should always inform clinical decision making.
- In emergencies, when treatment is necessary to save a life or to prevent imminent serious harm, the law "presumes" that consent would have been granted by the patient.
- The patient's safety must be secured throughout the assessment process. Patients at high risk for suicide may injure themselves in the ED or may elope. Preventive safety measures must be anticipated and instituted, when indicated.
- Psychiatrists who work in or consult with the ED should have knowledge of the mental health resources available in the community.

- Patients at risk for suicide who are discharged from the ED should be provided with follow-up instructions and, when possible, provided appointments for early evaluation and treatment.
- Evaluations, clinical interventions, suicide risk assessments, risk-benefit determinations, and the clinician's decision-making process should be thoroughly documented.
- Be aware of and follow EMTALA mandates requiring appropriate screening examination, stabilization, and transfer or discharge of anyone seeking emergency services. EMTALA applies to all physicians.

REFERENCES

American Psychiatric Association: The Principles of Medical Ethics With Annotations Especially Applicable to Psychiatry. Washington, DC, American Psychiatric Association, 2001

Appleby L, Dennehy JA, Thomas CS, et al: Aftercare and clinical characteristics of people with mental illness who commit suicide: a case-control study. Lancet 353:1397–1400, 1999a

Appleby L, Shaw J, Amos T, et al: Suicide within 12 months of contact with mental health services: national clinical survey. BMJ 318:1235–1239, 1999b

Bonner MT, Bonner J: Characteristics and six-month outcome of patients who use suicide threats to seek hospital admission. Psychiatr Serv 47:871–873, 1996

Breslow RE: Structure and function of psychiatric emergency services, in Emergency Psychiatry. Edited by Allen MH. Washington, DC, American Psychiatric Publishing, 2002, pp 1–31

Currier GW, Allen MH, Serper MR, et al: Medical, psychiatric, and cognitive assessment in the psychiatric emergency service, in Emergency Psychiatry. Edited by Allen MH. Washington, DC, American Psychiatric Publishing, 2002, pp 35–74

Dhossche DM: Suicidal behavior in psychiatric emergency room patients. South Med J 93:310–314, 2000

Elliott RL: Patient dumping, COBRA, and the public psychiatric hospital. Hosp Community Psychiatry 44:155–158, 1993

Fawcett J, Scheptner WA, Fogg L, et al: Time-related predictors of suicide in major affective disorder. Am J Psychiatry 147:1189–1194, 1990

Forster PL, Wu LH: Assessment and treatment of suicidal patients in an emergency setting, in Emergency Psychiatry. Edited by Allen MH. Washington, DC, American Psychiatric Publishing, 2002, pp 75–113

Heikkinen ME, Aro HM, Lonnqvist J: Recent life events, social support and suicide. Acta Psychiatr Scand Suppl 377:65–72, 1994

Hillard JR, Ramm D, Zung WW, et al: Suicide in a psychiatric emergency room population. Am J Psychiatry 140:459–462, 1983

Kessler RC, Borges G, Walters EE: Prevalence of and risk factors for lifetime suicide attempts in the National Comorbidity Survey. Arch Gen Psychiatry 56:617–626, 1999

Maltsberger JT, Hendin H, Haas AP, et al: Determination of precipitating events in the suicide of psychiatric patients. Suicide Life Threat Behav 33:111–119, 2003

Mills v Rogers, 478 F. Supp. 1342 (D. Mass. 1979), *aff'd in part, rev'd in part,* 634 F.2d 650 (1st Cir. 1980), *vacated and remanded,* 457 U.S. 291 (1982), *on remand,* 738 F.2d 1 (1st Cir. 1984); *see also* Rogers v Commissioner of Dep't of Mental Health, 390 Mass. 489, 458 N.E.2d 308 (1983), *cert. denied,* 484 U.S. 1010 (1988)

Mishkin B: Determining the capacity for making health care decisions. Adv Psychosom Med 19:151–166, 1989

Ostamo A, Lonnqvist J: Excess mortality in suicide attempters. Soc Psychiatry Psychiatr Epidemiol 36:29–35, 2001

Quinn DK, Geppert CMA, Maggiore WA: The Emergency Medical Treatment and Active Labor Act of 1985 and the practice of psychiatry. Psychiatr Serv 53:1301–1307, 2002

Reid WH, Balis GU: Evaluation of the violent patient. Psychiatry Update 6:49–57, 1987

Rennie v Klein, 476 F. Supp.1294 (D. N.J. 1979), *aff'd in part, modified in part, and remanded,* 653 F.2d 836 (3d Cir. 1980), *vacated and remanded,* 458 U.S. 1119 (1982), 720 F.2d 266 (3d Cir. 1983)

Schloendorff v Society of New York Hosp., 211 N.Y. 125, 105 N.E. 92 (1914), *overruled by* Bing v Thunig, 2 N.Y.2d 656, 143 N.E.2d 3, 163 N.Y.S.2d 3 (1957)

Simon RI: Taking the "sue" out of suicide: a forensic psychiatrist's perspective. Psychiatr Ann 30:399–407, 2000

Simon RI: Psychiatry and Law for Clinicians, 3rd Edition. Washington, DC, American Psychiatric Publishing, 2001

Simon RI, Goetz S: Forensic issues in the psychiatric emergency department. Psychiatr Clin North Am 22:851–864, 1999

Slovenko R: Psychiatry in Law/Law in Psychiatry. New York, Brunner-Routledge, 2002

Swartz MS: What constitutes a psychiatric emergency: legal dimensions. Bull Am Acad Psychiatry Law 15:57–68, 1987

The Emergency Medical Treatment and Active Labor Act of 1986, as Amended. 42 U.S.C.A. § 1395dd (1995)

Underwood v United States, 356 F.2d 92 (5th Cir. 1966)

Weber R: Underusing overdose as a method of suicide: a trend analysis. American Association of Suicidology News Link 28:3, 8, 2002

Wheeler AM: EMTALA: what is it? how does it affect psychiatrists today? Psychiatric Practice and Managed Care 7:3–4, 2001

Wingerson D, Russo J, Ries R, et al: Use of psychiatric emergency services and enrollment status in a public managed mental health plan. Psychiatr Serv 52:1494–1501, 2001

Yates BD, Nordquist CR, Schultz-Ross RA: Feigned psychiatric symptoms in the emergency room. Psychiatr Serv 47:998–1000, 1996

Zealberg JJ, Santos AB: Comprehensive Emergency Health Care. New York, WW Norton, 1996

8

SUICIDE AFTERMATH: DOCUMENTATION, CONFIDENTIALITY, AND SURVIVOR CARE

Give sorrow words; the grief that does not speak
Whispers the o'er-fraught heart and bids it break.

William Shakespeare, *Macbeth*, Act IV, Scene 3

INTRODUCTION

Careful documentation and maintenance of confidentiality of the patient's records support good clinical care. They also provide a sound defense in malpractice litigation as well as in administrative and ethics proceedings. After a patient's death, the duty to maintain confidentiality of the patient's record continues, unless a court decision or statute provides otherwise. Suicide aftermath presents the clinician with conflicting tensions between maintaining patient confidentiality, providing support to the suicide survivors, and implementing risk management principles that limit liability exposure. Although documentation, confidentiality, and suicide aftermath are addressed as separate topics, they inevitably overlap.

CASE EXAMPLE

Mr. Pitts, the 45-year-old chief financial officer (CFO) of an energy conglomerate, commits suicide while under the outpatient psychiatric care of Dr. Rowe. Mr. Pitts was treated with a selective serotonin reuptake inhibitor (SSRI) antidepressant and weekly individual psychotherapy. His diagnosis was major depression, single episode, moderate without psychotic features. Mr. Pitts's depression began after a governmental agency initiated an investigation of his company's financial reporting, following allegation of irregularities in accounting methods. Mr. Pitts was a main target of the investigation.

Mr. Pitts had been a very successful CFO with another company prior to assuming the CFO position with the energy conglomerate. His move was considered by industry watchers to be a professional coup, placing Mr. Pitts on the "fast track" to become the chief operating officer of the conglomerate. When allegations of wrongdoing were made against Mr. Pitts, he became acutely depressed and sought the help of Dr. Rowe. At the first session, Dr. Rowe reassured Mr. Pitts that the psychotherapy was confidential. During a treatment session, Mr. Pitts discussed officers of the company by name who he believed were involved in covering up fraud. Dr. Rowe, who kept detailed records, documented Mr. Pitts's statements.

During the course of the investigation, a national newspaper reported that Mr. Pitts would soon be indicted on criminal charges of fraud in his position as CFO. Throughout the therapy, Dr. Rowe systematically assessed Mr. Pitts's risk of suicide. Mr. Pitts revealed that he had occasional "fleeting" thoughts about "being out of this situation" but adamantly denied active suicide intent or a plan. The therapeutic alliance appeared to be a protective factor. Other protective factors included his family's support and his strong religious beliefs.

Following the newspaper article about alleged corporate scandal and Mr. Pitts's expected criminal indictment, he went to a motel and committed suicide by handgun. He left the following suicide note to his wife:

> *Dear Pris—I cannot bear the personal shame and the scandal inflicted on you, the children, and our parents by any criminal proceedings. I am totally innocent of wrongdoing. I know you will take good care of the kids. I will miss all of you terribly. I am so sorry.—Dave*

Dr. Rowe notes in the patient's record, "The suicide was a total surprise. Mr. Pitts adamantly denied any intent or plan to kill himself. Ongoing systematic suicide risk assessment revealed an unchanging low to moderate risk." The bereaved wife requests an appointment with Dr. Rowe, which he grants. She wants to know why her husband committed suicide, why his suicide was not prevented, and why she was not warned. Dr. Rowe responds to the wife's questions in a nondefensive and supportive manner, revealing only enough information to answer her questions. Dr. Rowe understands that confidentiality continues after a patient's death, but he feels that it cannot be absolute in responding to questions from the survivors of suicide. Dr. Rowe does not make any self-serving or self-incriminating statements. The session goes well. Mr. Pitts's wife does not make any threats or even intimate that she will sue.

Dr. Rowe reports the suicide to his professional liability insurance carrier within 30 days, as required by his policy. The insurance company assigns an attorney to meet with Dr. Rowe. The attorney reviews Dr. Rowe's treatment records on Mr. Pitts carefully and finds them to be complete. It is Dr. Rowe's practice to dictate his notes after each patient session. The notes are transcribed and stored in the patient's computer file.

The attorney, however, expresses concern about a portion of Mr. Pitts's record that documents accusations of fraud against named individuals of the conglomerate. The attorney feels certain that the investigating agency will obtain a court order requiring copies of Mr. Pitts's psychiatric records. The attorney informs Dr. Rowe that a legal cause of action may exist against him when words contained in a patient's medical record defame those who are living. She explains that unless a privilege exists to make disclosures, mental health professionals are responsible for statements made, even though the views are purported to be those of the patient. In addition to the deep sorrow over the suicide of his patient, Dr. Rowe spends sleepless nights worrying about the possibility of being sued for malpractice and a legal action for defamation of character by officers of the conglomerate named by the patient.

DISCUSSION

The clinical, ethical, and legal principles governing patient documentation, confidentiality, and record keeping that are in place during a patient's life continue after his or her death. The following discussion examines these principles in relation to suicidal patients and patients who committed suicide.

DOCUMENTATION

Documentation is an integral part of patient care. It encourages the practitioner to sharpen clinical focus and clarify decision-making rationale. The record becomes an active clinical tool, not just an inert document. The clinician treats the patient, not the chart. Documentation as a risk management tool supports good clinical care.

When patients are at risk for suicide, it is necessary for psychiatrists to document all clinical interventions and their rationales. Documentation should address the following basic questions: what was done, the reason(s) for doing it, and the rationale for rejecting alternative interventions or treatments (Slovenko 2002). Suicide risk assessments should be recorded when performed. Psychiatrists who perform adequate suicide risk assessments may not necessarily record them.

In outpatient settings, suicide risk assessment and contemporaneous documentation usually take place at the time of the initial interview, at the emergence of suicidal ideation or behavior, and when a significant regression occurs in the patient's clinical condition. On inpatient units, important points of documentation of suicide risk assessments occur at admission, changes in safety supervision levels, ward changes, the issuance of passes, marked changes in the clinical condition of the patient, and evaluation for discharge (Simon 2000). Suicide risk assessment is a process, never just an isolated event (see Chapter 2, "Suicide Risk Assessment").

If a malpractice claim is brought against the psychiatrist, contemporaneous documentation of suicide risk assessments assists the court in evaluating the many clinical complexities and ambiguities that exist in treatment and management of patients at risk for suicide. Some courts may conclude that what is not recorded has not been done. For example, in *Abille v. United States* (1980), a psychiatrist failed to maintain contemporary notes, orders, or other records that adequately explained the management decisions for a patient who committed suicide. The psychiatrist transferred the patient from suicide status to a status appropriate for less dangerous patients. At the time of the transfer, no notation was made by the psychiatrist explaining the transfer, even though he usually made such notes. Such documentation was required by hospital regulations. The court acknowledged that a reasonable psychiatrist might have determined that the patient could be reclassified with safety, but without notes there was concern that the decision was made negligently. *Abille* underscores the court's need to know the decision-making process of the psychiatrist. A psychiatrist's best friend in court is a carefully documented record that contemporaneously details the provision of reasonable care.

Generally, in the absence of corroborating records, an assertion in court that certain actions were taken is a question for the fact finder who must consider the issue of proof. When an adequate record exists, the possibility of proving that an action (e.g., treatment or procedure) was undertaken is significantly enhanced. Moreover, lawsuits often are brought many months or even several years from the time of the alleged negligence. The psychiatrist may not remember the patient or the treatment that was provided. Without an adequate record, the defendant clinician is less able to mount an effective legal defense. The absence of adequate documentation does not necessarily indicate the absence of appropriate care. However, at deposition or trial, testimony by the clinician that adequate treatment was provided the patient is much less convincing without supporting documentation.

Integrated interdisciplinary behavioral records are used in many clinical settings. On inpatient units, notes by the psychiatrist, treatment team members, consultants, and other mental health professionals are documented sequentially (see Chapter 6, "Inpatients"). Adequate documentation by the psychiatrist provides others with access to his or her ongoing decision-making rationale. Adequate documentation permits the treatment team to review the psychiatrist's clinical reasoning across hospital staff shifts. In *Brandvain v. Ridgeview Inst.* (1988/1989), the admitting physician failed to document in the admission history information from the patient's wife about the patient's intense suicidal ideation and recent suicide attempt. The treating psychiatrist judged a hanging attempt on the psychiatric unit to be an "incident." The treating psychiatrist did not document his reasoning in concluding that the suicide attempt was a "gesture." Moreover, he did not order suicide precautions. The treating psychiatrist was unaware of the patient's suicide attempt prior to hospitalization. The two clinical attendants who rescued the patient during the suicide attempt made no entries in the patient's record. The incident was known to the staff but was not documented in the interdisciplinary notes. At the change of nursing shifts, no record was kept that a nurse had placed the patient on 15-minute checks. The nurse on the next shift was unaware of the suicide precautions and did not continue the checks. Shortly thereafter, the patient hung himself by his shirt from a shower head. A jury found the psychiatrist and hospital to be negligent.

Adequate documentation of suicide risk assessments also assists utilization reviewers to substantiate the necessity for continued treatment of suicidal patients. It is equally important for the psychiatrist to carefully read the notes entered by others in the patient's records throughout the hospital stay. It is standard clinical practice to write a progress note at each patient hospital visit. Hospital bylaws and regulations usually require the psychiatrist to see the patient each day of hospitalization and to enter daily progress notes. At the time of patient discharge, the decision for discharge, including the risk-benefit assessments for continued hospitalization versus discharge, should be documented. Detailed follow-up arrangements made with the patient for outpatient care also should be recorded.

In high-volume, rapid-patient-turnover inpatient units, documentation may be given short shrift. The adequacy of documentation also may be influenced by diagnostic factors, the assessment process, the patient's clinical condition, and the ability to cooperate with the examiner. For example, an acutely psychotic, agitated patient may not be able to cooperate with the psychiatrist in providing a coherent history. Thus, documentation may also vary according to the nature of the patient, assessment methods used, and the clinical setting. Malone et al. (1995) found that documentation of suicidal behavior was less accurate in the physician's discharge summary compared with documentation at the intake assessment, which utilized a semistructured format for recording clinical information. They counseled that the discharge summary must accurately document suicidal behavior to help identify high-risk patients for appropriate outpatient care.

Documentation should be careful, concise, complete, contemporaneous, and clear (legible). Legible handwriting facilitates good clinical care of the patient. Illegible writing creates the impression of carelessness, haste, and the provision of substandard clinical care. Illegible doctor's orders can lead to management mistakes that a patient may exploit to commit suicide. Illegible orders are a common cause of drug errors that can seriously harm patients (see Table 8–1). The risk of suicide also may be increased if the patient receives the wrong medication, which could delay critical treatment during a short-stay hospitalization.

Table 8–1. Examples of potential drug brand-name errors

Ambien—Amen
Celexa—Celebrex –Cerebyx
Lamictal—Lomotil—Lamisil
Luvox—Levoxl
Remeron—Zemuron
Zyprexa—Zyrtec

Source. Adapted from Cohen MR: Zyrtex–Zyprexa Mix-Up. AHRQ Web M&M [Online journal: http://webmm.orhq.gov], April 2003. Used with permission of AHRQ Web M&M.

At deposition or trial, the clinician's inability to decipher his or her handwriting is an embarrassment. The clinician loses credibility, raising doubts about his or her competence in other areas of the patient's care.

The use of abbreviations poses the risk of misinterpretation and harm, especially for patients at risk for suicide. For example, the shorthand "D/C" is confusing. Does it mean "discontinue" or "discharge"? A D/C order intended to discontinue suicide precautions for a patient at risk for suicide could be misinterpreted as an order to discharge the patient. Patient orders should be written out, not abbreviated.

Whether the patient is treated as an outpatient or an inpatient, the psychiatrist should document the treatment plan, the clinical reasoning as it pertains to specific treatments and interventions, and any communication with prior treaters and significant others. Pertinent telephone calls from the patient or family need to be documented. Detailed medication records should be kept. When consultations are obtained, a written consultation report should be requested and included in the patient's record. When the psychiatrist will be away from his or her practice, coverage instructions to the patient require documentation.

A psychiatric record that carefully documents the psychiatrist's suicide assessments and decision-making process provides a formidable legal defense by supplying the psychiatrist and the expert witness with specific information on which to base their testimony. The psychiatrist's testimony is made credible and the expert's testimony is shown not to be based on second-guessing (Laub 2001).

Adequate documentation also permits the treatment team to review the psychiatrist's clinical reasoning across hospital staff shifts. Failure to adequately document suicide risk assessments, treatment, and safety interventions for patients at risk for suicide may not be the cause of a patient's suicide. However, the standard of care requires that the clinician maintain adequate patient records. When a psychiatrist sees an inpatient briefly, does not discuss clinical assessments with staff, and does not document suicide risk assessments and treatment interventions, the legal defense against a claim of malpractice for the patient's suicide is made difficult. Although inadequate documentation by the psychiatrist or clinical staff may not be the cause of a patient's suicide, it may be part of an overall pattern of substandard care. The careful documentation of substandard care is disastrous if a claim of malpractice is filed against the psychiatrist.

CONFIDENTIALITY

The duty to maintain confidentiality of patient records follows the patient in death, unless a specific court decision or statute in a particular jurisdiction provides otherwise. The Ethics Committee on the Principles of Medical Ethics (American Psychiatric Association 2001a, Section 4-K) contains the following question and answer raised by a psychiatrist on this very point:

> Question: Can I give confidential information about a recently deceased mother to her grieving daughter?
> Answer: No. Ethically, her confidences survive her death. Legally, this is an unclear issue varying from one jurisdiction to another. Further, there is a risk of the information being used to seek an advantage in the contesting of a will or in competition with other surviving family members.

Information may be requested after a patient's death. As a general rule, written authorization should be obtained from the executor or administrator of the deceased patient's estate before a copy of the medical records is released. If the estate has been settled and an executor or administrator no longer exists, a *copy* of the medical records should be released only to properly appointed legal representatives (American Psychiatric Association Committee on Confidentiality 1987).

Criminal investigations, will contests, inquiries by the Internal Revenue Service, life insurance investigations, and families seeking information about the deceased patient as part of the grieving process are some of the reasons for postmortem information requests. When a patient commits suicide, family members may request a meeting with the treating psychiatrist to try to understand the suicide. This is a very stressful time for the family and for the psychiatrist. In this situation, the psychiatrist may feel defeated, guilty, and defensive. The family invariably feels bewilderment, guilt, and anger.

In these difficult circumstances, the psychiatrist may reveal too much information. Additional painful details of the patient's life that are not relevant to the inquiry must not be released to the family. Discussing the patient's suicide with colleagues, friends, or a spouse may violate patient confidentiality. The immediate priority should be to console the family and assist them in their grief, as was done by Dr. Rowe in the case example. The psychiatrist should not refuse to see the family, unless litigation has been threatened or instituted by the family against the psychiatrist.

If it is necessary to reveal confidential information after the patient's death, the psychiatrist may minimize legal risks by providing just enough information for the task at hand. Details of the patient's therapy are rarely if ever required. Relevancy is the guiding rule (Simon 1992). As Dr. Rowe discovered to his chagrin, documenting information learned from the patient about third parties may be legally dangerous. The dead or their survivors cannot sue for defamation or the invasion of privacy because these are personal rights that die with the individual (Slovenko 1983). Even if a person is defamed while alive, the cause of action under common law dies with the person. However, a cause of action may exist when words contained in a medical record independently reflect on and defame those living. Slovenko wrote that "one who divulges an allegation by another may find himself liable although he did not indicate his own belief in the truth of the statement" (p. 126).

As explained by the lawyer in the case example, unless privilege exists to make disclosures, mental health professionals are responsible for statements made, even though the views are purported to be those of the patient. Documenting a deceased patient's inflammatory comments about third parties is seldom necessary for the purposes of record keeping (e.g., to facilitate ongoing treatment or to supply information to be available in the future for other physicians, for research, or for legal purposes). Dr. Rowe discovered that detailed documentation of clinically irrelevant information may expose the psychiatrist to legal liability.

States have created confidentiality provisions in professional licensure laws or in confidentiality and privilege statutes. Some patient access statutes contain provisions that allow the right of access to be exercised by third parties after a patient's death (Macbeth et al. 1994). A subpoena of the psychiatrist or the patient's records is not by itself sufficient legal compulsion to breach confidentiality. Furthermore, the physician-patient privilege does not expire on the patient's death. The privilege continues after the patient's death and may be claimed by the deceased patient's next of kin or legal representative. The physician-patient privilege seeks to protect the patient from embarrassment, which could extend to family members after the patient dies (Slovenko 1983).

Before releasing any information, the psychiatrist should consider obtaining the advice of legal counsel. Psychiatrists must be careful not to make unauthorized extrajudicial or statutorily prohibited disclosure of patient records, unless the disclosure is justified by overriding public interest. A majority of states have enacted legislation subjecting physicians to loss of their licenses for the unauthorized release of medical records. In addition, such a release could constitute the basis for a lawsuit.

The Principles of Medical Ethics With Annotations Especially Applicable to Psychiatry (American Psychiatric Association 2001b) states, "A psychiatrist may release confidential information only with the authorization of the patient or under proper legal compulsion" (Section 4, Annotation 2). A major controversy was created when disclosures were made by the treating psychiatrist following the suicide of the American poet Anne Sexton (Goldstein 1992). This case underscores many of the complex legal and ethical issues surrounding after-death release of confidential information.

The American Psychiatric Association's Guidelines on Confidentiality are explicit concerning disclosure of information by a psychiatrist after the death of a patient:

> Psychiatrists should remember that their ethical and legal responsibilities regarding confidentiality continue after their patients' deaths. In cases in which the release of information would be injurious to the deceased patient's interests or reputation, care must be exercised to limit the released data to that which is necessary for the purpose stated in the request for information. (American Psychiatric Association Committee on Confidentiality 1987)

Patients have new statutory rights regarding the release of health information mandated by the Health Insurance Portability and Accountability Act of 1996 (HIPAA). The final version of the privacy rule regulation applies, unless superseded by state privacy regulations that are more stringent ("HHS Final Modifications" 2002). Psychiatrists and other health care "providers" who electronically transmit information qualify as covered entities under HIPAA.

The privacy rule is complex, establishing psychiatrists' duties and patients' rights regarding confidentiality and the management of patients' records (Vanderpool 2002). Psychiatrists must provide patients written notice of how they can use, keep, and disclose patients' health information. Except for psychotherapy notes, patients must be able to obtain copies of their records and request amendment, within specified time limitations.

The rules governing patients' access to their own psychiatric records are complicated and vary considerably by jurisdiction. Under HIPAA and many state laws and regulations, patients have the right to obtain copies of the psychiatric record and to request amendments. When a patient requests a copy of the psychiatric record, if possible, the contents of the record should be discussed with the patient so that he or she can ask questions. Clinical judgment must be used so that the implementation of HIPAA or state requirements does not increase the risk of suicide in an already vulnerable or unstable patient. Under HIPAA, all disclosures are permissive, except for mandatory disclosures to the Secretary of

Health and Human Services for enforcement and to the patient. The rule does not require other disclosures. Appelbaum (2002) noted that an important exception to the privacy rule applies when the requested access is likely to endanger the life or physical safety of the individual or another person. The privacy rule *permits* "providers," within certain guidelines, to disclose information without patient's authorization (e.g., in emergencies) (Vanderpool 2002).

Patients at risk for suicide may have a variety of reasons for requesting review and amendment of their records. For example, a patient may be coerced by anxious family members to demand his or her psychiatric records from the psychiatrist. The suicidal patient may become destabilized by reading the psychiatric records or by conflict with insistent family members who want to see the patient's record. Destructive family dynamics may facilitate suicidal behaviors. Although patients are entitled to their records under HIPAA and by law in many jurisdictions, a current patient's request for his or her records or amendments to the records should be taken up initially as a treatment issue and the reasons for the request explored.

The psychiatrist is not required to respond automatically to the privacy rule or other statutory requirements if compliance would endanger the patient. The HIPAA provision allowing the patient to restrict disclosure of protected health information does not prevent the psychiatrist from obtaining the support of significant others, for example, when a patient is in a suicidal crisis. Maintaining professional discretion is key. Amending records at the patient's request may have liability consequences if a malpractice suit is brought against the psychiatrist. For example, in order to obtain life insurance, a patient with episodic suicidal ideation may request that the clinician amend the record by expunging any reference to suicide. If the clinician acquiesces and the patient subsequently commits suicide, the clinician would be defenseless against a malpractice claim without a factual record. Much more commonly, patients ask that certain diagnoses, especially schizophrenia, be expunged from their records. Patients also request that errors be corrected, such as when the patient's record reads, "The patient has a history of marijuana" instead of "a history of migraine" (D. Vanderpool, personal communication, December 2002). Amending the patient's record has potentially serious implications. Consideration should be given to consulting with legal counsel or referring to the Professional Risk Management Services online resource manual, "HIPAA Help: The Privacy Rule" (available at http://www.psychprogram.com).

The patient's record should not be amended unless it is inaccurate or incomplete. The psychiatrist may deny a request for record amendment if the patient's record is accurate and complete. As noted previously, many states already allow for amendment requests. Unlike the procedure for correcting errors, which is discussed later, nothing should be crossed out. Instead, an addendum should be placed in the patient's record acknowledging an error and indicating any additions or corrections that were made. When a lawsuit is filed against a psychiatrist, every state permits the patient, legal guardian, or surviving family members to subpoena the records. In this situation, only a *copy* of the record should be provided.

HIPAA does not provide individuals with a right to sue in order to enforce privacy rights. Apart from the privacy rule, psychiatrists must comply with similar or more stringent case law, regulations, state and federal statutes, and ethical requirements. However, the privacy rule makes it easier for patients to sue or bring complaints before a licensure board because it sets a standard for the protection of patient information.

Finally, maintaining confidentiality after a patient attempts or commits suicide on the psychiatric unit is a difficult if not impossible task. Other patients know what has occurred (e.g., rescue, ambulance, code, activity, patient removal). Discussions should be held with patients regarding only the fact of the incident and their feelings. It is unnecessary to delve into details about the patient or about the suicide. The patient's confidentiality should be protected as much as possible. It is important to reassure patients that the staff is in control and to deal with their fears, guilt, and misconceptions.

The discussion by staff members during a clinical staff conference about the patient's suicide may not be privileged information in the event of a lawsuit. However, the confidentiality of staff members' deliberations during quality assurance and other peer review meetings is likely protected. It is unlikely that confidentiality exists for informal discussions between the clinical staff or between staff members and patients.

PATIENT RECORDS

The clinician must keep an adequate—not a perfect—record. A patient's record should document major decisions in the assessment, treatment, and management of the patient's suicide risk. For example, all suicide risk assessments need to be documented. In addition, medication records should accurately reflect the amount of medication prescribed, instructions given for taking the medication, and any information issued to the patient regarding the benefits, risks, and side effects associated with a medication. Overdosing on prescribed medications is a common method of attempting or committing suicide.

Nonadherence to psychiatric treatment, including failure to take prescribed medications or to take them as prescribed, is important to note. Keeping copies of actual prescriptions or a log of prescriptions is good clinical practice. Including in a patient's record the clinician's risk-benefit assessments and reasoning in making important treatment and management interventions, as well as the informed consent obtained from the patient and waivers of confidentiality, represents sound clinical risk management. In litigation, good patient records can be the psychiatrist's best friend. Inadequate or no records can be the psychiatrist's worse enemy.

Errors in psychiatric diagnosis and treatment are not per se actionable. Good records can go a long way in showing that although an error was made, the psychiatrist used reasonable skill and diligence in arriving at treatment and management decisions.

Writing self-serving statements in the medical record after a patient's suicide in the hope of exonerating oneself damages the clinician's credibility. Attorneys read every word in the patient's record. The clinician will be subjected to searching cross-examination. The discrepancy between testimony developed in court and self-serving information recorded in the psychiatric record may deal a severe blow to the clinician's case.

Medical records should never be altered. An altered record will be interpreted by opposing counsel as an admission of fault. If an error is made, the incorrect portion of the record should be crossed out, initialed, and dated and the word *error* written in the margin. If clarification of the error is necessary, it should appear in proper sequence and also be dated. Postincident written statements by the psychiatrist must be dated contemporaneously. Other than the use of the word *error* in correcting a mistake, margins should be kept free of writing. Spaces should not be left between items of documentation. Any existing spaces should be crossed out.

Generally, state laws and administrative regulations require that patient records be kept. Destruction of records when the intent is to prevent disclosure at a judicial proceeding is forbidden. As noted above, failure to adequately document suicide risk assessments, treatment, and safety interventions for patients at risk for suicide is not usually the cause of a patient's suicide. However, the standard of care requires that the clinician maintain adequate patient records. State licensing and certification laws also may contain record-keeping requirements. Some state regulations and statutes specify the number of years that medical and hospital records must be held. Professional organizations may provide specific guidelines for record keeping. Moreover, state licensing and certification laws may incorporate record-keeping guidelines and principles of a state or national professional organization. Violations of the record-keeping requirements may lead to suspension or loss of the practitioner's license.

Psychiatrists should consider keeping their patients' records indefinitely. Each state, through its statute of limitations, defines the length of time for bringing a malpractice action. Generally, the statute of limitations for malpractice claims is 2 or 3 years from the time of the alleged injury or the patient's discovery of an injury. It is longer for breach-of-contract actions, usually 6 years from the last date of treatment. If the patient is a minor, the statute of limitations for malpractice may not begin to run until the patient reaches the age of majority.

The statute of limitations is tolled (i.e., suspended) when a person is under a legal disability at the time that the alleged injury arises. Legal disability is defined broadly as the lack of legal capacity to perform an act. Thus, a minor or mentally incompetent person is considered to be incapable of initiating a lawsuit in his or her own behalf. No time limit exists for ethical charges to be filed by former patients or by professional organizations. Licensing authorities do not follow the same time limitations established for legal actions.

Medical records may be kept in written form, on microfilm, on audiotape, or on a computer disk. Appropriate security measures must be taken in storing confidential information. All paper records should be physically secured. Electronic files located in computers, laptops, or other storage devices need to be secured physically and electronically against theft or access by unauthorized individuals (Professional Risk Management Services 2003). The psychiatrist should be in compliance with state and federal laws and regulations applicable to the creation, use, and storage of computerized patient records (Simon 1992). Ordinarily, the psychiatrist will not be liable for entrusting confidential reports to secretaries or secretarial services for typing (Slovenko 1973). However, by extension, they are under the same obligation to maintain confidentiality as the psychiatrist.

SUICIDE AFTERMATH

Suicide aftermath often presents conflicting concerns, roles, and responsibilities for the clinician (Kaye and Soreff 1991). Certain risk-management steps should be taken after a suicide occurs (American Psychiatric Association 1985). The patient's records should be complete and up to date. Any notes should be kept. Lengthy entries should be avoided where previously shorter notations were made. To avoid any suggestion of impropriety, all entries made after the incident should be correctly dated.

As a general rule, the psychiatrist should consult with an attorney before making any oral or written statements or before releasing patient records. It is appropriate to release information necessary for the care and follow-up of a patient who attempts suicide, after patient authorization. A detailed account of a patient's suicide or statements apportioning responsibility should not be made before consultation with an attorney. Details revealed to the hospital about the patient's suicide, unless privileged, may later be used as evidence against the psychiatrist, if the hospital attempts to shift responsibility for the suicide.

A complete and candid reporting of a patient suicide should be made immediately to the malpractice insurance carrier, even if no lawsuit is anticipated. A detailed report may be requested by the insurance carrier that will be helpful in obtaining the best possible legal defense or settlement, if a malpractice claim is filed against the psychiatrist.

In inpatient and clinic settings, when an inconsistency exists with another professional's notes (e.g., nurse's notes), a meeting with that professional and his or her supervisor should be considered. If litigation has been threatened or initiated, it may be necessary to include the psychiatrist's attorney. The inconsistencies should be discussed to see if they can be resolved. If resolved, the corrections should be made in a jointly prepared memorandum that fully describes the circumstances. It should be signed by all parties and placed in the patient's file. The memorandum may be made available to the plaintiff via discovery, if litigation should arise. It is important to not withhold discussions that were held, unless protected from discovery by law (e.g., quality assurance or peer review). The psychiatrist's efforts to resolve inconsistencies demonstrates that the patient's record is read carefully. It also shows that the psychiatrist works closely with the treatment team.

Conversations with family members may be appropriate and can allay grief and assist family members in obtaining help. As noted earlier, care must be exercised not to reveal confidential information about the patient and to avoid making self-incriminating or self-exonerating statements. However, the maintenance of absolute confidentiality of the deceased patient is usually not possible. To do so would defy common sense and may appear evasive to suicide survivors (Slovenko 1998). A discussion employing general principles of psychiatry rather than specific disclosures about the deceased patient may be sufficient. Defensive statements may further distress the family and provide a spur to litigation. A psychiatrist's meeting with bereaved family members after a patient's suicide is invariably stressful for both sides. The balance between maintaining confidentiality of the deceased patient and responding openly and empathically to surviving family members' questions and feelings can be a daunting task for the clinician.

The psychiatrist may decide to send a letter or card of condolence. Attending the wake or funeral of a patient who committed suicide can be very important for the psychiatrist and for the family. However, the psychiatrist must be prepared to encounter extreme emotional distress if there is a viewing. Psychiatrists are not accustomed to dealing with death, much less a viewing or even a closed casket. The feelings engendered in the psychiatrist will likely be heightened by the family's intense grief, which may include feelings of anger toward the psychiatrist. A memorial service may be less emotionally traumatic, but not necessarily. Nonetheless, attending the patient's funeral may be a positive, healing experience for both the clinician and the family. The family may express appreciation for the care provided by the psychiatrist to a severely or chronically mentally ill patient, whom they feel is finally at peace.

The perceptions of 71 suicide survivors regarding clinicians who treated their loved ones at the time of death were surveyed by Peterson et al. (2002). The results indicated that only 11% of the sample reported that the clinician attempted to contact them before the death. The respondents cited failure to involve the family in the patient's treatment as the second most frequent mistake made by clinicians. The most common clinician mistake cited by suicide survivors was medication decisions.

The responders noted that the most helpful response of clinicians after the patient's death was to make contact with the family (21%). However, 20% indicated that nothing was helpful. Most survivors who were not contacted by the clinician (74%) wanted to speak with the clinician and attempted to make contact. A clinician who is in emotional distress and conflict over a patient's suicide may withdraw from survivors. However, 48% of those who had contact believed that the clinician was holding back information to be self-protective. The data suggest that survivors value various types of contact with clinicians following their loss. Half of the respondents wished that the clinician would have attended the funeral. Offers of sympathy, attendance at the funeral, and expressions of condolence were noted as helpful.

The survivors who did not consider suing the clinician found meetings with the clinician to be meaningful. They also believed that the clinician was open and straightforward. Moreover, survivors who saw the clinician as grieving the loss of their loved one were more likely not to bring a lawsuit. Survivors who felt blamed by the clinician were more likely to consider bringing a lawsuit.

Through a condolence telephone call, the family's wishes regarding the psychiatrist's presence at the funeral can be ascertained. This avoids an unpleasant situation where the psychiatrist's presence is unwanted or, even worse, where the psychiatrist is verbally or even physically attacked. The psychiatrist should have reasonable control of his or her feelings when meeting with suicide survivors or attending a deceased patient's funeral. Expressions of sorrow and grief are appropriate. However, uncontrollable crying, defensiveness, or expressions of self-doubt may create the impression that the psychiatrist is admitting fault for the patient's suicide. Good judgment is necessary in deciding how to handle these matters. After consideration of a number of personal and situational (e.g., legal) factors, the clinician may decide that sending a condolence card or attending the funeral of a deceased patient may not be appropriate.

Liability exposure may be heightened for the psychiatrist who has a "good" relationship with family members. In this situation, the psychiatrist may reveal too much information, breaching the deceased patient's confidentiality, or make self-incriminating statements about the care of the patient. Even family members who are initially appreciative of the psychiatrist's care may later change their minds and sue. Maintaining one's professional bearing is supportive both of suicide survivors and of sound risk management.

AFTERCARE FOR SUICIDE SURVIVORS

Suicide aftercare is a clinically based outreach effort to survivors of a patient's suicide. It is an important aspect of suicide aftermath management. The term *suicide survivors* refers to family, friends, significant others, and loved ones of the individual who commits suicide. Clinicians who lose patients to suicide are not ordinarily considered suicide survivors; however, they usually carry a lifelong emotional burden. Aftercare is also appropriate for clinicians who have lost a patient to suicide. It is estimated that each suicide intimately affects at least six other people. The number of survivors of suicides in the year 2000 was more than 176,000. The number of survivors of more than 738,000 suicides between 1976 and 2000 is estimated to be 4.4 million, or one of every 62 Americans in 2000 (U.S.A. Suicide 2003).

The survivors of suicide are at increased risk for suicide themselves (Ness and Pfeffer 1990). They are more vulnerable to physical and psychological disorders. Depression, posttraumatic stress disorder, shame, guilt, and somatic complaints occur in suicide survivors (Seguin et al. 1995). These reactions are more severe in parents of young or adult children who commit suicide (Brent et al. 1996). The outcome for bereaved adults studied up to 10 years following suicide indicated that significant psychiatric symptoms may last up to 3 years (Saarinen et al. 2000). Approximately 63% of bereaved adults adapted over this time period.

Gutheil recommends postsuicide family outreach by the clinician as crucial for the devastated family members following a suicide (T.G. Gutheil, personal communication, October 1989). This recommendation, which is based primarily on humanitarian concerns for survivors, has important risk management implications. Gutheil points out that "bad feelings" combined with a bad outcome often lead to litigation. The persons who lived with the patient before the suicide not only currently experience intense emotional pain but also shared it with the patient before death. As mentioned earlier, some lawsuits are filed because of the clinician's refusal to express, in some way, feelings of condolence, sympathy, and regret for the patient's death.

In Massachusetts, an "apology statute" exists that renders various benevolent human expressions such as condolences, regrets, and apologies "inadmissible as evidence of an admission of liability in a civil action" (Mass. Gen. Laws ch. 233, § 23D [1986]). Slovenko (2002) noted that Texas and California enacted legislation similar to that in Massachusetts. The highest courts of Georgia and Vermont provided apology protection by judicial opinions in 1992. However, Regehr and Gutheil (2002) stated that "the current empirical evidence is insufficiently solid to support the proposition that apology by oppressors, perpetrators, and a defendant is a panacea leading to healing of trauma under all circumstances" (pp. 429–430).

A fine line exists between a psychiatrist's apology and the perception by others that fault is being admitted. Admissions of wrongdoing may void insurance coverage (Slovenko 2002). Moreover, another party may be found ultimately at fault in litigation, not the psychiatrist. A skillful lawyer may take feelings of genuine sympathy and turn them against the psychiatrist as an admission of fault. To say "I am sorry" is certainly the appropriate human response, but in a litigation context, it may backfire. The psychiatrist must be guided by good judgment, not by guilt-driven feelings or masochistic impulses.

Attorneys advise psychiatrists in different ways about suicide aftercare. Following a bad outcome, many attorneys recommend that the case be sealed and no communication be established with the family. However, some attorneys encourage judicious communication, consultation, or even treatment of family members. The treatment of family members by the psychiatrist who treated the patient before his or her suicide is likely doomed from the start by insurmountable transference and countertransference reactions. The family should be referred for treatment. However, if treatment of family members is undertaken, the psychiatrist should focus on addressing the feelings of family members rather than the specifics of the patient's care.

Suicide aftercare is similar to any other grief-related therapy or consultation. The clinician may justifiably worry that contact with survivors of suicide will increase the risk of a lawsuit. Nonetheless, the value of such consultation in healing grief is great enough for clinicians to consider providing humanitarian support to the survivors of patient suicide. Outreach to survivors of patient suicides should not be undertaken primarily for risk management purposes. No easy answers exist for managing the complex and often conflicting tensions between suicide aftercare and risk management.

Most practicing psychiatrists can expect that a patient suicide will occur during their years of practice. Psychiatrist reactions to a patient's suicide often include shame, guilt, anger, avoidance behaviors, intrusive thoughts, questioning of one's competency, and litigation fears (Gitlin 1999; Hendin et al. 2000). The American Association of Suicidology's Clinician Task Force makes available a number of resources to clinicians who have had patients commit suicide (see http://www.suicidology.org).

CLINICALLY BASED RISK MANAGEMENT

- Careful documentation supports good clinical care.
- Maintaining adequate treatment records is standard psychiatric practice.
- Documentation of clinical interventions should answer what was done, the reason(s) for doing it, and the rationale for rejecting alternative interventions or treatments.
- Systematic suicide risk assessment should be recorded when done.

- In malpractice litigation or administrative or ethics proceedings, an adequately documented, legible patient record is the clinician's best friend.
- Illegible documentation is of no assistance to other caregivers who are also responsible for the care of the patient. It gives the impression of carelessness, haste, and the provision of poor clinical care.
- Illegible doctor's orders are a common cause of drug and other errors that can seriously harm patients, possibly increasing their suicide risk.
- In malpractice litigation, some courts have concluded that what is not recorded was not done.
- Documentation should be careful, concise, complete, clear, and contemporaneous.
- Dates and times of documentation should always be noted.
- The duty to maintain confidentiality of patient records follows the patient in death, unless provided otherwise by a specific court decision or statute.
- The physician-patient privilege that protects confidentiality does not end with the patient's death. It may be claimed by the deceased patient's next of kin or a legal representative.
- Written authorization should be obtained from the executor or administrator of the deceased patient's estate before a *copy* of the medical records is released.
- If it is necessary for the psychiatrist to reveal confidential information about a deceased patient, legal exposure may be minimized by providing only enough information for the matter at issue.
- It is rarely, if ever, necessary to record a patient's inflammatory comments about a third party. The psychiatrist may be held legally accountable for the documented statements made, even though the psychiatrist does not indicate a belief in the statements.
- Standard procedures should be followed for correcting errors and misunderstandings. Postincident written statements must be accurately dated.
- There should be no tampering, deletions, changes, or destruction in patient records after a patient's suicide.
- Patient records should be kept at least for the length of time that malpractice claims can be brought according to the statute of

limitations. The clinician should consider keeping patient records indefinitely for future treatment purposes and for administrative, licensure, or ethical proceedings that are not governed by the statute of limitations.

- The aftermath of suicide presents the clinician with conflicting roles and concerns between outreach to suicide survivors and risk management.
- Consideration should be given to consulting with an attorney before making any oral or written statements regarding a patient's suicide or suicide attempt or before releasing patient records, unless it is to assist in the clinical care of a patient who has attempted suicide.
- The appropriateness of sending a condolence card or attending the deceased patient's funeral should be considered by the clinician case by case.
- Suicide aftercare is a clinically based outreach effort to survivors of suicide, including clinicians who lose patients to suicide. No easy answers exist for handling the complexity of suicide aftercare and risk management. Case-by-case decisions are required.
- Following a patient's suicide, the clinician should inform the professional liability insurance carrier immediately.

REFERENCES

Abille v United States, 482 F. Supp. 703, 708 (N.D. Cal. 1980)

American Psychiatric Association: Legal Consultation Plan. Washington, DC, American Psychiatric Association, 1985

American Psychiatric Association: Opinions of the Ethics Committee on The Principles of Medical Ethics With Annotations Especially Applicable to Psychiatry. Washington, DC, American Psychiatric Association, 2001a

American Psychiatric Association: The Principles of Medical Ethics With Annotations Especially Applicable to Psychiatry. Washington, DC, American Psychiatric Association, 2001b

American Psychiatric Association Committee on Confidentiality: Guidelines on confidentiality. Am J Psychiatry 144:1522–1526, 1987

Appelbaum PS: Privacy in psychiatric treatment: threats and responses. Am J Psychiatry 159:1809–1818, 2002

Brandvain v Ridgeview Inst., 188 Ga. App. 106, 372 S.E.2d 265 (1988), *aff'd,* 259 Ga. 376, 382 S.E.2d 597 (1989)

Brent DA, Moritz G, Bridge J, et al: The impact of adolescent suicide on siblings and parents: a longitudinal follow-up. Suicide Life Threat Behav 26:253–259, 1996

Gitlin MJ: A psychiatrist's reaction to a patient's suicide. Am J Psychiatry 156:1630–1634, 1999

Goldstein RL: Psychiatric poetic license? Postmortem disclosures of confidential information in the Anne Sexton case. Psychiatr Ann 22:341–348, 1992

Hendin H, Lipschitz A, Maltsberger JT, et al: Therapists' reactions to patients' suicides. Am J Psychiatry 157:2022–2027, 2000

HHS final modifications to health privacy rule. Fed Regist 67:53182–53273, August 14, 2002

Kaye NS, Soreff SM: The psychiatrist's role, responses and responsibilities when a patient commits suicide. Am J Psychiatry 148:739–743, 1991

Laub MJ: Suicide: psychiatric malpractice implications. Rx for Risk 9:1, 6–7, 2001

Macbeth JE, Wheeler AM, Sithers J, et al: Legal and Risk Management Issues in the Practice of Psychiatry. Washington, DC, Psychiatrist's Purchasing Group, 1994

Malone KM, Szanto K, Corbitt EM, et al: Clinical assessment versus research methods in the assessment of suicidal behavior. Am J Psychiatry 152:1601–1607, 1995

Ness DE, Pfeffer CR: Sequelae of bereavement resulting from suicide. Am J Psychiatry 147:279–285, 1990

Peterson EM, Luoma JB, Dunne E: Suicide survivors' perceptions of the treating clinician. Suicide Life Threat Behav 32:158–166, 2002

Professional Risk Management Services. Rx for Risk 11:4, 2003

Regehr C, Gutheil TG: Apology, justice and trauma recovery. J Am Acad Psychiatry Law 30:425–429, 2002

Saarinen PI, Hintikka J, Viinamaeki H, et al: Is it possible to adapt to the suicide of a close individual? Results of a 10-year prospective study. Int J Soc Psychiatry 46:182–190, 2000

Seguin M, Lesage A, Kiely MC: Parental bereavement after suicide and accident: a comparative study. Suicide Life Threat Behav 25:489–492, 1995

Simon RI: Clinical Psychiatry and the Law, 2nd Edition. Washington, DC, American Psychiatric Press, 1992

Simon RI: Taking the "sue" out of suicide: a forensic psychiatrist's perspective. Psychiatr Ann 30:399–407, 2000

Slovenko R: Psychiatry and Law. Boston, MA, Little, Brown, 1973

Slovenko R: The hazards of writing or disclosing information in psychiatry. Behav Sci Law 1:109–127, 1983

Slovenko R: Psychiatry and Confidentiality: Testimonial Privileged Communication, Reporting Duties, and Breach of Confidentiality. Springfield, IL, Charles C Thomas, 1998

Slovenko R: Psychiatry in Law/Law in Psychiatry. New York, Brunner-Routledge, 2002

U.S.A. Suicide: 2000 official final data. Available at: http://www.iusb.edu/njmcintos/usa2000summary.htm. Accessed January 3, 2003

Vanderpool D: HIPAA privacy rule: an update for psychiatrists. Psychiatric Practice and Managed Care 8:5–12, 2002

INDEX OF LEGAL CASES AND STATUTES

SUBJECT INDEX

*Page numbers printed in **boldface** type refer to tables or figures.*